Jane Addams

Jane Addams. (University of Illinois at Chicago's University Library. Jane Addams Memorial Collection)

Sandra Opdycke

Jane Addams
and Her Vision for America

THE LIBRARY OF AMERICAN BIOGRAPHY

Edited by Mark C. Carnes

Prentice Hall

Boston Columbus Indianapolis New York San Francisco Upper Saddle River Amsterdam
Cape Town Dubai London Madrid Milan Munich Paris Montréal Toronto Delhi
Mexico City São Paulo Sydney Hong Kong Seoul Singapore Taipei Tokyo

Editorial Director: Craig Campanella
Executive Editor: Ed Parsons
Editorial Project Manager: Rob DeGeorge
Editorial Assistant: Alex Rabinowitz
Director of Marketing: Brandy Dawson
Senior Marketing Manager: Maureen E.
    Prado Roberts
Marketing Assistant: Marissa C. O'Brien
Senior Managing Editor: Ann Marie
    McCarthy

Operations Specialist: Renata Butera
Creative Art Director: Jayne Conte
Cover Designer: Karen Noferi
Cover Art: The Granger Collection, New York
Full-Service Project Management: Chitra Ganesan
Composition: PreMediaGlobal
Printer / Binder: Edwards Brothers
Cover Printer: Lehigh Phoenix
Text Font: Times New Roman

Credits and acknowledgments borrowed from other sources and reproduced, with permission, in this textbook appear on appropriate page within the text.

Many of the designations by manufacturers and seller to distinguish their products are claimed as trademarks. Where those designations appear in this book, and the publisher was aware of a trademark claim, the designations have been printed in initial caps or all caps.

Library of Congress Cataloging-in-Publication Data
Opdycke, Sandra.
Jane Addams and her vision for America / Sandra Opdycke.
   p. cm.
Includes bibliographical references and index.
ISBN-13: 978-0-205-59840-3 (alk. paper)
ISBN-10: 0-205-59840-4 (alk. paper)
1. Addams, Jane, 1860-1935. 2. Women social workers--United States--Biography.
3. Women social reformers--United States--Biography. 4. United States--Social
conditions--19th century. 5. United States--Social conditions--20th century. I. Title.
HV28.A35O63 2012
361.92--dc22
[B]   2011000319
10 9 8 7 6 5 4 3 2 1

Prentice Hall
is an imprint of

ISBN-13: 978-0-205-59840-3
ISBN-10: 0-205-59840-4

www.pearsonhighered.com

*Jane Addams' friend Lillian Wald always
began her letters to Addams: "Beloved Lady."*

*This book is dedicated to my seven beloved
ladies:*
Robin   Brooke   Megan
Emma   Luciana   Ada   Luna

Contents

Editor's Preface

We remember Jane Addams as a good person in a Progressive age that enshrined do-gooders. A major reason why is the book for which she was justly famous, *Twenty Years at Hull House,* which chronicled her struggles to improve the lives of poor immigrants in Chicago. By looking at her in this way, however, we reduce Addams to a caricature of virtue, someone whose thoroughly benevolent impulses render her irrelevant to the hard-hearted realities of our more cynical and materialistic world.

It is precisely because Addams endures more as burnished icon than as a flesh and blood person that Sandra Opdycke's humanely engaging biography is so important. Opdycke goes beyond the testimonials to reveal Addams's complexity. Though brilliant, Addams was plagued by doubts. Though committed to the selfless service of mankind, she was driven by unquenchable ambition. Though capable of innumerable kindnesses towards the people she sought to help, she often resorted to a paternalistic rhetoric that demeaned them. And though she ceaselessly championed women's special sensibilities and the benefits of maternal nurture, she never married or bore children. By viewing Addams through the clear, sharp prism of Opdycke's prose, we perceive someone who, however luminous, emerged from the clay shared by all humanity.

This biography also provides a broad window on the Progressive world. Addams was not just the driving force in the American settlement movement; she also was a major leader in the movements to promote peace, child welfare, women's suffrage, improved housing, education, juvenile justice, labor relations, and civil liberties, and the reform of urban and state politics. Because these causes have subsequently become institutionalized in so many international, federal, or state agencies, it is easy to forget the difficult struggles that were fought to achieve them a century ago.

The ultimate institutionalization of such movements, however, makes it easy to assume that these achievements were inevitable. As Opdycke makes clear, however, the aging Adams perceived that her vision of a social order built upon "sympathetic understanding" was still far from realization. The persistence of injustice, the unprecedented slaughter of the Great War, and the approach of another one cast a shadow over her final years. Even today, Opdycke notes, Addams's vision remains unfulfilled, for

> we know very well what it is to live in neighborhoods divided from each other by income and race. . . we have seen differences over politics and religion and personal life-choices rip communities apart. And like her, we have watched overseas conflicts rooted in old hatreds explode across the landscape. Even though Addams' ideas were developed in response to other quarrels and other wars, the need for 'sympathetic understanding'. . . is as evident today as it was when she called for it a century ago.

MARK C. CARNES

ANN WHITNEY OLIN PROFESSOR OF HISTORY

BARNARD COLLEGE, COLUMBIA UNIVERSITY

Acknowledgments

My greatest debt as the author of this book is to Jane Addams herself, for writing so extensively, so vividly, and so thoughtfully about her own experiences and ideas. Despite her intensely busy schedule, Addams managed to produce 11 books during her lifetime as well as several hundred shorter pieces—nearly all of them thought-provoking and some of them truly memorable. Addams wrote primarily to communicate with her contemporaries—to enlighten them and change their thinking about public issues of the day. But her formidable literary output is a gift to us as well. Speaking as her biographer, I am grateful to have had the chance to hear her voice so clearly and to see, close-up, how she perceived the world around her.

I am also grateful to the scholars who assembled the major archives documenting Addams' life—the Jane Addams Collection at Swarthmore College, the Jane Addams Memorial Collection at the University of Illinois at Chicago, and the Jane Addams Papers on microfilm. The individuals who created these collections—as well as the historians and biographers who have drawn upon them—have left a rich legacy for those of us who follow.

On a more personal note, I would like to thank my friend and colleague Mark Carnes. It was he who first suggested that I undertake this book, and as the editor of this series, he provided me with valuable advice and counsel as my work proceeded. I also appreciate the helpful support I have received from Ed Parsons at Pearson.

In addition, I would like to pay tribute to my dear associates and longtime collaborators, Marque Miringoff and her late husband Marc. My special interest in Jane Addams began in the 1970s, when Marc introduced me to *Democracy and Social Ethics*. And now, 35 years later, Marque has sustained the family connection to Addams through her perceptive comments on this manuscript. It has always been a privilege to work with the Miringoffs because of their shared conviction—articulated by Addams a century ago—that the purpose of social research is not simply to acquire abstract knowledge but to inform the public, foster constructive debate, and improve the conditions of American life.

These acknowledgments end where my fondest feelings begin—with my family. All of them—from my grandchildren to my dear husband Leo—have encouraged me on this project. In particular, Leo has been endlessly supportive, reviewing each chapter with his authoritative English teacher's eye and cheerfully enduring the many months when it seemed that "Jane" had become a third member of our household. To express my appreciation, let me borrow a line from *Twelfth Night*: "I can no other answer make but thanks, and thanks, and ever thanks."

Introduction

A hundred years ago, Jane Addams was the most famous woman in America. Celebrated for her achievements in the field of social reform, she was so universally admired that—years before women were even allowed to vote—there were those who suggested she might become America's first female president. Addams' fame also extended overseas, and in her later years, she became the first woman ever to win the Nobel Prize for Peace. "Is she really the only woman in America?" asked an Australian visitor. "She is the only one our newspapers quote."

The path of Addams' career followed a series of ever-widening circles. Having started out working with immigrant families in one poor Chicago neighborhood, she became increasingly active in city, state, and national advocacy efforts—to the point that it is hard to think of a single major campaign for social reform during the early 20th century in which she did not play a part. Then, in her mid-50s, Addams expanded her horizons still further and began working with women around the world for the cause of peace. This initiative, which started as an effort by female pacifists to bring World War I to a halt, evolved into the Women's International League for Peace and Freedom, which Addams led for 15 years.

Today, more than 75 years after Addams' death, we still live in a world that she helped to create through the causes she championed and the people she inspired. Although some of the changes she worked for were not achieved during her lifetime, she and her allies helped prepare the ground for many of the reforms we take for granted today—including Social Security, the prohibition of child labor, women's suffrage, the minimum wage, juvenile justice, collective bargaining, adult education, and occupational safety standards. In addition, as leader of the Women's International League for Peace and Freedom, Addams articulated the case for pacifism in a way that commanded serious attention in her own time and continues today to offer a compelling argument against war. More than a social worker, more than a reformer, more than a peace activist, Addams was one of America's great public citizens.

Jane Addams' career began in 1889, when, at the age of 29, she rented space in a rundown section of Chicago and, with her friend Ellen Starr, established Hull-House—one of the first settlement houses in the United States. Inspired by the pioneering Toynbee Hall in London, Hull-House was a new kind of social institution—a place where young college graduates could live together in a poor urban district while providing services and outreach to the surrounding community.

Within a year after Addams and Starr established themselves at Hull-House, other college graduates started joining them there, attracted by the chance to serve society, to establish friendly relations across the divide of class and ethnicity, and to supplement their academic training by—as Addams put it—"learning of life from life itself." The Hull-House residents were enthusiastic young reformers, many of whom had professional training as lawyers, teachers, economists, or physicians. Among them were Julia Lathrop, who became a major figure in the social welfare field and later served as the first head of the U.S. Children's Bureau; Florence Kelley, a leading social activist, researcher, economist, and labor advocate; and Alice Hamilton, whose groundbreaking research played a major role in establishing the field of occupational medicine. Over the years, each of Hull-House's many residents made a distinct contribution to the work of the settlement, and nearly all of them developed new capacities and interests as a result of their experience there.

As Addams and her fellow residents learned more about their immigrant neighbors' lives, they continually enlarged the

Hull-House program to address their needs. To make this possible, Addams spent virtually all her own money on the settlement and also built a circle of donors who provided generous support. With their help, Hull-House gradually expanded to fill an entire block, offering social and educational clubs, sports programs, a kindergarten, art classes, concerts, plays, a music school, and the most stimulating lecture series in the city. Besides these formal programs, the settlement workers assisted their neighbors with many personal problems, helping them deal with deaths and births, unemployment and runaway husbands, injuries on the job and troubles with the law. News of what was being done in Chicago began to spread, and Hull-House soon found itself hosting a steady stream of visitors— scholars, public officials, social thinkers, and activists—from around the country and around the world.

Addams loved her work at the settlement, and she remained deeply committed to it for the rest of her life. But living in such an impoverished neighborhood also opened her eyes to all the problems that Hull-House could *not* solve. Thus began her career in the wider field of social advocacy. For example, seeing the inadequate street-cleaning services in the neighborhood drew her and her fellow residents into the politics of municipal reform. The terrible conditions in local factories and sweatshops led them to start lobbying for stronger labor laws. And Addams' special concern for the children of the neighborhood inspired her to start working for school reform as well as helping to establish the first juvenile court in the United States.

Addams had the great advantage of working for social change during one of the most intense periods of reform activity in American history. The opening of Hull-House coincided with the early years of the so-called Progressive Era, a period that was noteworthy for the breadth and energy of reform initiatives throughout the country. During this era, which lasted until World War I, thousands of reform-minded professionals—working closely with labor leaders, enlightened businessmen, and dedicated volunteers—set out to transform America into a more modern, more just, and more humane society.

Addams participated wholeheartedly in these efforts, deriving stimulation, support, and encouragement from the opportunity to collaborate with people who shared her social concerns. From local and state initiatives, she moved on to work at the national level, and by the early 20th century, she had emerged as a major figure in the progressive movement—active particularly in the campaigns for women's suffrage and the prohibition of child labor.

Throughout the Progressive Era, Addams promoted reform not only through her organizational work but also through her writing and public speaking. Besides writing innumerable magazine articles, she traveled across the country lecturing to civic groups, women's clubs, and college students. She also published five books during these years: her famous memoir, *Twenty Years at Hull-House* (1910), as well as *Democracy and Social Ethics* (1902), *Newer Ideals of Peace* (1907), *The Spirit of Youth and the City Streets* (1909), and *A New Conscience and an Ancient Evil* (1912). In all these ways, Addams sought to inspire the public with her own vision of what American democracy could be.

Addams expected that the reform enthusiasm that was so visible during the Progressive Era would continue for many more years. But in 1914, the outbreak of World War I in Europe changed everything. Convinced that war represented the very antithesis of social progress, Addams threw herself into the effort to stop the fighting. She gave speeches, wrote articles, served as chair of the Women's Peace Party, and, in the spring of 1915, helped organize an international women's campaign for peace. The war continued, however, and in 1917, the United States joined the hostilities.

As soon as the United States became a combatant, most American peace advocates dropped their opposition to the war or at least stopped expressing their opposition in public. However, Addams continued to speak out for peace, and she suffered years of ostracism for doing so. Even after the war ended in 1918, she and her fellow pacifists continued to be condemned as traitors. Because they supported disarmament, they were now accused of trying to render the United States defenseless against Soviet Russia. Throughout these difficult years, Addams made frequent trips abroad as chair of the Women's International League for Peace and Freedom. She was generally welcomed in other countries as a renowned spokesperson for peace, but the warmth of that reception hardly made up to her for the hostility she faced at home.

It was only toward the end of Addams' life—in the 1930s—that the American political climate eased, and she found herself once again treated as a revered public citizen. In her final years, she received numerous awards—most notably, the Nobel Peace Prize. In addition, she took great pleasure in seeing Franklin Roosevelt's New Deal begin to enact many of the reforms that she had worked for throughout her life. She died in 1935.

Echoing the pattern of Addams' own career, this book starts with an account of her early years and the founding of Hull-House and then works outward to trace her growing involvement in city, state, national, and finally international advocacy. Part 1, "Inventing a Life of Service," describes how—during the first 35 years of her life—Addams developed the sense of vocation, the ideas, and the methods that would define her career as a social reformer. Chapter 1 covers her early life and the launching of Hull-House, while Chapter 2 recounts how the settlement developed into a flourishing institution, embodying Addams' commitment to bridging the divisions of class and ethnicity that fractured American society. Chapter 3 discusses the rise of progressivism and shows how the movement intersected with Addams' pursuit of her own pre-eminent goal: to make the nation's democratic ideals manifest in the reality of everyday life. Chapter 4 explores the vital role that collaboration played in her career, describing her work with the community of residents at Hull-House, the settlement movement, the academic world, the social work profession, and reform-minded businessmen.

Part 2, "Working for Progresssive Reform," treats Addams' activities during the Progressive Era thematically. Throughout this section, it will be observed how often her experience with problems in the Hull-House neighborhood led her into large-scale campaigns for reform. This pattern is illustrated in discussions of her work with three different groups: women (Chapter 5), children (Chapter 6), and the labor movement (Chapter 7). The peak years of progressivism as a national movement are described in Chapter 8, which culminates with an account of Addams' participation in Theodore Roosevelt's campaign for president on the Progressive Party ticket in 1912.

In Part 3, "Broader Horizons," we see Addams move into the role of an international spokeswoman for peace. Chapter 9 explores her involvement in the peace movement during World War I and the political price she paid for it. Chapter 10 discusses the continuing hostility she encountered during the 1920s in the United States—both as a pacifist and as a believer in progressive values that were no longer in fashion—compared with her recognition overseas as an international spokeswoman for peace. Chapter 11 discusses her bittersweet final years during the 1930s, while Chapter 12 describes how Addams has been remembered since her death and identifies some key themes in her life and work.

Reflecting on Addams' career, one is particularly struck by the remarkable variety of her activities. Few women, after all, can claim to have been both a neighborhood garbage inspector and a Nobel Prize–winner—not to mention a settlement worker, author, lecturer, women's club member, lobbyist, teacher, political campaigner, and community organizer. Of course, if Addams had seen each one of her many activities as a separate undertaking, she could never have achieved so much. But to her, they were all part of one overarching vision, which was to apply democratic ideals to the realities of American experience.

The proof of our democracy, Addams insisted, does not lie in waving flags or making patriotic speeches; it lies in the familiar transactions of ordinary life. How fairly do employers treat their workers? What kind of future can immigrant children look forward to? Can low-income families find safe and adequate housing? Are women treated as full citizens? Can we trust our political leaders? Does the United States deal respectfully and responsibly with other nations? Only by testing ourselves against standards like these, said Addams, can we be sure that we are a truly democratic society. This is the philosophy she lived by, and this is the philosophy that inspired so many of the people whose lives she touched during the course of her long career.

Late in Addams' life, at a dinner in her honor, her friend Charles Merriam captured both the improbability and the great significance of what Addams had achieved in her life. He said:

> More than any other woman in America she has . . . understood how to speak to what Lincoln called the better angels of our nature. If you say it is not possible for any one to be at once a statesman without a portfolio, a professor without a chair, and a guiding woman in a man made world, I answer that it is not possible. But—here she is!"

Inventing a
Life of Service

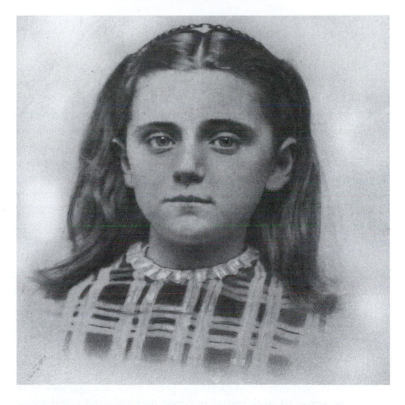

Jane Addams, age eight, 1868. (University of Illinois at Chicago's
University Library. Jane Addams Memorial Collection)

1

Finding the Path

When Jane Addams was a child, she had the same dream night after night. In this dream, the grownups had disappeared, and somehow the fate of the whole world depended on her building a wagon wheel. It was a formidable task for a six-year-old, and the weight of the challenge stayed with her even after she woke up. So, her autobiography tells us, she would hover at the door of the village wheelwright, anxiously studying every move he made. Then, daunted by the task she faced, she would turn away with a sigh, "bearing my responsibility as best I could."

Did this dream occur exactly as Addams described it? It is impossible to be sure. Besides being a world-famous reformer, she was an accomplished writer, and she often reshaped her experiences to give power to the story she was telling. But whatever the literal truth, there are certainly elements in this account that reappeared again and again in her life—the sense of social obligation, the self-doubt, the touch of sadness. Addams also had many other qualities; as an adult, she was admired for her organizational ability, her writing, and her political skills. But what gave her career depth and meaning— what made her one of America's great public citizens—was that same sense of high moral purpose that haunted her dreams when she was six years old.

Her Father's Daughter

Jane Addams was born in Cedarville, Illinois, on September 6, 1860. Her father, John Addams, had moved into the area as a young miller 16 years earlier, when northern Illinois was still pioneer country. Over time, as the prairie town grew, he became one of Cedarville's leading citizens—a banker, a significant property owner, and a state legislator. He was the dominant figure of Jane's childhood, her revered source of guidance, and the person whose approval she valued most in the world.

One reason that Jane's father loomed so large in her life was that she lost her mother when she was only two years old. Sarah Addams died at the age of 46 after bearing her ninth child. The baby was stillborn and the fourth of her children to die at or near birth. There was another death in the Addams household four years later, when Jane's sister Martha died of typhoid. These family losses were paralleled in the surrounding community. Jane never forgot the experience of standing on the wintry prairie with her schoolmates to watch a friend's mother being lowered into her grave. For weeks afterward, a question that Jane had overheard at the funeral reverberated through her head: "Whatever will the children do?"

There was a larger context for this sense of death in the air. The Civil War began just a few months after Jane was born, and the effects of the war were clearly visible in Cedarville throughout her childhood: the black-garbed widows, the disabled veterans, the portraits of fallen heroes, and the annual ceremonies of remembrance. Moreover, because Abraham Lincoln had been a friend of her father, Lincoln's anguished presidency and tragic death gave the war an even more personal meaning. Jane's childhood included many happy times, but death was there too, and her experience seems to have taught her very early that grief and loss are a fundamental part of living.

Within the Addams family, Sarah's death—followed by Martha's in 1867—left John as a 45-year-old widower with four children to care for: Mary (age 22), Weber (15), Alice (14), and seven-year-old Jane. Mary did her best to mother her younger siblings and in the process forged a bond with Jane that would last the rest of their lives. But more was needed, and in 1868, John transformed his family's life by marrying Anna Haldeman, a handsome and high-spirited widow with two sons.

When we try to picture Jane at the time of her father's remarriage, the challenge is to balance the available evidence against her own conviction that she was homely. She had a slight curvature of the spine, and in her recollections, this disability overwhelmed everything else about her appearance. She once recalled that as a child, she would try to avoid walking beside her handsome father so no one would connect him with "the ugly, pigeon-toed little girl, whose crooked back obliged her to walk with her head held very much to one side." But those who grew up with her had little to say about the curved back. What they remembered was her "spiritual," almost "dreamy" appearance. A picture of her taken the year her father remarried shows a pretty eight-year-old with a sweet, slightly sad expression, long brown hair pulled behind the ears, and huge dark eyes. It is hard to believe that this child looked plain to anyone but herself.

Whatever Jane's inner concerns, she faced additional challenges with the arrival of her new stepmother. Anna Haldeman Addams was an emotional and self-involved woman, with a mercurial temper; her granddaughter later remarked that the children in the Addams household "felt both the storm and the sunshine of Anna's gracious but complicated character." People often found her difficult, and many Cedarville residents considered her grand manners off-putting. Nevertheless, she brought verve and color to the Addams household by introducing the whole family to the pleasures of art and music, drama and poetry, good design and good food.

Anna also brought Jane a new playmate: her son George, who was just a year younger than Jane. Anna's older son Harry was already in college at the time of the marriage, and within a few years, Jane's brother and sisters were also out on their own. This left Jane and George as the only children in the house. The two became fast friends, playing together for hours on end throughout their childhood. Even after they became teenagers, they remained close companions, sharing games of chess and cards, sledding and snowballing, music lessons and poetry reading.

Jane Addams was educated in the small public school in Cedarville. She was a star student, but the work was not very demanding, and she took little pleasure in it. Her real intellectual stimulation came from her father. He gave her challenging books to read, encouraged her to discuss them, and talked with her thoughtfully about ethics and religion and politics. In an era when women were widely considered to be mentally inferior to men, Jane Addams was fortunate to have a father who treated her as a valued intellectual companion and took pleasure in helping her develop her mind.

One of the most important ways that Addams' father expressed his faith in women's potential was by sending all three of his daughters to college. When Addams finished high school in 1877, she went off to nearby Rockford Seminary, as her sisters had done. It has sometimes been asserted that her father prevented her from going to her first choice—the more prestigious Smith College—but historian Victoria Brown has shown that the courses available to Addams in Cedarville would not have qualified her for admission to Smith. She did hope to transfer there later on, and she took a number of extra courses while she was at Rockford in order to prepare herself for the Smith admission exams. But in 1877, Smith was beyond her grasp. Nevertheless, we must remember that at a time when just 1 percent of American women were graduates of any college at all, going to Rockford represented a significant opportunity.

Addams and Rockford were never a perfect fit because of the school's intense emphasis on religion. The school director, Anna Sill, was a devout Protestant of the evangelical type, and under her leadership, Rockford dedicated itself to preparing young women to be foreign missionaries. This was not the kind of religious orientation that Addams had absorbed from her father. He was a member of the Rockford board of trustees and a regular churchgoer, but his own version of Christianity focused much more on ethical behavior than on promoting conversions. Addams followed his lead, and throughout her four years at the seminary, she firmly held out against the pressure to embrace a more evangelical form of religion.

Despite being out of step with Rockford in religious terms, Addams flourished during her time there. Within a few weeks of her arrival, she was elected class president, and she was re-elected every year thereafter. She joined the debate team, wrote for the campus magazine, and helped found a scientific association. In addition, she took every difficult course she could find, read voraciously, and extracted as much as she could from Rockford's relatively weak science offerings. One college friend recalled: "We all loved to go to her room. We just knew there was always something 'doing' where she was, and that however mopey it might be elsewhere there was intellectual ozone in her vicinity."

One characteristic that separated Addams from most of her classmates was her total lack of interest in the male sex. In fact, the diaries she kept during these years scarcely mentioned boys, except to note how foolish it was for girls to lose their heads over them. This is not to say that some boys may not have been interested in her. One young man who saw her give a speech at Rockford later wrote: "As she stood up to speak, she was slight and pale, spirited and charming. I have to confess that I fell in love with Jane Addams that day and never got over it." But although he and perhaps others were drawn to her, there is no indication that she felt attracted in return.

Addams did not even engage in the sentimental relationships between girls that were so common in the late 19th century. She had no real intimates at Rockford, and it may be significant that of her two closest college friends, Sarah Anderson was a teacher, which automatically established a certain distance between them, and her classmate Ellen Starr left Rockford after freshman year, so their relationship had to be sustained mainly by correspondence. Starr made it clear in her letters that her feelings for Addams ran very deep, but Addams rarely responded in kind, and if Starr pressed her too strongly, Addams tended to back away. Young people express their sexuality in different ways, and perhaps Addams did feel some of the pangs and attractions that are typical of late adolescence. But if she did, there is no hint of it in the record.

With her heart in safekeeping, Addams was free to enjoy the other pleasures of college life, and in her senior year, she did so to the hilt, juggling academic work and extracurricular activities at a ferocious pace. Addams drove herself to take the full load of courses required for a bachelor of arts degree despite the fact that Rockford—which was technically a seminary—could not at that time grant college degrees. (A year later, when Rockford did officially become a college, Addams was invited back to receive the first bachelor of arts degree the institution ever granted.)

Racing through the hectic activities of her senior year, Addams also looked ahead to what would come next. Her plan was to take an extra year at Smith College and then go to medical school. Medicine was not an easy field for women to enter in the 1880s. Only a handful of medical schools even accepted female students, and numerous obstacles blocked any female doctor's path to licensure and a successful career. But Addams had two consuming desires: She wanted to serve society, and she wanted to count for something in the world. Being a physician promised to fulfill these goals. She felt that spending an extra year at Smith would give her a solid background for her medical studies.

At the Rockford commencement in June 1881, Addams' valedictory address laid out the road she hoped to pursue. The speech hailed women for their time-honored gift of intuition, but it also warned that if they limited themselves to that kind of knowledge, they would find themselves in the position of Cassandra, who correctly predicted the fall of Troy but was ignored by those around her. To command attention, Addams said, women must supplement their intuitive gifts with the analytic powers of science.

As Addams left the podium, she must have felt that she was taking the first step on the very road she had described. But within a month, her hectic final year at college caught up with her, and she suffered a physical collapse, with severe pain in her back as well as general exhaustion. Under orders from her doctor, she gave up the idea of going to Smith that fall.

Then, in August came a far more devastating blow. On a family trip to Wisconsin, her beloved father suffered an attack of appendicitis and died within a few days. As Addams wrote Ellen Starr, it was "the greatest sorrow that can ever come to me." For as long as she could remember, she had depended on her father to support her with his unconditional love and to inspire her with his faith in what she could achieve. Now he was gone. Just at the time when she would be facing intense pressure to settle for the genteel existence of a middle-class spinster, she had lost the one person who believed most firmly in her potential. Eight long years would pass before she regained her bearings.

The Years of Uncertainty

Between 1881 and 1889, Addams engaged at various times in travel, cultural activities, independent study, family caretaking, social life, churchgoing, charity work, and medical study. Many of these experiences were diverting, and some were enlightening, but none seemed to provide the full and valuable life she longed for. So, although the money she had inherited from her father made her financially independent, the restrictions imposed by custom, by her family, and by her own self-doubt still hemmed her in. Throughout this troubled time, Addams searched for the path forward, wondered if such a path existed, and blamed herself for not finding it.

The first stop in Addams' odyssey was Philadelphia. Several years earlier, her sister Alice had married their stepbrother—Anna's older son Harry Haldeman. In the fall of 1881, Alice and Harry moved to Philadelphia so he could study medicine. Welcoming the chance to spend the winter somewhere more stimulating than Cedarville, Anna decided to follow them, and Addams dutifully tagged along. Then, because the Woman's Medical College of Philadelphia was nearby, she began taking courses there.

In theory, starting medical school was the realization of Addams' long-held dream. But in practice, although she earned good grades, she found her studies disappointingly dull. Perhaps no activity could have made her happy during that grief-stricken fall, but in truth, she had always been more interested in the idea of being a doctor than in the actual details of medical practice. On top of that, she found it difficult to combine her studies with the full-time task of being Anna's companion: socializing with her at home and going about with her to a round of parties and cultural events. It was a killing schedule, and when Addams was felled by back pain and general fatigue that winter, she dropped out of medical school—never to return.

Another longtime dream was abandoned a few months later. Early in the fall of 1882, Addams went to Northampton, Massachusetts, in order to take the entrance exams for Smith College. While she was there, she received a letter from her sister Alice in Iowa, where Harry had established his practice. Alice reported that her husband was prepared to perform a new type of operation on Addams that could cure her back problems. Closing the door on Smith (forever, as it turned out), Addams left for Iowa immediately. Harry went ahead with the operation, and for the next six months, Addams remained flat on her back in the Haldemans' house, immobilized by a cast. When it was all over, Harry pronounced the operation a success, and Addams agreed that she felt better. Some historians have questioned whether the procedure was actually helpful because Addams continued to have periods of ill health the rest of her life. But relatively few of these episodes involved back trouble, so perhaps the surgery was as effective as Harry claimed.

By the time Addams returned to Cedarville after the operation, two discarded dreams lay behind her: Smith College and a career in medicine. It is also possible that the operation may have closed another door in her life. People within Addams' family have suggested that one of the reasons she never married was because her back surgery left her unable to bear children. The operation may indeed have made pregnancy impossible or inadvisable for her, although there is no evidence that that was the case. But it would be hard to point to anything Addams said or did—even before the operation—that suggested she was interested in getting married.

There was a powerful context for Addams' disinclination to marry. During the 1870s and 1880s, young women like her were for the first time in American history being admitted to higher education in significant numbers. But they knew that if they used their education to build professional careers, it would be nearly impossible for them to fulfill their duties as wives according to the expectations of society (and most husbands). As Addams herself explained later in her life, "Women could not fulfill the two functions of profession and home-making . . . until public opinion tolerated the double role."

So, this was the choice that female college graduates like Addams faced: They could get married or they could have professional careers, but they could not count on doing both. Weighing the options, half the college women of Addams' generation—an unprecedented proportion—chose to remain single. In Addams' case, it does not seem to have been a great sacrifice. But even if it had, she might still have chosen the same course because of her drive to make her mark in the world—to perform some important service to society.

However strong Addams' drive to do something worthwhile, she still lacked direction. So, once again, she settled into a life focused on ministering to Anna's needs and helping to resolve family crises, including her brother Weber's increasing mental problems. Finally, in August 1883, feeling the need for a "radical change," she reported to Ellen Starr: "I have accepted the advice given to every exhausted American, 'go abroad.'" Shortly thereafter, Addams set sail for Europe with her stepmother and four other women, two of them family members.

For the next two years, they roamed the continent in search of culture and picturesque scenery, traveling from England to Italy and back again. At one level, reflected in Addams' cheerful letters to her family, she passed the time very pleasantly. At another level, expressed in her diaries and in occasional anguished letters to Ellen Starr, Addams felt she was getting nowhere. "I have been idle for two years just because I had not enough vitality to be anything else," she wrote Starr. "I have constantly lost confidence in myself, and have gained nothing and improved in nothing."

Besides chafing at her own uselessness, Addams was struggling to resolve her feelings about religion. She had always been put off by doctrinal rigidity; even as a child, she was deeply troubled when she heard some neighbors whispering that a much loved doctor who had recently passed away could not possibly be going to heaven because he had never joined the church. Later, at Rockford, while refusing to join Sill's ranks of missionaries, Addams struggled to define what she did believe in. At one point, she tested her faith by going three months without praying. She found that the most frightening part of the experiment was that it seemed to make no difference at all. Sometimes, she seemed to have come to a kind of resolution; at 19, she wrote Starr that her whole theology now boiled down to a simple creed: "Be sincere & don't fuss." But a few months later, she was back to agonizing, and the subject of religion continued to trouble her throughout her 20s.

Addams' running debate with herself did not seem to be based on any wish to smooth her own path into heaven. Rather, she felt that the right kind of religious faith would help her work more effectively to make life better here on Earth. As she explained to Starr: "If I could fix myself with my relations to God and the universe . . . I could use my faculties and energy so much better." Now and then, she got a glimpse of what she had in mind; for example, during her stay in Rome, she spent time studying the history of the early Christians, and she came to love them for their willingness to "share the common lot" and their "joyous simplicity." But how was a young college graduate from Cedarville to put those ideas into action? She was still not sure.

Addams returned to the United States in the spring of 1885—this time to Baltimore, where Anna was living while her son George went to medical school. Addams would later write that the next two years were the "nadir of my nervous depression and sense of maladjustment." Once again, she spent her time making social and cultural rounds with her stepmother, caring for whichever sibling was in trouble, and mediating the periodic family fights. Meanwhile, Anna was growing steadily more difficult, partly out of loneliness and partly from her worries about her sons—Harry, who was drinking heavily, and George, who was becoming more and more eccentric. At one point, Anna seems to have concluded that the solution to George's problems would be for Addams to marry him. Addams' steadfast refusal to do so became one more point of conflict in a contentious household.

Throughout these troubled years, what Addams must have found most disturbing was the realization that this unsatisfying way of life—based on tending to everyone's needs but her own—was not an aberration; it was exactly what society expected of the family spinster. If she did not deliver herself from this deadening routine, it could very well claim the rest of her life. Little by little, she began taking small steps toward independence; she did her first charity work—at a shelter for elderly black women—and in 1886, she became the youngest member of the Rockford board of trustees. Then, in December 1887, she set sail for a second trip to Europe—this time, with no family members along—just her two closest friends from Rockford: Ellen Starr and Sarah Anderson.

The three women spent most of their 18 months abroad doing the same kind of cultural tourism that Addams had engaged in with Anna on her earlier trip. In most respects, this trip was more rewarding because Starr and Anderson were more stimulating intellectual companions, and Addams herself was a more experienced and thoughtful traveler. Nevertheless, Addams became increasingly convinced that she must stop simply absorbing the past and preparing herself for some nameless something in the future. It was time to act. And she was beginning to think she knew how.

Before leaving home, Addams had read a magazine article about a new venture in cross-class understanding called Toynbee Hall. Canon Samuel Barnett, an Anglican clergyman, had established this "settlement house" in the slums of London's East End and invited a group of young university graduates to live there. Using Toynbee Hall as a base, these privileged young men were working to establish friendly relations with the neighbors while providing them with cultural and educational opportunities that would not have been available to them otherwise.

Addams must have mulled over the article for months, but during her final months in Europe, her ideas became clearer. As she later described it, she "gradually became convinced that it would be a good thing to rent a house in a part of the city where many primitive and actual needs are found." But instead of staffing her house with men, as Toynbee Hall did, she would seek out young women who, like herself "had been given over too exclusively to study" and who could benefit from a chance to "learn of life from life itself."

One night during the final weeks of the trip, Addams hesitantly broached her idea to Starr. When Starr said that she not only loved the idea but that she wanted to be part of it, Addams felt that a great hurdle had been leaped. Just a few weeks later, Addams, Starr, and Anderson were in London visiting Toynbee Hall. The settlement was inspiring and so was the ferment of social reform then under way in London. More clearly than ever before, Addams sensed how Christian values could be linked to the pursuit of social justice. Sailing back to America in the summer of 1888 and happily thinking over her plans, Addams recognized that many obstacles lay ahead. But she was convinced that "the period of mere passive receptivity had come to an end."

Becoming Saint Jane

Before Addams and Starr even reached home, they agreed that their settlement would be established in Chicago. So, in January 1889, they rented an apartment there and set out to make their dream a reality. There were practical reasons for choosing Chicago: It was the closest large city to Cedarville, and Starr had been teaching there for some time. But it was more than a convenient location; in many ways, it was America's quintessential industrial metropolis. After nearly being wiped out by the Great Fire of 1871, the city had bounced back more boisterous than ever. By 1889, when Addams and Starr arrived to look for a settlement location, Chicago had re-established itself as a city of clattering railroads, vast warehouses, the famous Stockyards, huge factories, and humming financial markets. The city's population had surged since the fire, rising in 20 years from 300,000 to 1 million. By 1910, it would hit 2 million.

In Chicago, as in many other American cities during these years, a handful of industrialists were amassing huge fortunes while hundreds of thousands of their employees were earning barely enough to feed their families. American labor leaders had struggled for years to build a workers' movement strong enough to combat these inequities. Factory owners ferociously opposed their efforts, and because the laws and the courts strongly favored capital over labor, few unions managed to last very long. Nevertheless, throughout the late 19th century, there were periodic explosions of working-class militance that sent shock waves around the country.

One of the most famous of these episodes was the Haymarket Affair—so called because it took place at an anarchist rally in 1886 in Chicago's Haymarket Square. It happened during a tempestuous week, when labor demands for the eight-hour day sprang up across the country, inspiring at least 350,000 workers to walk off their jobs. Chicago was hit harder than any other city, with about 30,000 workers out on strike and another 30,000 joining them after work for marches and demonstrations. The protests went on for days, and in a skirmish at one strike location on May 3, two workers were shot by the police. The anarchists were only one group among many involved in these events, but the movement had gained international notoriety because some of its adherents were committed to political assassination; just five years earlier, one had managed to kill the Russian czar. Accordingly, when the anarchists scheduled a rally in Haymarket Square on May 4 to protest the killing of the strikers the previous day, the gathering drew a sizable police presence.

The event was peaceable, the night was drizzly, and people had already started to leave when the police marched out into the square, demanding that the meeting be shut down. Suddenly, a bomb exploded right in the midst of the advancing police. In response, the jittery police opened fire directly into the crowd. By the time the shooting stopped, 50 police and an unknown number of bystanders had been wounded, and eight policemen lay dead. In addition, at least four civilians died later of their wounds. Nearly all the injuries had been caused by the gunfire, but it was the bomb that captured the public imagination. A spasm of fear swept across the country, and in Chicago, the hostility to anarchists approached hysteria. Although no individual was actually shown to have thrown the bomb, hundreds of anarchists—most of them foreign-born—were rounded up, and eight (six of them foreign-born) were indicted for murder.

This furor seared into the public mind an association between foreign birth and terrorism, and for generations thereafter, law-abiding immigrants would periodically find themselves tarred with the same brush. Such feelings were common in many American communities, but they had particular implications for Chicago's social fabric because immigrants were so vital to the city's welfare. They had played a major role in Chicago's economic expansion, and so huge were their numbers that by the time Addams arrived in 1889, immigrants and their children represented more than three-quarters of the city's population.

The ethnic groups that had come to Chicago the earliest—such as the Germans and the Irish—had managed to climb a few rungs up the economic ladder by 1889, but the newer arrivals—especially the Italians and the Jews—were still at the bottom. As a result, they endured all the worst aspects of industrial labor in late 19th century America: dangerous working conditions, low wages, long hours, and sporadic unemployment. In addition, because the cheapest housing was close to the factories, most of the city's immigrants had to live in the same grim industrial districts where they worked.

Beyond Chicago's prosperous central business district stood blocks and blocks of industrial slums that contained both the factories that gave the immigrants their jobs and the broken-down tenements where they lived. A British journalist visiting the city a few years after Addams arrived described Chicago's slum neighborhoods this way: "Street stretches beyond street of little houses, mostly wooden, begrimed with soot, rotting, falling to pieces. The pathways are of rickety and worm-eaten planks. . . . The streets are quagmires of black mud."

This is the world that Addams and Starr entered when they set out to find a place to establish their settlement. From January to

May 1889, they prowled Chicago's immigrant districts, guided by a variety of new acquaintances who volunteered to show them around. Meanwhile, Addams was also making the rounds of privileged Chicago to spread the word about her project. She gave speeches and press interviews, attended luncheons and teas and dinner parties, visited churches and missions and women's clubs—tirelessly describing her plan. Starr even wrote a friend: "Jane thirsts very much for the anarchists. She is going to hunt up their Sunday schools."

Addams proved to be a persuasive campaigner, particularly when she made it clear that she was seeking moral support and volunteers for the settlement but not money. (She planned to cover the initial expenses out of the money she had inherited from her father.) One mark of her effectiveness is the fact that the most influential women's group in the city, the Chicago Woman's Club, embraced the project, allowing her to make several appeals for volunteers at the club and commending her work to the membership.

How did Addams make so many converts? For one thing, she had a way of speaking that somehow combined passion for her subject with a gentle nonthreatening manner. Her appearance was also reassuring. One admirer described her as "a frail sensitive girl . . . anything but the reforming extremist type." As for her message, her emphasis on cross-class understanding spoke to the many Chicagoans who were troubled about the social divisions they saw in their city. Furthermore, at a time when charitable work was too often associated with an attitude of condescension toward the poor, she went out of her way to insist that the new program would do as much for the settlement workers as for those they served. This message appealed strongly to the type of young women Addams hoped to attract as volunteers.

It must be acknowledged that the idea of mutual benefit did not communicate itself very clearly to the press. Reporters were fascinated by the fact that a privileged young woman like Addams was planning to make her home in an immigrant slum. Trying to make sense of the unlikely story, the press insisted on portraying Addams as a selfless martyr who was sacrificing her own comfort and pleasure for the good of the poor. Anyone who knew her understood very well that she got much more pleasure from the work she was doing than from making the social rounds. But it was a picturesque version of the truth, and it probably helped to bring good will to the project.

Throughout these months of publicizing their plans, Addams and Starr also continued to look for a place to establish their settlement. At last, in May 1889, they found what they had been looking for: a handsome old house on Halsted Street, located in the 19th Ward on the city's Near West Side. Once prosperously middle class, the neighborhood had been swallowed up by factories and tenements. The house, too, was sadly run down, with a saloon and a furniture factory on the ground floor. But it was spacious and, to Addams and Starr, full of potential. Furthermore, it was located in exactly the kind of immigrant district the women had been seeking. On investigating, they learned that the house had been built in 1856 by a wealthy businessman, Charles Hull, and had recently been inherited by his cousin and secretary, Helen Culver. Within weeks, Addams arranged to rent the entire second floor as well as one large room downstairs.

Over the summer, while the house was being renovated, Addams went home to Cedarville to report on her project. Her sisters were delighted with her news, but to her stepmother, Addams' plan represented only a heartless abandonment of her family duties. Anna remained opposed to the project for the rest of her life and always refused to support it financially. We can recognize Addams' progress in becoming her own woman when we observe that instead of deferring to her stepmother as she might once have done, she simply took note of her disapproval and proceeded with the project exactly as she had planned. A few months earlier, Addams had written her sister Alice: "There's power in me, and will to dominate which I must exercise, they will hurt me else." For years, she had lived her life according to other people's expectations, now she was determined to chart her own course.

On September 18, 1889, just a few days after Addams' 29th birthday, she and Starr moved into their new quarters. Savoring the significance of the occasion, Addams wrote later: "Probably no young matron ever placed her own things in her own house with more pleasure than that with which we first furnished Hull-House." In the years ahead, she would travel widely in the United States and around the world. And as she aged, she would often spend extended periods of time living elsewhere with friends. But for the rest of her life, Halsted Street would be her emotional home.

Once the settlement was open, it was time to launch their program. But how does one appeal to people who are poor, overworked, uneasy with strangers, and uncertain about their English? Curiosity brought in a few visitors, but more would be needed to build a real presence in the neighborhood. Accordingly, Addams started paying neighborly visits on the women who lived nearby. She said that the experience was "sad and amusing, humbling and inspiring, but always genuine and never wearisome."

Observing these women's lives, and hearing heart-breaking tales of children left alone while their mothers were working, Addams and Starr concluded that their first formal offering should be a kindergarten. Within a month, two volunteers were caring for 24 children every morning, and 70 more children were on the waiting list. One program led to the next. As older children began stopping in to see what was happening, Addams and Starr organized three clubs for them. The kindergarten mothers formed a women's group, and attendance at the social and cultural evenings increased steadily.

In May 1890, eight months after they opened, Addams and Starr received a welcome vote of confidence: Charles Hull's cousin agreed to give them the whole house on Halsted Street, rent-free, for the next four years. From then on, their project had a name: Hull-House. Wryly linking the name change to the free rent, Starr wrote to a friend: "Connect the two facts in any delicate way that your refined imagination suggests. It was growing inconvenient not to have a name, &—it is very convenient to have four years rent."

With room to grow, the program expanded rapidly. Addams and Starr developed a variety of activities for young working people, ranging from concerts and dances to reading clubs and art lessons. Women's activities also increased. The men of the neighborhood were the wariest, but even they gradually began to appear, especially for evenings of ethnic culture or political discussion. Addams and Starr each ran a few of the activities themselves and recruited dozens of volunteers to provide the rest of the program. The indefatigable Mary Keyser, who had been with them from the start, did the housekeeping.

By the end of its second year, the Hull-House program was outgrowing the whole building. Thanks to skillful cultivation by Addams, a local merchant gave Hull-House its first major financial donation: $5,000 for a new art building. The Butler Building (named for the donor) was constructed on a nearby lot that Addams persuaded Culver to let them use rent-free. Soon, programs were humming in every available space, and about 75 volunteers were coming in from outside to help with the program. Meanwhile, four more young women came to live at Hull-House as "residents."

Throughout this heady period, the only thing that did not improve was the relationship between Addams and Starr. In their younger years, their relationship had thrived on long separations, short visits, occasional trips, and heartfelt correspondence. Starr had helped Addams get Hull-House launched, and after it opened, she taught several classes while also enlivening the settlement with her enthusiasm and high ideals. But as Hull-House evolved from a brave experiment to a flourishing institution, Starr became increasingly dissatisfied. This place was Addams' dream, not hers, and she began to feel the need for a consuming passion of her own. Also, on a personal level, as Addams' fame increased and her circle of friends widened, Starr felt more and more dispensable. She confided to a friend that it was sometimes disheartening to feel that Addams' love for her now included the whole 19th Ward. Starr continued to live at Hull-House until the 1920s, and she and Addams remained friends for life, but their years of intimate association were over.

Meanwhile, someone new had entered Addams' life. Mary Rozet Smith came to Hull-House at the age of 20 to help run the kindergarten. Wealthy and beautiful, she seems to have charmed everyone who encountered her; Hull-House resident Alice

Hamilton called her "the most universally beloved person" she had ever met. Starting in 1890, Smith did a variety of volunteer jobs at Hull-House and became one of its most generous donors. More importantly, as her relationship with Addams flowered, she made Addams' comfort and happiness her career.

Were Smith and Addams lovers in the 21st-century sense of the word? It is impossible to know. During the late 19th century, female friendships were often very emotional and demonstrative. For example, it was not unusual for heterosexual women who were close friends to address each other in romantic terms, to hug and kiss each other, and to sleep in the same bed. Perhaps this was the extent of Addams' intimacy with Smith, or perhaps it went further. But whatever their physical relationship, they were emotional partners for more than 40 years. Their friendship was, as Addams' nephew James Linn observed, "the highest and clearest note in the music of Jane Addams' personal life."

Over the next two decades, with Mary Smith's support, Addams expanded Hull-House until it filled an entire city block, bustling every day with residents, volunteers, and flocks of visitors. Presiding over this whirlwind was Addams herself, modestly titled "head resident" but widely recognized as the emotional heart of everything that happened there. Indeed, she attracted such rapt admiration in some circles that her fellow residents sometimes referred to her as "Saint Jane," gently poking fun at her sanctified image.

Saint or not, what Addams achieved at Hull-House during these years was remarkable. This was not the first settlement in the United States; two others also inspired by Toynbee Hall had opened slightly earlier in New York City. Furthermore, in the 20 years after Hull-House opened, several hundred more settlements were established in cities all around the United States, so by the early 1900s, it was possible to speak of a settlement movement. Nevertheless, Hull-House stood out from the rest because of its size and its imaginative energy. This is the subject of the next chapter: how, through the development of Hull-House, Addams sought to enrich the lives of her new neighbors in the 19th Ward.

2

Reaching Out
to the Neighbors

Imagine you are standing at the corner of Halsted and Polk streets in Chicago on a wintry night in 1894. The dark streets are piled high with grimy snow, the nearby factories stand silent in the shadows, and lights glimmer fitfully in the ramshackle houses up and down the street. But on the corner in front of you stands a cluster of buildings ablaze with life. This is Hull-House.

Snatches of music spill into the street as doors open and close. Through the lighted windows of the central building you can see pictures on the walls, shelves full of books, and humming activity in every room. Tonight, people from the neighborhood are attending classes on Dante, Bohemian history, cooking, English literature, and letter writing. There is a group reading French, and one of the girls' clubs is having its weekly meeting. Some German families are having a party upstairs while a group of Italians is gathered in the downstairs parlor. Hull-House is the embodiment of Addams' early ambition to build a settlement in an immigrant district and to make it "easily accessible, ample in space, hospitable and tolerant in spirit."

Hull-House may have begun as a dream in Jane Addams' head, but by its fifth anniversary in 1894, it had developed into a living, breathing institution—imitated by a growing number of settlements around the country and famous around the world. House resident Alice Hamilton used to say that visitors came to Chicago to see just three things: the University of Chicago, the Stockyards, and Hull-House. But for the people who lived in the 19th Ward, the settlement was something more important than a tourist attraction. As a girl who grew up nearby explained, it was an "oasis." It was "the university, the opera house, the theater, the concert and lecture hall, the gymnasium, the library, the clubhouse of the neighborhood."

Enriching the Neighbors' Lives

When Addams first began to explore the 19th Ward, one of the things that struck her most forcefully was how bleak life was for her immigrant neighbors, who were exiled from their own culture and excluded from the best features of their new country. She hoped that Hull-House could provide the cultural stimulation they were lacking, and at the same time draw them into social fellowship. "If it is natural to feed the hungry and care for the sick," she wrote, "it is certainly natural to give pleasure to the young, comfort to the aged, and to minister to the deep-seated craving for social intercourse that all men feel."

Addams hated to hear Hull-House described as a social laboratory; she thought of it as "something much more human and spontaneous than such a phrase connotes." But she did see it as a testing place for American values. If the words of Jefferson and Lincoln meant anything, then Americans of different classes had to be able to communicate with each other and to learn from each other. Hull-House existed to foster this exchange—to "socialize democracy," as Addams put it—by building bridges between the privileged settlement workers and their poor immigrant neighbors, by supporting whatever social and cultural activities were already available, and by creating new opportunities based on the settlement workers' own education and experience. In this way, Hull-House might draw its neighbors more fully into the circle of American society and help them live richer, more satisfying lives.

It may seem strange, in such a poor neighborhood, that Addams chose initially to focus on language classes and social clubs rather than wage levels and mortality rates. It was not that she was unaware of the problems around her. "It seems sometimes as if we ought to drop everything else," she said, "and merely feed people, clothe people, [and] clean their houses, that they may live better." On another occasion, she wrote her stepbrother: "One is so overpowered by the misery . . . of so large a number of city people that the wonder is that conscientious people can let it alone." In future years Addams would address this kind of deprivation more directly. But at first, she did choose to "let it alone"—apparently convinced that poverty and hard work could destroy the soul as well as the body and that Hull-House's best chance to make a contribution would be by ministering to its neighbors' souls through social and cultural programs.

Designing these social and cultural programs was not a simple undertaking because the neighborhood contained so many different nationalities—19 of them, according to a ward census in 1895. There were large numbers of Bohemians as well as Germans, Italians, Greeks, and Russian Jews. Summing up the programs that Hull-House offered this diverse community, Addams explained that they had come "from no preconceived notion of what a Social Settlement should be, but . . . increased gradually on demand." For example, to the Bohemians, Hull-House offered the holiday festivities they said they missed from the Old Country. Many of the German immigrants felt out of touch with their American-born children, so for them, the settlement provided family-style evenings, which perpetuated their culture and at the same time helped to ease the generation gap.

The Hull-House residents met a number of older neighbors who were well-educated but living in straitened circumstances— either because of financial setbacks or simply because they were immigrants. For these people, the settlement's clubs and classes represented an opportunity to revive interests and talents they had given up hope of ever using again. Then there were adults who had had relatively little formal schooling but who welcomed the chance to flex their mental muscles. And there were the young people, many of whom gained at Hull-House their first dreams of reaching beyond the limits of their immediate circumstances. All in all, by the time of Hull-House's fifth anniversary in 1894, the settlement was attracting several hundred participants every week.

Building an Institution

As the Hull-House program expanded, so did the staff and the physical plant—from Addams and Ellen Starr in a few rooms in 1889 to several dozen residents and more than a hundred volunteers in a campus filled with interconnected buildings by 1910.

The residents—most of them women—played a particularly important role in the development of Hull-House as an institution. They included Florence Kelley, a dedicated reformer and labor activist and later the founding director of the National Consumers' League; Julia Lathrop, a leading social worker who in 1912 became the first head of the U.S. Children's Bureau; Alice Hamilton, a pioneer in the field of occupational medicine; Edith Abbott, the first female dean of an American graduate school (the School of Social Service Administration at the University of Chicago); her sister Grace Abbott, who led the Immigrants Protective League during her Chicago years and later succeeded Julia Lathrop as head of the U.S. Children's Bureau; Alzina Stevens, an early union leader with the Knights of Labor and the first probation officer of the Cook County Juvenile Court; Sophonisba Breckinridge, the first female graduate of the University of Chicago's law school and an important figure in social work education; and Mary Kenney, the first woman to serve as a full-time organizer for the American Federation of Labor.

To supplement the efforts of the residents, scores of volunteers—also mostly women—came in regularly to help with the Hull-House program. Some of these volunteers found the environment too depressing and dropped out after a few visits. (One complained that the neighborhood air was bad for her carriage horses.) Others melted away when Addams began speaking out on such controversial topics as immigrants' rights. But a remarkable number remained loyal and helpful for decades, contributing thousands of hours to the settlement every year.

Many of these volunteers were also financial donors. With their backing and that of other supporters, Addams worked tirelessly to organize the continual renovations and construction needed to house the growing institution. Gradually, new buildings filled the Hull-House block on Halsted Street—each one connected to the others by a maze of corridors and passageways. The Butler Building went up in 1891, containing an art gallery, a branch of the Chicago Public Library, and a studio. Two years later came the coffeehouse and the gymnasium. The drawing room in the main house was also renovated at this time to make a lecture hall. In subsequent years Addams found donors for a children's building, a theater, a Woman's Club building, a music school, a co-operative apartment house for working women, and a home across the street for male residents. As the physical campus took shape, so did the dream. As Addams said, the settlement's buildings "clothed in brick and mortar and made visible to the world that which we were trying to do."

Hull-House was indeed impressive from the outside, but what neighbors especially remembered about it in later years was the inside. As soon as Addams moved in, she filled the building with family antiques, fine carpets, reproductions of famous paintings, and curios from her travels. She believed that these handsome interiors would help local people learn to appreciate beautiful things. They would also convey Hull-House's social message: that her immigrant neighbors were worthy of the very best she had. The atmosphere she created did indeed make a profound impression on the people who came there. One local girl recalled: "At Hull-House, everything was beautiful. Clean, fresh, never slipshod or second-rate."

Despite the fine furnishings, local people seem to have felt comfortable at Hull-House. One man from the neighborhood says that the first time he went there, as a teenager, "the door was open and I walked in." After he sat in the front room for a while, Addams happened by. She offered him a magazine that she thought he might enjoy and urged him to come back often. So many people responded to this welcoming atmosphere that "toting" visitors—greeting them, showing them around, helping them find what they were looking for—became a regular assignment for Hull-House residents. But the most important aspect of Hull-House's appeal was not its attractiveness or its friendliness but something more profound: "You walked through the door," says a neighbor, "and things happened."

In 1897, a Hull-House resident wrote an account of a typical day at the settlement. It began about 6 a.m., when the first parent dropped a baby off at the nursery. By 7:30 a.m., the coffeehouse was bustling, with House residents coming in for breakfast and neighbors stopping by for a cup of coffee or some fresh-baked bread. Soon, the office across the courtyard began to fill with people looking for work or seeking temporary assistance, and toddlers' voices could be heard in the kindergarten. About 9 a.m., the visiting nurse left for her rounds in the neighborhood, and Hull-House residents who worked elsewhere during the day headed off for their jobs. In the afternoon, one could hear the chatter of voices from a Woman's Club meeting in Bowen Hall, the laughter of the girls' basketball team practicing in the gymnasium, and the music of the children's chorus rehearsing for a concert. At 6 p.m., the residents ate dinner together, after which "a riot of young people" bustled in, heading for the evening's classes, rehearsals, sports, and club meetings. Finally, around midnight, the whole complex settled down for the night.

Sharing the Arts

From the day Hull-House first opened its doors in 1889, arts activities were a major part of the program. Addams was convinced that the arts provided an avenue for expressing the highest and best that people had in them. She did believe that privileged young college graduates sometimes allowed cultural pursuits to insulate them from the essential task of experiencing "life as it is." But in a neighborhood like the 19th Ward, where people were battered day in and day out by "life as it is," the arts provided exactly what they needed: understanding, beauty, delight, and inspiration. Ellen Starr had a particularly deep interest in broadening access to the arts, and she played a major role in developing the arts program at Hull-House.

During the 1890s, working-class people had little access to formal arts activities. Concerts and plays and lessons were too expensive, while museums were few and located far from poor neighborhoods. Many reformers of the period embraced the concept that art should be available to all, but few put the idea into practice as vigorously as Hull-House. This was the goal: to ensure that, as Addams put it, the benefits of the arts would be "incorporated into our common life and have free mobility through all elements of society."

Addams and Starr took their first plunge when they invited some of the Italian women in the neighborhood to come and hear the first chapter of George Eliot's novel *Romola* (set in Florence) read aloud in Italian. After the reading, the group had coffee and looked at stereopticon slides of Florentine art. It must have struck some of the guests as an odd way to spend an evening, but the very rarity of such an event—combined with the women's curiosity about the house—ensured a good turnout. As the group continued to meet each week to hear another chapter, Addams and Starr personalized the proceedings by inviting two different members each week to come early and have dinner with them and then help wash the dishes and clear the table for the evening's meeting.

The arts program expanded steadily in the years that followed. The settlement's first picture exhibit attracted more than 4,000 people in the first 10 days—partly because the gallery stayed open late in the evening (as did the library) to accommodate working people's hours. From then on, Hull-House presented two or three major exhibits a year—each one drawing large crowds and concluding with mass participation in the vote for favorite painting. The settlement also established a lending library of pictures so the neighbors could have works of art to enjoy at home.

Hull-House encouraged its neighbors to make art as well as look at it. Several local artists were provided with studio space in exchange for giving classes in painting. Two residents began teaching crafts at the settlement, and Starr studied bookbinding so she could pass that skill on to her students. The culmination of all this activity was a display of everyone's artwork once a year in a big well-attended exhibition.

Meanwhile, on the musical front, Hull-House developed two choruses—one for adults and one for children—and a regular schedule of free concerts on Sunday afternoons. There was also a large music school, where participants were taught to compose music as well as to perform. Hull-House residents frequently suffered the disappointment of watching gifted young musicians leave school for jobs which, as Addams wrote, "so sap their vitality that they cannot carry on serious study in the scanty hours outside factory work." But the joyous participation in the Christmas music recital every year made clear that many lives were being enriched by the Hull-House program.

Perhaps the settlement's greatest innovation in the arts was its theater program. At the time, opportunities to see live theater outside New York City were almost entirely confined to large downtown auditoriums. The settlement broke new ground by establishing its own troupe—the Hull-House Players—and presenting serious drama in its own small auditorium. This initiative was one of America's very first "little theaters" and the spiritual ancestor of the small theater companies that exist all over the United States today.

When Hull-House's theater program first began, Addams thought of it primarily as an opportunity for participants to learn poise and diction. (This did happen; one local woman said that her whole life was changed when acting in plays at Hull-House cured her of her stutter.) But as the program developed, Addams began to take more seriously the impact of the plays themselves—their capacity to show fundamental emotions at work in a way that captured the imagination of a broad democratic audience.

The democratic significance of the theatrical experience was enhanced because Hull-House often produced plays drawn from the neighbors' own heritage. A Chicago reviewer described attending a production of *Odysseus* in an auditorium "packed too closely for comfort with the most cosmopolitan crowd I have ever seen." For a while, he wrote, "all distinctions were forgotten—the millennium was here. . . . We were all brothers and sisters again." As for the Greek actors, after participating in this noble expression of their own culture, "they seemed to feel that they had come into their own. They were set right at last in our eyes."

Addams has sometimes been accused of trying to "Americanize" her immigrant neighbors. There were certainly times when her comments about their "simplicity" sounded condescending. And she did tend to define a person of good taste as someone who shared her reverence for the major achievements of western European civilization. But she was open to new experience, and within a few years of moving to Hull-House, she became convinced that part of the settlement's mission must be to help her neighbors preserve their own cultural traditions.

The production of *Odysseus* mentioned above was just one example of the many ways that Hull-House celebrated its neighbors' culture. The settlement held a huge St. Patrick's Day dance every year, celebrated Italian patriot Mazzini's birthday with the Society of Young Italy, encouraged its Russian neighbors to present plays in Russian, helped Mexicans in the neighborhood build a small business creating traditional pottery, put on the first production in North America of Sophocles' *Ajax* (in Greek), and preserved and performed many folk songs that had never before been written down.

Of all the Old World traditions that Addams saw carried on around her, she particularly valued the crafts practiced by women in the neighborhood: weaving, spinning, embroidering, and lace-making. She recognized that such accomplishments might receive a cold welcome in the United States, where people seemed to prefer what was new and machine-made. She also knew that many of these women's American-born children were embarrassed to see their mothers clinging to the "old ways." But Addams herself treasured these traditional female arts—both for their beauty and for the link they provided to generations of human history.

This enthusiasm gave rise in 1900 to a new Hull-House project: the Labor Museum, in which neighborhood women demonstrated their traditional crafts. Within a few years, three women were working regularly in the "shops," with the cost of the program offset by sales of the fabric they wove. Seeing these women at work, thought Addams, was instructive for everyone who visited the museum. As for the women themselves, it preserved their ancient skills, gave them a chance to show off their expertise to people who appreciated it, and allowed them to appear before their children, for once, as respected experts rather than ignorant "greenhorns."

Education Tailored to the Neighborhood

Although Addams loved the Labor Museum and all the other traditional activities at Hull-House, she knew very well that her neighbors' path to a better life in the United States lay primarily through education, not through ancient crafts. Like many progressives, she had an almost mystical faith in the power of education—not only because of its power to open occupational doors but also because she believed it was the best way to help each individual achieve all that was in him or her.

Addams also agreed with philosopher John Dewey that education was the most promising way to move the country beyond its current social divisions toward a more cohesive whole. Many of their contemporaries were convinced that education should achieve this goal simply by training immigrants to adapt to America's Anglo-Saxon way of life. Addams and Dewey resolutely opposed that idea. In a democracy, said Dewey, true education involved "assimilation to one another" rather than forcing every newcomer to assimilate to "Anglo-Saxonism."

In this context, it is interesting to speculate about the emphasis Addams placed on observing national traditions at Hull-House—a custom that would seem to foster separatism rather than unity. Historian Rivka Shpak Lissak is probably correct in suggesting that Addams saw this celebration of national identity as an intermediate step that was designed to give her neighbors' cultural practices the respect they deserved at a time when most Americans had little use for them. However, Addams clearly hoped that, in the long run, the immigrants would be integrated into a more inclusive American society—one that they themselves would help to shape.

Addams was certain that education had the potential to play a vital role in helping immigrants move toward this larger role in American society. But she knew there were significant barriers that kept education from fulfilling its promise. For example, she asked, who currently benefitted from the rich resources of the nation's colleges and universities? Only a privileged few. Here was a situation, she thought, in which settlements like Hull-House could make a difference. They could "bring into the circle of knowledge and fuller life, men and women who might otherwise be left outside."

On her visit to England in 1887, Addams had been impressed by a new approach to education called the college extension course. Programs like this gave workers access to college-level work but in accessible community locations. Such an approach was almost unknown in the United States, so Hull-House broke new ground when it launched its own college extension program in 1891. The University of Chicago opened soon afterward, and from then on, Addams recruited most of the settlement's college extension teachers from there.

Within a few years, Hull-House was offering 35 courses a semester to about 200 students, most of whom lived in the neighborhood. The curriculum covered topics such as Roman history, music, German, Shakespeare, rhetoric, drawing, and mathematics. The majority of students were young men hoping to build professional careers, but there were also some factory workers eager for an intellectual challenge as well as more educated people who welcomed an opportunity to continue their studies.

Another pioneering effort at democratizing higher learning began when Addams launched a working women's summer school at her alma mater, Rockford College. Each summer, 90 women—most of them immigrants or the daughters of immigrants—followed their college extension work at Hull-House with a two- or four-week stay at Rockford. The students paid $2 a week; Addams, Starr, and other volunteers taught the courses; the college donated the use of the buildings; and Addams found contributors to cover the rest of the expenses. The Rockford Summer School is believed to have been the first program in which an American educational institution provided a residential college experience for working women.

By the early 1900s, Hull-House had established itself as a leader in the move to give immigrant workers access to higher education. But even while the program was expanding, Addams was starting to ask herself whether it was fully meeting her neighbors' educational needs. The college courses were clearly useful to some local people, but as she observed, "they leave quite untouched the great mass of the factory population." Look at the dutiful hardworking lives the men lead, said Addams. "They give all their wages to their wives, they have a vague pride in their superior children, but they grow prematurely old and stiff in all their muscles, and become more and more taciturn."

What should Hull-House be doing for these men—and for their wives, many of whom were factory workers themselves? It should not be focusing simply on reproducing "the college type of culture." Instead, it should base its educational program on the realities of life in the 19th Ward, including the fact that the typical worker—male or female—had little hope of advancing to a professional career. To meet this wider need, Hull-House began offering such practical courses as English, cooking, dressmaking, and training in various trades. It also added some very basic introductory courses on such topics as government and American history.

Yet Addams was still dissatisfied. Whatever Hull-House's educational efforts, she knew that the majority of her neighbors would spend most of their lives doing grueling repetitive work, functioning as tiny cogs in the vast machinery of American industry. What could be done to make their lives more satisfying? She conceived the idea that they might take more pride in their work—and hence in themselves—if they understood more about the overall process of which they were a part. The Labor Museum was an early effort in this direction; to Addams, the garment factories around the 19th Ward were the direct descendants of the ancient needlework that the neighborhood women had done in the Old Country. She was convinced that if garment workers could visualize the whole historical development of their industry and if they understood its current workings better, they would gain a new appreciation of their own "industrial and social value."

Addams continued to think and write about this idea for the rest of her life. It was never fully fleshed out in terms of actual courses, but the mere process of giving so much thought to her neighbors' difficult work lives contributed to a gradual transition in the way she perceived the Hull-House mission. Social, artistic, and educational activities would always be a major part of the settlement program. But over time, Addams' sympathetic response to the realities of life in the 19th Ward raised searching new questions in her mind about how Hull-House could best serve its neighbors. What should it be doing about their more basic needs? Where did simple assistance come into the picture?

Helping People in Need

Addams always shied away from the term *charity* because she associated it with the kind of patronizing handout that elevated the donor and demeaned the recipient. She also associated it with the most hopeless and destitute segment of urban society. In a formulation that came perilously close to the Victorian distinction between the "worthy" and "unworthy" poor, Addams often stressed the fact that her neighbors were not candidates for charity because they were self-respecting working people. They might lead hard lives, but they did not want "philanthropy" (another word she disliked).

But there were more humane ways to provide assistance. Addams enormously admired the warmth with which her neighbors helped each other. This relationship became her model, and as the settlement was irresistibly drawn into aiding people in need, Addams tried always to keep the interaction as human and direct as that of one neighbor helping another. For example, there is a Hull-House legend about the night she awoke to find a burglar climbing in her bedroom window. Instead of screaming, she asked him why he was there. When he said he was unemployed and his family was desperate, she said, "If you really want a job, come back tomorrow morning and I will help you find one." Then, as he turned back toward the window, she said, "Don't go out that way; you might fall. Let yourself out the front door."

Most neighbors did not, of course, announce their problems by climbing in the bedroom window. The local Italians came to Hull-House first for the social evenings. Then, once they were sure they were welcome, they began asking for help with various difficulties: lawsuits, family vendettas, sickness, wayward children, and language troubles. Other Hull-House participants followed suit, and Addams heard about more troubles as she made her social rounds in the neighborhood. Soon, she and other Hull-House residents were helping in a great variety of ways, including babysitting, nursing the sick, getting compensation for injured workers, preparing the dead for burial, washing new babies, sheltering women from their abusive husbands, visiting relatives in prison, retrieving furniture after it had been repossessed, and getting widows their pensions.

Helping the neighbors became a much more serious undertaking when the city was hit by a devastating depression in the fall of 1893. The World Columbian Exposition of 1893 had attracted huge crowds to Chicago, thus providing local people with jobs and drawing many more workers from around the country. Then the fair ended, leaving large numbers of people unemployed at exactly the same time that—by coincidence—the whole national economy went into a tailspin; by late fall, 100,000 Chicagoans had lost their jobs. The effect on the 19th Ward was horrendous. People began coming to Hull-House not just for social activities and culture but for jobs, rent money, and food. Starr wrote a friend: "We are sunk under a mass of the unemployed morning, noon, and night." The settlement began by allocating $100 a month to provide street-sweeping jobs. By the fall of 1893, it was spending $600 a month and still not meeting the need.

At the mayor's request, Addams served on a city committee that initiated a program of public jobs and meal tickets; it too was soon besieged with applicants. Meanwhile, making home visits in the Hull-House neighborhood, Addams encountered poverty beyond anything she had seen in previous years, compounded by people's fear of debt, their humiliation before their children, and their terror of starving to death. Addams recalled later that throughout this period, she was haunted by shame "that I should be comfortable in the midst of such distress." She was also assailed by a sense that everything she had tried to do at Hull-House was "futile and superficial." Perhaps the whole idea of living among the poor was just playacting, as long as the actual conditions of her life were so different from those of the people around her.

This dark winter marked the end of Addams' belief that Hull-House could serve its neighbors solely by concentrating on social and cultural programs. Reaching for new ideas, she began what she later called "the most serious economic reading I have ever done." She also sought out more inspirational sources, most notably the Russian writer and philosopher Leo Tolstoy. Born to great wealth, Count Tolstoy had decided as a young man that he could not live a life of luxury that depended on the toil of oppressed Russian peasants. He therefore gave up his fortune and retired to a small farm, where he spent the rest of his life living by his own labor. Addams turned repeatedly to Tolstoy's writing during the difficult winter of 1893–1894. And a few years later, when she was vacationing in Europe, she traveled to Russia to meet him.

The visit did not go particularly well. The great man showed little interest in Hull-House, teased Addams a bit about the fact that she was fashionably dressed, and expressed surprise that she drew part of her income from farm mortgages—in other words, from the labor of others. For Addams, who was used to being praised for her selflessness, even this gentle criticism must have stung a bit—particularly when it came from someone she admired so much. She promised herself that as soon as she returned to Chicago, she would make at least a gesture toward purifying her life: She would draw on her heritage as a miller's daughter and start baking her own bread every day.

Addams' resolve evaporated almost as soon as she got home. Besieged by all the usual demands on her time, she concluded that it would be perverse to put off her many obligations simply to tend to her own soul in the kitchen. The bread-baking plan was abandoned. Nevertheless, although Addams was unwilling to model her life on Tolstoy's, she never forgot the example he provided—of someone who chose to live every day according to his highest ideals of fellowship with the poor. During the next few years, shaken by the depression, moved by her neighbors' suffering, and stimulated by her visit to Tolstoy, Addams continued to brood over the challenges and pitfalls of what she called "the charitable relationship."

The problem of the charitable relationship was on many people's minds during these years. Over the previous century, numerous private agencies had grown up in every city to give aid to the poor. The result was a considerable overlap in services and some opportunity for fraud because it was possible for a single family to get assistance from several different agencies without their being aware of it. Critics of the system began calling for better coordination of charitable care. In addition, many asserted that assistance was being provided too freely, thus promoting dependency. It was much better, these critics argued, to break the cycle of poverty by helping the poor live more productive lives.

These concerns gave rise to what came to be known as "organized charity," an approach designed to systematize the provision of care to the poor. Typically, the core agency involved was a Charity Organization Society (COS), which served as a clearinghouse for private charitable services within a given city. Besides establishing a centralized list of recipients and fostering better administration in the various agencies, the most distinctive COS activity was its use of "scientific investigation" to determine why each applicant family was poor and what could be done to help them out of their poverty. At its best, this approach—which its supporters described as "organized love"—meant giving the families individual attention, wise counsel, and helpful referrals.

At its worst, it meant subjecting them to the intrusive visits of an outsider who sometimes seemed more interested in forcing them off the assistance rolls than in helping them improve their lives. The case against the COS method was put most memorably by poet John Boyle O'Reilly:

> The organized charity, scrimped and iced,
> In the name of a cautious statistical Christ.

Addams took a more favorable view of COS than O'Reilly. She recognized the value of good administration, and she admired Julia Lathrop, a longtime Hull-House resident who was active in the COS movement. Indeed, when Lathrop succeeded in getting a Bureau of Organized Charities established in Chicago in 1893, the young man appointed to run it became a Hull-House resident himself. But there was an important difference between the settlement's approach to serving the poor and that generally used by COS. Hull-House residents sought to build a continuing relationship with their neighbors, while agencies like COS rarely dealt with the poor except when they were in trouble.

To illustrate the value of the settlement approach, Addams described being invited to dinner by a family she had helped through a financial crisis two years earlier. The mother said she could not bear to have Addams remember her as she had been at that low point of her life; she said it was as if her guest had seen her only when she was misshapen with rheumatism. To Addams, this incident confirmed the settlement's wisdom in determining to know its neighbors "through all the varying conditions of life, to stand by when they are in distress, but by no means to drop intercourse with them when normal prosperity has returned."

One of the benefits of having a relationship that lasted through good times and bad, Addams thought, was the fact that when help was needed, the interaction could be more sympathetic and democratic than that between a COS charity visitor and a family applying for assistance. Crystallizing her ideas by putting them on paper, as she often did, Addams wrote an essay in 1899 entitled "The Subtle Problem of Charity," in which she described the quandaries faced by a charity visitor in dealing with one of her client families.

Showing some charity herself, Addams gave the young visitor credit for having misgivings about the method she had been trained to follow. For example, she described the woman's discomfort at having to focus so single-mindedly on the family's capacity to make money—even to the point of encouraging them to take their young son out of school and put him to work. The charity worker felt particularly awkward about making this demand because she herself had never been self-supporting; after all, observed Addams, "our democracy has taught us to apply our moral teaching all around." Looking at the interaction from the family's viewpoint, Addams described how difficult it was for them to square the visitor's apparent good intentions with her unwillingness to give them the help they obviously needed. And how unrealistic—even cruel—she sounded when she ignored their obligations to their friends and relatives and insisted that any money they earned must be kept for themselves.

This essay, although gently expressed, offered a powerful critique of an approach to charity that, in Addams' words, too often substituted "a theory of social conduct for the natural promptings of the heart." She continued to develop these ideas, and as her influence expanded in the early 20th century, she won increasing support for her conviction that the poor should be treated not with "kindly contempt" but with a sense of "democratic obligation."

Addams' dedication to building these sustained relationships with the poor helps to explain her conviction that she and her Hull-House colleagues had to live on Halsted Street as well as work there. "We need the thrust in the side," she said, "the lateral pressure which comes from living next door to poverty." That "thrust in the side" continually inspired Addams to broaden and deepen her view of the settlement mission. One day, as she and a neighbor stood watching the construction of yet another Hull-House building, Addams asked the woman if she thought they were spreading out too fast. "Oh no," the woman answered, "you can afford to spread out wide, you are so well planted in the mud." She was referring, in part, to the muddy street where they were standing. But she was also acknowledging the profound connection that Hull-House had managed to establish with the neighborhood it served.

Hull-House was not, of course, universally admired. There were conservatives who insisted that urban immigrants were too foreign or too poor or too ignorant to benefit from the settlement approach. And within the neighborhood, there were always plenty of people who remained uninterested in the programs offered or suspicious of an institution dominated by philanthropic Protestant women.

Even some progressives had their doubts about Hull-House. Writer Walter Lippmann found it very appealing as a utopian experiment, but he maintained that the "industrial forces" arrayed against it were too strong to make it a realistic model for replication. Just as a single planter could not end slavery by giving his own slaves their freedom, said Lippmann, so "Hull-House cannot remake Chicago. A few hundred lives can be changed, . . . for the rest it is a guide to the imagination." But in a sense, providing a guide to the imagination was precisely what Addams hoped to do at Hull-House. She knew as well as Lippmann that the settlement could not solve all the problems of Chicago or even of the 19th Ward. Nevertheless, as Lippmann suggested, "if Hull-House is unable to civilize Chicago, it at least shows Chicago and America what a civilization might be like."

3

Putting Democracy into Practice

By the mid-1890s, Jane Addams was increasingly focusing her attention on how to link her work at Hull-House more closely to her larger aspirations for American society. This broader emphasis coincided with a new stage in her own personal development. Addams had finally resolved the religious uncertainties of her younger years. She continued to place a spiritual value on leading an ethical life, she went to church from time to time, and she sometimes used Christian imagery in her books and speeches. But the primary faith that guided her life as an adult was a "civic religion" based on the ideals and promise of American democracy.

In order to understand Addams' perspective on democracy, it is helpful to remember that she belonged to the emerging school of American philosophy known as pragmatism. (In fact, Addams' own ideas helped to shape this body of thought through her close association with John Dewey, a leading figure in the movement.) Pragmatists place little value on rigid codes of belief. Instead, they see life as an extended dialogue between thinking and acting. People form ideas based on their experience. They continually test those ideas in real-life situations, and if they are wise, they reflect on what they have learned and adjust their ideas and their actions accordingly. Pragmatism is sometimes crudely summarized as a call for doing "whatever works." But such a simplification hardly does justice to the subtle interplay between thought and action that makes this philosophy so distinctive. Although pragmatism focuses less than some schools of thought on precisely defining "the good," it is intensely concerned with how to give life to one's principles in the changing conditions of the real world.

How does this apply to Addams' views on democracy? She was devoted heart and soul to the core ideals expressed in the Declaration of Independence and the Constitution. But she thought that over time, the country had failed to "enlarge those ideals in accord with our . . . experience of life." The problem, she said, was that America had inherited from the Founders a relatively narrow approach to applying the ideals they expounded—expressed almost entirely through the vote. Addams believed that the limitations in this purely electoral approach to democracy had mattered somewhat less in the 18th century, when rural life fostered informal connections to fill in the gaps. But in the diverse urbanized world of the 1890s, social divisions tended to harden—between rich and poor, between employers and workers, and between citizens and their government. Increasingly, those who held power—whether political, economic, or social—made the decisions, while the rest simply acquiesced.

Addams did not blame the Founders for the situation in which America found itself. They had based their ideas on the best wisdom of their time. Now the people of her own time must do the same. The central purpose of the reforms Addams championed was to reconceptualize the ideals of American democracy for a new era, reflecting the critical importance of collective obligation and responsive government in a complex industrial society.

Joining the Progressive Movement

There was a wider context for the evolution of Addams' ideas about democracy. Throughout her first 25 years at Hull-House, her efforts were stimulated and sustained by her participation in a wave of reform activity that came to be known as the progressive movement. Seldom in American history have there been such widespread efforts to achieve so many different kinds of economic, political, and social reform. Indeed, progressivism had such an impact on American public life that the period from about 1890 to World War I is often called the Progressive Era.

Who exactly were the progressives? At the heart of the movement was a large cadre of middle-class reformers, including politicians, journalists, social workers, historians, philosophers, teachers, settlement workers, clergymen, women's club members, and some forward-looking businessmen. Labor unions also played an important part. They had their own priorities, but they worked closely with the reformers on many issues, and they helped shape the progressive agenda.

As a group, the progressives shared a broad set of overlapping principles and goals rather than a single well-defined creed. They disagreed sharply among themselves on many key issues of the day, such as immigration and race relations. But they were united by their faith in human progress and by their conviction that they could analyze contemporary conditions and institute reforms that would benefit the whole society. This, they believed, was the way to achieve social progress.

Another point of agreement among the progressives was the conviction that American society was being undermined by what Herbert Croly described in *The Promise of American Life* (1910) as "chaotic individualism." The progressives understood that individual rights were essential in a democracy, but they believed that in a complex industrial society, these rights had to be tempered by concern for the public interest. In fact, the only way to remain a democracy was to prevent the most powerful members of society from trampling on the rights of others.

In suggesting that the rights of the powerful needed to be curtailed, presumably by government, the progressives were challenging two very strongly held American ideas: admiration for individual success and wariness of governmental power. Both ideas had a long history in the United States. And during the so-called Gilded Age of the 1870s and 1880s, they were given "scientific" reinforcement by a body of thought that came to be called social Darwinism (so named because it was popularly—although incorrectly—believed to reflect Charles Darwin's theory of evolution).

The principles of social Darwinism were derived from the writings of British philosopher Herbert Spencer, among others, and were popularized in the United States by sociology professor William Sumner. According to this school of thought, unfettered competition was essential to human progress because it weeded out the "unfit" members of society, leaving those who were most qualified to carry on the race. Thus, according to social Darwinism, reforms intended to help the weak or control the strong were not only futile but destructive because they interfered with the upward march of humanity. The only rational approach was to accept society as it was and trust the gradual process of evolution to resolve any difficulties.

Government policies during this period were quite consistent with social Darwinist teachings. To understand what a small role the government played in American life at this time, it is important to remember that this was an era before Social Security, federal housing programs, antipollution laws, workers' compensation, unemployment insurance, the interstate highway system, federal aid to education, the Securities and Exchange Commission, the Federal Reserve Board, the Centers for Disease Control, the National Labor Relations Board, food stamps, Medicare, or Medicaid.

In economic matters, legislators and judges during the late 19th century adhered to a policy of non-intervention known as *laissez-faire* (from the French, meaning "Let events take their course" or "Leave it alone"). Some of them took this course because of a philosophical reluctance to expand the reach of government, some from a determination to keep taxes low, and some because they opposed all constraints on private business. This laissez-faire approach was reinforced by a strong legal precedent: the Supreme Court's decision in the Slaughterhouse cases in 1873, which defined corporate rights so broadly that hardly any form of business regulation could be considered constitutional. Overall, the public policy that probably had the greatest impact on Americans' daily life—starting in the Gilded Age and lasting well into the Progressive Era—was the tendency of the government *not* to intervene in economic and social matters, thus allowing the forces of individual power and privilege to operate unchecked.

The progressives maintained that excessive individualism and limited government were doing real damage to American society.

They acknowledged that these values might have been appropriate in the past, but they insisted that they were drastically wrong for the present. They pointed out that since the end of the Civil War, the United States had gone through a period of sweeping change. Industrial capitalism had transformed the economy. The country's population had tripled, augmented in part by the arrival of nearly 25 million immigrants. Twelve western states had entered the Union. And the number of American cities with populations over 100,000 had risen from 9 to 114. But here was this huge urbanized industrial country, still trying to manage its affairs by means of laws and institutions designed for a bygone era.

And what was the result? The signs of dysfunction were all around: in the crowded dirty cities, the rapacious behavior of the country's leading corporations, the bloody conflicts between labor and management, the corruption of urban politics, the miserable lives of millions of immigrants, and the growing chasm between rich and poor. Clearly, the unregulated pursuit of individual interests was tearing America apart. A new standard was needed, in which the actions of each sector of society—business, politics, the professions, even the church—would be judged by how much they contributed to or detracted from the common good.

What kinds of behaviors were most harmful to the public interest, and how should they be corrected? Here, the progressives diverged, with some stressing economic regulation, some political reform, and some social justice.

To such economic progressives as Richard Ely, Theodore Roosevelt, and Henry Demarest Lloyd, one of the most troubling features of contemporary society was the rise of corporate power. Year by year, huge firms had established near-monopoly control over their respective industries, so traditional competition had been virtually eliminated. In his influential book *Wealth Against Commonwealth* (1894), Lloyd argued that this concentration of economic power was bad for the American economy and that the inequality it fostered was a threat to democracy itself. "Our great money-makers have sprung in one generation," he wrote, "into seats of power kings do not know." The economic progressives did win a few legislative victories—most notably the Sherman Antitrust Act

(1890). But the fight to get these laws enforced and expanded continued for many years.

For those progressives who concentrated primarily on political reform, the greatest area of concern was the poor quality of state and local government. In particular, the cities were notoriously ill-run, thanks to a corrupt alliance between dishonest politicians and their cronies in the business world. Some political progressives showed their ethnic and class bias by blaming the whole problem on the rising number of immigrant voters in the cities. They therefore tried in various ways to limit the number of such voters or dilute their influence in elections. Meanwhile, other progressives were participating in an even more pernicious version of "reform"—the successful campaign to disenfranchise virtually all African American voters in the South.

On the positive side, many political progressives sought more constructive ways to improve and democratize American political life, including measures such as the secret ballot, fairer corporate taxes, municipal ownership of utilities, civil service laws, and women's suffrage. They also worked—often in collaboration with the labor movement—to elect reform candidates to office. Tammany Hall boss George Washington Plunkitt liked to describe these politicians as "morning glories" because they "looked lovely in the mornin' and withered up in a short time, while the regular machines went on flourishin' forever, like fine old oaks." Nevertheless, a considerable number of progressive politicians— including Tom Johnson of Cleveland, Samuel "Golden Rule" Jones of Toledo, Hazen Pingree of Detroit, Robert LaFollette of Wisconsin, and John Peter Altgeld of Illinois—established distinguished records. And the reforms they instituted often outlasted their own terms in office.

While some progressive groups were trying to regulate business or clean up American politics, another wing of the movement was devoting its attention to social problems. These social progressives insisted that a modern democracy had an obligation to protect society, not simply by preventing crime and assisting the destitute, but also by helping to ensure adequate living conditions for all its citizens. This was the aspect of progressivism in which Addams herself was most involved.

Indeed, says historian Maureen Flanagan, in the field of social progressivism, "wherever one looks . . . one finds Jane Addams."

Throughout the Progressive Era, Addams and her allies in settlement houses, women's clubs, and civic organizations worked to expand the range of government into such areas as public health, housing, recreation, family services, and child welfare. In addition, social progressives called for changes to benefit what reform politician Robert F. Wagner described as "this most precious asset, the workers." They defended the rights of unions and lobbied for laws to improve factory conditions, end child labor, limit women's working hours, and eliminate sweatshops. They achieved relatively little national legislation during the Progressive Era, but they did manage to get many reforms enacted at the state and municipal levels.

Besides calling for more government action, social progressives also worked to promote reform in the private sector—establishing hundreds of new organizations and encouraging old ones to broaden their missions. Progressive lawyers (such as Louis Brandeis), economists (such as Richard Ely), and physicians (such as Hull-House resident Alice Hamilton) demonstrated through their own careers how much the different professions could contribute to society. Meanwhile, in the Social Gospel movement—often spoken of as the religious wing of progressivism—theologian Walter Rauschenbusch led the effort to make the Protestant church more socially conscious. Rauschenbusch insisted that instead of concentrating on preparing souls for heaven, the church should be working for reforms that would establish the Kingdom of God right here on Earth.

The progressives maintained that individual citizens should also be rethinking their public obligations. Hammering this message home was a group of crusading journalists called muckrakers, who published blistering exposés of evil-doing in fields as diverse as meat-packing, city politics, the patent medicine industry, and the U.S. Senate. By one estimate, the muckrakers produced more than 2,300 books and articles between 1903 and 1912. These works, by such authors as Lincoln Steffens, Ida Tarbell, and Ray Stannard Baker, revealed plenty of sin in high places, but the muckrakers continually reminded their readers that public apathy was also a sin. For example, in *The Shame of the Cities* (1905)—based on a series of articles in *McClure's*, the leading muckraker magazine— Steffens asserted that the shame of urban corruption belonged primarily not to the politicians who took money for favors but to the "respectable" businessmen who offered the bribes, and to the voters who let this evil system go unchallenged.

Other progressives also sought to keep the public informed and engaged. For example, the National Child Labor Committee promoted its cause for years through speeches, statistical reports, legislative testimony, public exhibits, magazine articles, conferences, and the compelling photographs of Lewis Hine. Even poets lent their voices, as in these haunting lines by Sarah Cleghorn about children working in a textile mill:

> The golf links lie so near the mill
> That almost every day
> The laboring children can look out
> And see the men at play.

In campaigns like these, the progressives worked hard to highlight the unfairness of existing conditions. But at the same time, they stressed the idea that improving these conditions would benefit all Americans, not just the underprivileged. For example, they argued that the country would do better economically if its poor children were better educated, that making prisons more humane would reduce crime, that there would be fewer destructive strikes if working conditions improved, and that eradicating diseases in the slums would prevent citywide epidemics.

At one level, this line of argument represented a purely rational appeal to people's self-interest. At another, it suggested a more provocative idea: that American life need not be a Darwinian struggle, with the strong continually trampling the week underfoot. Rather, the progressives suggested, true prosperity depended on everyone's doing well. This was what Addams meant when she observed that "without the advance and improvement of the whole, no man can hope for any lasting improvement in his own moral or material individual condition."

The progressives were not without their faults. Even well-regarded reformers such as Theodore Roosevelt, theologian Josiah Strong, settlement worker Robert Woods, and economist John R. Commons mixed their social ideals with an unpleasant streak of racism and/or nativism. Others, including birth control advocate Margaret Sanger, called for discriminatory measures against the disabled in the name of "race improvement," or eugenics.

More generally, the progressives were vulnerable to the argument made by historians such as Michael McGerr that their fundamental goal was simply to remake the world according to their own middle-class tastes. This seems too sweeping an interpretation, but it is true that even the most enlightened reformers had a tendency to overestimate their own objectivity—simply assuming that everyone shared their predominantly middle-class, predominantly Protestant view of the world. As a result, they sometimes paid too little attention to the genuine conflicts of interest that divided American society, optimistically insisting that every clash of interests could be reasoned away.

Despite these flaws, however, there are lessons that every generation can learn from the progressives' eagerness to confront the issues of their time and their conviction that humans have the capacity and indeed the obligation to reshape their world. Whatever their specific reform interests, the activists of the Progressive Era were inspired, as Addams observed, by a "faith in human volition as a power which may really direct and shape social conditions."

In the years between 1890 and 1914, Addams constantly collaborated with other progressives, gaining both inspiration and organizational support from her association with them. The growth of the movement helped create the climate within which her own work went forward. And as her influence increased, she played an important role in shaping and articulating the aspects of progressivism that were most important to her: collective obligation, government's social responsibility, and the conviction that people working together can foster social progress.

Building Social Connections

One of Addams' most significant contributions to the body of progressive thought was her insistence that social reform must take place not only at the institutional level but also at the level of personal relationships—that a critical test of democracy lies in how we treat each other every day. Exploring this idea in one of her best-known books, *Democracy and Social Ethics* (1902), Addams called for a new system of social relations that would revivify the ideals of American democracy under the conditions of industrial society. She observed that democracy had to represent more than the passive "sentiment" of wishing all men well and more than the abstract "creed" of believing in human dignity. It had to operate as a practical "rule of living."

To suggest how this might be done, Addams devoted each of the six chapters in *Democracy and Social Ethics* to a different relationship typical of contemporary life: charity visitor and client, parent and adult daughter, mistress and servant, employer and factory worker, teacher and student, urban boss and voter. Addams portrayed each of these relationships as a kind of moral battleground in which old hierarchical ways of relating to each other were being challenged by newer, more democratic approaches.

One idea pervades all six chapters in *Democracy and Social Ethics*: the importance of broadening our sympathies so we understand how the world looks to other people. "The identification with the common lot," wrote Addams, "is the essential idea of Democracy." What does it feel like to be a factory worker? Or a housemaid? Or an immigrant voter? If we close such people out of our minds and hearts, said Addams, "we not only tremendously circumscribe our range of life but limit the scope of our ethics." We can achieve real democracy only by reaching beyond our separate little worlds and "mixing on the thronged and common road where all must turn out for one another, and at least see the size of one another's burdens."

To Addams, the need for mutual understanding was one of the most crucial elements of democratic society. And one of the most obvious obstacles to that understanding—particularly in cities like Chicago—was the division between the classes. It was concern over the gulf between the rich and the poor that first drew Addams into settlement work, and she devoted much of her life to combating it. Moreover, she recognized that the immigrants of the 19th Ward were isolated not only by their poverty but also by their unfamiliarity with American life and their difficulties with English. To illustrate the point, she described an Italian woman who had lived in the 19th Ward for six years. This woman, she said, expressed amazement one day when she saw a vase of roses in the Hull-House parlor. She assumed they must have come from Italy, having no idea that there was a florist just ten blocks away.

Addams felt she saw the same level of ignorance—and with less excuse—on the Americans' side. Except for the labor contractors and slumlords and sweatshop operators who exploited the immigrants so cruelly, few native-born Americans had any contact with the newcomers at all. The typical recent male immigrant was able to vote thanks to the pressure of urban political machines. But otherwise, said Addams, we "dub him with epithets deriding his past life or present occupation, and feel no duty to invite him to our houses." How can we function as a democracy, she asked, when we know—and care—so little about our fellow citizens?

It is worth noting that Addams had much more to say about insensitivity toward immigrants than about racial discrimination. And although she actively supported a number of social programs in predominantly black neighborhoods, she does not seem to have objected to the informal segregation that sometimes occurred within Hull-House's own clubs. Compared to her contemporaries, Addams was quite enlightened about racial issues. She contributed her name to the announcement launching the National Association for the Advancement of Colored People, stirred up a media storm by inviting the officers of the National Council of Colored Women to lunch at Hull-House, was a close friend of African American activist Ida Wells-Barnett, and welcomed the outspoken W.E.B. DuBois to the settlement's weekly lecture series. Nevertheless, because there were relatively few African Americans in the Hull-House neighborhood until after World War I, she did not have to grapple with the issue of race prejudice on a daily basis. Perhaps the fairest summary would be to say that

Addams embraced racial tolerance as a personal virtue, but she never fought for it with the focus and passion that she brought to issues such as child labor and women's suffrage.

If Addams acted less decisively than she might have on racial issues, she did work wholeheartedly to address the kinds of social injustice she observed firsthand in the 19th Ward. Reaching out to share her concerns with the American public, she established a virtual second career as a public interpreter of urban social conditions, writing 11 books in the course of her life as well as several hundred speeches, essays, book reviews, and newspaper columns,

Addams also established herself as a lecturer on social issues, traveling around the country to address civic and business groups, reform organizations, women's clubs, and college students. To take one example, in the busy month of February 1899, she gave speeches in New York, Massachusetts, Vermont, Pennsylvania, Virginia, and South Carolina. These lectures—as well as her books and articles—represented an important source of income for Addams, since because by then, she had spent most of her modest inheritance on launching Hull-House. But however useful these financial benefits were, Addams was primarily on a moral mission, seeking to foster democratic social connections across American society.

Asking More of Government

Addams' commitment to democratic relationships never diminished. But she knew that the citizens of a well-functioning democracy must also be assured a basic level of material well-being. And like many progressives, she became convinced that to bring that about would require the help of government. The depression of 1893–1894 brought this lesson home with painful clarity. The urgent level of need throughout the 19th Ward led Hull-House to increase its own charitable services, but at the same time, it compelled Addams to recognize that private philanthropy by itself was, as she said, "totally inadequate to deal with the vast numbers of the city's disinherited."

Conditions in Chicago were particularly difficult that winter because in addition to the financial depression, the city was hit by a smallpox epidemic. To Addams, the bravery and unselfishness of the county smallpox officials—whom she saw going house to house in the 19th Ward—symbolized the government's obligation "to carry on the dangerous and difficult undertakings for which private philanthropy is unfitted."

But however indispensable public services were, Addams was under no illusion about their quality. Again and again she heard from her neighbors how disagreeable it was to apply for public relief, how grim conditions were in the county insane asylum, and how much they dreaded ending their days in the poorhouse. Responding to situations like these, Hull-House residents joined a number of campaigns designed to improve the quality of government services.

The settlement also launched a number of pilot projects designed to demonstrate the need for the government to move into new fields. For example, despite the lack of indoor plumbing in poor neighborhoods like the 19th Ward, women's groups had trouble persuading skeptical city officials that the residents would use public bathhouses if they were available. Then, Addams made the demand visible by installing three public baths at Hull-House. The overwhelming response from her neighbors helped change minds in City Hall and led to the opening of Chicago's first public bathhouse in 1894; a dozen more were built in the years that followed. Similarly, when Hull-House created Chicago's first public playground, its popularity helped persuade the city to build many more—all maintained and staffed with public funds.

Addams believed that encouraging government to provide needed services like these would not only improve living conditions in immigrant neighborhoods, but it would also strengthen democracy by giving local residents a stronger sense of connection to their government. No wonder, she said, that they poured their energies into such voluntary organizations as unions and benefit societies; those institutions were the only ones that were dealing with the issues that really mattered in their lives. People almost always skimp on their "civic duty," she pointed out, "when government fails to address the issues closest to their hearts.

Not all progressives shared Addams' enthusiasm for broad political participation; a good number of them believed that government would function better if political action was limited to the more enlightened members of society. But Addams was convinced that broad community involvement was essential if the improvements achieved by Hull-House were to be sustained. In cities like Chicago, she said, public officials were "always waiting to be urged to do their duty." This tendency was a problem wherever it occurred, but it was "fatal in a ward where there is no initiative among the citizens." Accordingly, besides trying to improve material conditions in the 19th Ward, Hull-House worked continually to train its neighbors to assert their rights and hold government to its rightful obligations.

Addams always stressed what she called "practical citizenship," inviting her neighbors to participate in such advocacy projects as getting a street paved, a gambling house closed, or a popular police sergeant reinstated. Thus, said Addams, "through such humble doors, perchance the immigrant will at last enter into his heritage in a new nation."

Taking on the Bosses

By far the most famous of Hull-House's ventures into "practical citizenship" took place in 1895, when Jane Addams was named garbage inspector for the 19th Ward. At the time, the city's arrangements for garbage collection involved precisely the kind of backroom deals that progressive reformers often criticized. Garbage contracts were awarded as political favors, and although the designated firms were meant to make their rounds in each neighborhood at least three times a week, many of them showed up only once or twice a month. Conditions were particularly bad in such industrial neighborhoods as the 19th Ward, where the uncollected garbage included not only household refuse but the waste from local factories and stables. On hot summer days, the stench of the overflowing garbage boxes could be overpowering.

In 1892, the Chicago Woman's Club helped launch a citywide project for voluntary street inspection as part of a larger campaign to highlight underfunded public services. This was a classic example of Progressive Era reform, designed not only to improve the functioning of the municipal government, but also to expose corrupt city contracts, raise the quality of urban life, and protect public health. Hull-House resident Florence Kelley joined the campaign immediately, organizing a phalanx of voluntary inspectors in the 19th Ward. In just one month, they deluged the city with more than a thousand complaints. But conditions hardly changed at all.

Addams was drawn into the fray later—and by a more personal event. When her older sister Mary Addams Linn died in 1894, Addams was named guardian of Mary's two youngest children: 14-year-old Esther and 11-year-old Stanley. (Addams was also devoted to Mary's two older boys—John and James—but since they were over 18, they did not require a guardian.) Addams initially hoped that Stanley, whose health was fragile, could come live at Hull-House, while Esther went to boarding school. But looking with a fresh eye at the garbage-clogged streets of the 19th Ward, Addams concluded that this was no place for her delicate nephew. So, reluctantly, she sent Stanley off to boarding school as well. And then, ashamed that she had ignored the problem until it affected her own family, she threw herself into the fight for cleaner streets.

Her first approach was to submit her own bid for garbage removal, which would have put her in charge of hiring sub-contractors to do the actual collection. Typically, she researched the topic exhaustively, gathering information about the most modern methods used in other cities. Her proposal, which she submitted with two local businessmen, was more comprehensive than the other bids but also more expensive. In the end, her bid did not even receive formal consideration, as it was thrown out on a technicality. But it did attract considerable media coverage, which provided a good chance to educate the public about the issues involved.

Six months later, a different opportunity presented itself. Seeking to reverse years of public apathy toward corruption in municipal politics, the progressive-minded Civic Federation (on whose board Addams served) backed an entire slate of insurgent candidates in the city elections of 1895. The reformers won handily, taking the mayoralty and a dozen City Council seats. One outcome of their victory was a reformed approach to garbage collection. The new Commissioner of Public Works appointed seven new garbage inspectors. And thanks in part to the publicity surrounding Addams' earlier bid, she was selected as inspector for the 19th Ward. This appointment represented two firsts: the city's first female garbage inspector and Addams' first paying job. (Her work at Hull-House carried no salary.)

From then on, three days a week, Addams and her assistant rose at 5 a.m. and spent the next four hours following in a cart as the contractor's wagons made their rounds and proceeded to the reeking city dump. Addams also spent many hours hounding landlords and factory owners about their waste disposal methods, reminding tenants to do their own part, giving children prizes for picking up litter, and starting a recycling effort that delivered discarded tin cans to a nearby factory that made sash-cord weights. On one occasion, she even persuaded the mayor to come and admire what she had found under 18 inches of packed-down garbage: a perfectly good paved street. In short order, the crusading lady inspector became every newspaper's favorite story.

Perhaps it was all too good to last. By the end of Addams' first year in office, the ward's powerful alderman had grown uncomfortable at seeing a reformer (and a woman at that) causing such a stir and holding so lucrative a city job. He quietly arranged for garbage collection to be combined with street maintenance and directed by a "ward superintendent"—a new civil service position for which women were not eligible. Thus ended Addams' career as a public servant—and as a wage earner. But she felt she had given her neighbors a useful example of a dedicated officeholder in action. She observed that one often heard pleasing rhetoric about officials' obligation to serve the public, but "we credit most easily that which we see."

The alderman who put Addams out of the garbage business was Johnny Powers, a major figure on the Chicago City

Council. Powers was the very prototype of the urban bosses whom progressives were fighting in cities around the country; he combined shameless graft with an array of favors to his constituents that made him hugely popular in the 19th Ward. Nevertheless, the reformers prepared to run a candidate against Powers in 1896.

Progressives all over Chicago were eager to see Powers defeated, but the job would have to be done by the voters of the 19th Ward. Hull-House threw itself into the campaign, rallying neighbors to the cause, sending out mailings, organizing meetings, and scheduling speakers to promote the man they were supporting against Powers. So, the voters went to the polls. On the morning after the election, the count showed that in the rest of the city, the reformers had done very well, winning 18 out of 24 contests. But in the 19th Ward, Powers had trounced them, winning twice as many votes as they did.

Two years later, the reformers again tried to unseat Powers, and they were defeated again—by an even larger majority than before. The outcome was a disappointment to Addams, who had thought the reform candidate had a real chance this time. But she should not have been surprised because even while the campaign was heating up, she was working on an essay entitled "Why the Ward Boss Rules."

Seeking as always to understand other people's view of the world, Addams used the essay to explore the strong bond between bosses like Powers and their supporters. This required a prodigious leap of the imagination because in her eyes, Powers was an unprincipled rogue whose greed harmed both the city and his constituents. But she knew that many of her neighbors saw him differently, and she tried to understand why. Was Powers not a thief? Of course he was, they would answer; all politicians stole. But at least he was nice about sharing the proceeds. And he was an unfailing source of help when they needed a job or a personal favor. In fact, as Addams learned during the 1898 campaign, Powers was so helpful that 2,600 people in the 19th Ward had jobs on the public payroll.

To Addams, the relationship between Powers and his constituents represented a throwback to more primitive times, when peasants lived under the thumb of a feudal lord. In that society, the best the villagers could hope for was that their leader would protect them and that he would show them the same informal kindness they showed each other—but on a grander scale because of the greater resources at his command. When the heirs to this tradition—the immigrants in the 19th Ward—were faced with the uncertainties of life in industrial Chicago, it was natural for them to put their trust in a man like Johnny Powers—"this stalking survival of village kindness." He displayed exactly the characteristics they had learned to expect from a political leader: greed and generosity.

To say that Addams understood the bond between Powers and his constituents is not to say that she condoned it. She knew that his corrupt practices directly harmed the very people who saw him as a benefactor—for example, when he took bribes from the streetcar companies that overcharged his constituents. In addition, although Powers interceded frequently with public officials regarding individual cases, he actually did very little to improve city practices. The effect was to undermine people's faith in government because their experience with Powers taught them that no transaction with the city—not a court case or a request for relief or an application for a job—could be trusted to work out well unless the alderman "put in a word" for you.

But if Powers was a seriously flawed leader, he was still the one who spoke to the people's hearts. Addams was well-aware that, compared to him, progressive candidates could sound quite cold and unfeeling when they donned "the apparel of righteousness" and talked only about civic virtue and bureaucratic improvements. However archaic and even dishonest the ward boss might be, higher-minded politicians could learn a good deal from his visceral connection to his constituents' daily lives. Only when reformers paid sympathetic heed to the individual as well as the larger society, she wrote—only when they acknowledged their constituents' material needs as well as their more elevated aspirations—could America's political life truly give "social expression to democracy."

After the defeat in 1898, some Hull-House residents wanted to take Powers on again in 1900, but Addams said no. She believed the effort would be unproductive and that there were other ways to act on the lessons they had learned. In fact, her lifelong emphasis on government's obligation to deal directly and sympathetically with the most immediate concerns in people's lives owed not a little to the lessons she learned from battling Johnny Powers in the 19th Ward.

Free Speech, Free Thought

Addams' greatest objection to Powers was the fact that his corruption and his emphasis on personal intervention taught the neighbors that American democracy was a sham. By contrast, Addams worked continually to apply democratic principles as concretely as possible to the challenges and uncertainties of urban life. One of the most controversial ways she did this was to take the First Amendment literally—that is, to hold America to its promise of free thought and free speech.

Chicago was a particularly tricky place to do this because of the intense hostility to radical ideas that was still reverberating from the Haymarket Affair of 1886. When the progressive governor John Peter Altgeld chose in 1893 to pardon the three surviving anarchists convicted in the affair, his decision evoked a frenzy of hatred and fear. He was defeated in the next election, and even when he died nine years after making his Haymarket decision, the hostility toward him was still so intense that Addams was one of only three civic leaders in all of Chicago who was willing to speak at his funeral.

Addams believed that continually harking back to the Haymarket Affair provided a useful cover for the many Chicagoans who simply disliked immigrants and freethinkers. Thanks to Haymarket, all outsiders could be conveniently lumped together as anarchists and bomb-throwers. There were, of course, genuine radicals in Chicago, and many of them were foreigners. But the only way their ideas could cause harm, Addams believed, would be if people tried to suppress them. "Bottled up, there is a danger of explosion," she wrote. "Uncorked, open to the freeing process of the air, all danger is averted."

Addams was convinced that in any democratic society, people of all shades of opinion needed to hear and understand each others' views. Providing a setting for that exchange became an important part of the Hull-House mission. "From the very nature of the case," said Addams, "the settlement cannot limit its friends to any one political party or economic school." Instead, it should "give the warm welcome of an inn" to every viewpoint.

Hull-House's active involvement in the issue of free speech began in 1892, when a group of socialists asked Addams whether they could hold their meetings at the settlement. She suggested that they do something a bit more ambitious and form a Working People's Social Science Club. She told them that if—as part of that effort—they would organize a series of weekly public lectures, she would provide the funds. The series they established proved to be unlike anything else available in Chicago—remarkable for the distinction of its speakers, the range of subjects covered, and the diversity of the audience it attracted. Attendance rarely fell below 50, and sessions with particularly popular speakers, such as reformer Henry George, had to be moved into the gymnasium.

The evening's schedule was always the same. The group would elect a chair for the night, the guest speaker would talk for an hour, and then there would be an hour of discussion. British socialist Beatrice Webb noted irritably in her diary that when she and her husband spoke to the club, they were pestered with "innumerable questions." But most visitors were impressed by the acuity of this working-class audience. Listening to her neighbors' thoughtful comments, Addams reflected that "no one so poignantly realizes the failures in the social structure as the man at the bottom, who has been most directly in contact with those failures and has suffered most."

What with the Social Science Club lectures and various other visiting speakers, Hull-House presented its neighbors and the Chicago public with an extraordinary array of social thinkers, ranging from the Russian anarchist Prince Peter Kropotkin to philosopher John Dewey. Other speakers included union leader Samuel Gompers on collective bargaining, the Haymarket anarchists' lawyer on the American jury system, and Addams herself on child labor.

Addams admired many of the guest lecturers as individuals and found something to respect in nearly every radical gospel preached at Hull-House, although she endorsed none of them in full. For example, she valued the socialists' commitment to social justice and observed somewhat wistfully: "I should have been glad to have had the comradeship of that gallant company." But although she agreed with the socialists on the importance of economic issues and the flaws of unbridled capitalism, she opposed their stress on class conflict and could never consider herself one of their number. So it was for Addams with each of the ideologies presented so passionately at the Hull-House lectures. Critics often held her personally accountable for these speeches, assuming that she endorsed every dissenting word. But the dissenters knew better. In fact, as her nephew James observed, "about the only group who did not regard Jane Addams as radical were the radicals themselves."

Even the most controversial of Hull-House's speakers had a certain aura of respectability simply because they were well-known public figures. Addams waded into deeper waters of controversy when she began defending the rights of immigrant radicals from the neighborhood. For example, after anarchist Leon Czolgosz assassinated President William McKinley in 1901, the Chicago police immediately began rounding up the local anarchists. Among the detainees was the editor of an anarchist newspaper, Abraham Isaak, who had often visited Hull-House. Word soon went around the 19th Ward that Isaak was being held without bail and denied legal counsel.

Stung by hearing someone say that this just showed America was not so different from czarist Russia, Addams set out to see what she could do. Taking progressive lawyer Raymond Robins with her, she met with the jail officials, then the Mayor, then the prisoner himself. Ultimately, Isaak and most of the other detainees were released. Addams always insisted that her own involvement had made little difference, but many Chicagoans criticized her for even trying to help such a sinister character. As one editorial commented: "Miss Addams can find plenty to do for the lowly classes without bothering herself with the defense of avowed anarchists."

Addams knew that identifying Hull-House so vigorously with the cause of free speech and free thought opened the settlement to frequent criticism and also lost it some donations. "At many times," she said ruefully, "it seemed to me that we were destined to alienate everybody." But if part of the Hull-House mission was to help its neighbors understand America, then the most important task was to show them democracy in action. They could learn the theory of democracy in the settlement's citizenship classes but "nothing can possibly give lessons in citizenship so effectively . . . as the current event itself."

This drive to make democracy real by expressing it in action was Addams' abiding concern—her own way of acting on her progressive principles—whether her efforts took the form of interpreting immigrants to other Americans, monitoring garbage collection, battling Johnny Powers, or defending the rights of her anarchist neighbors. Giving life to democracy in neighborhoods like the 19th Ward would benefit the immigrants, she knew. But it would also demonstrate the vitality of the nation's ideals in the only way that mattered—by showing that they were, as Addams said, "secure for all and incorporated into our common life."

4

Choosing Collaboration

How did Jane Addams—a single woman of modest means—manage to achieve so much in her life? Her dedication and her hard work were certainly important parts of the story, but there was also another key factor: Addams almost never worked alone.

The Progressive Era was notable for the vitality and variety of its organizational activity. During these years, thousands of committees and associations were established to address issues of social and economic reform. Addams helped found a considerable number of these groups, and she participated in many more. Some of them focused specifically on the 19th Ward; some operated at the city, county, or state level; and some dealt with national or international issues. As for the range of topics these groups addressed, the elevator man at the Chicago City Club captured the situation nicely one morning when he saw Addams heading upstairs for yet another lunch meeting. Who was she eating with today, he asked, garbage or "the social evil [that is, prostitution]?" The meeting could have been about either one, or about any number of other issues that Addams worked on collaboratively during these years, including child labor, playgrounds, race relations, unemployment, women's suffrage, education, political campaigns, or labor strikes.

Addams was convinced that working with other people was the best and most democratic way of solving problems. She maintained that even if a given task could be completed more efficiently by oneself, "associated effort may represent a finer social quality and have a greater social value." The end product was likely to be better, she thought, and the participants would benefit personally from what she called "the joy of association." Individual achievement might be what drew public applause, but it was collaboration that really fostered social progress.

Acknowledging the occasional frustrations of collaboration, Addams liked to quote Ralph Waldo Emerson's observation that "the test of a real reformer is his ability to put up with the other reformers." She herself scored very high on that test. She not only put up with her fellow reformers—and with non-reformers as well—she seemed to find something to like and respect in each one of them.

This open-mindedness often drove her more partisan allies to distraction. Ellen Starr once exclaimed, "Jane, if the devil himself came riding down Halsted Street with his tail waving out behind him, you'd say, 'What a beautiful curve he has in his tail.'" Still, Addams' willingness to see all sides of a question was a definite asset in helping people of divergent views work together.

Critics sometimes maintained that Addams stuck to her middle course simply to perpetuate her image as "Saint Jane" or to protect Hull-House from controversy. But as we have seen, she could be absolutely fearless in defense of basic democratic principles, such as free speech. Her evenhandedness in organizational work was not based on timidity but on her conviction that the best results could be obtained through open debate and collective effort.

Building a Community

Of all the people Addams collaborated with during her long career, few played as important a role in her life as the group of residents she gathered around her at Hull-House. The initial idea for the settlement grew out of Addams' own personal response to Toynbee Hall, but Hull-House was a collective effort almost from the first. Ellen Starr, for one, was an indispensable partner in getting it launched. Volunteers also played a vital role in the life of the settlement by generously contributing both their time and their money to help the cause.

But above all, it was the Hull-House residents who served as the core of the program, directing many of the activities, managing the settlement in Addams' absence, and linking it to the larger community of Chicago progressives through their own professional and organizational activities. To understand the residents' significance in the life of Hull-House, let us consider the careers of three of them who made particularly important contributions: Julia Lathrop, Florence Kelley, and Alice Hamilton.

Julia Lathrop lived at Hull-House from 1890 until she left for Washington in 1912 to head the new U.S. Children's Bureau. Just a year older than Addams, Lathrop graduated from Vassar College and then earned a law degree. She was back home in Rockford, Illinois, living with her parents and working in her father's law office when she heard Addams give a speech. Inspired by what she heard, Lathrop left Rockford for Chicago and became a Hull-House resident. She soon began working as a County Visitor, making house calls on all the relief cases within 10 blocks of the settlement. A few years later, when she became the first female member of the State Board of Charities, Lathrop insisted on visiting every one of the 102 county almshouses in the state. At one facility, in order to test the safety of a fire escape built in the form of a slide, she astonished the local officials by tucking up her skirts and sliding from top to bottom.

As Lathrop widened her acquaintance among other reformers in Chicago, she drew Hull-House into progressive efforts all over the city, playing a major role in developing the Cook County Juvenile Court, the Juvenile Protective Association, the Immigrants Protective League, and the Chicago School of Civics and Philanthropy. Meanwhile, at Hull-House, her weekly Plato Club was one of the most popular groups in the program, famous for its rousing discussions. Handsome and witty, Lathrop was generally able to convey her strongly held views without leaving a sting. Addams' nephew James Linn recalled: "Her laughter was a good as an argument." A new resident later confessed that he had been skeptical when he first heard the rapturous cry go around the settlement one afternoon: "Miss Lathrop is coming! Miss Lathrop is coming!" But once he met her—"such force, such warmth"—he too became a disciple.

Florence Kelley was another distinguished Hull-House resident. About the same age as Addams and Lathrop, she graduated from Cornell University and then spent a number of years in Europe, where she became an economist and a socialist. One of the few Hull-House women to have been married, Kelley arrived on the settlement doorstep with her three children in 1891, fleeing her abusive ex-husband. Over the next eight years, she researched sweatshop conditions in the 19th Ward; helped lead a coalition to win passage of pioneering labor legislation in the state; and then for several years supervised the department responsible for carrying out all factory inspections in Illinois. When her term expired in 1897 and the new antireform governor declined to reappoint her, she moved to New York City to head the National Consumers League, which she built into a formidable voice for labor reform.

Kelley's fellow advocate, Josephine Goldmark, once said of her: "No other man or woman I have ever heard so blended knowledge of facts, wit, satire, burning indignation, prophetic denunciation—all poured out at white heat." During her Hull-House years, Kelley was a scintillating member of the settlement community, and her fast-paced debates with Lathrop over the dinner table delighted all who witnessed them. Beyond the fireworks, most historians agree that she was the person most responsible for awakening the Hull-House residents—including Addams—to the importance of economic issues and the need to act aggressively for the reforms that were needed.

Alice Hamilton (the sister of the classicist Edith Hamilton) came to Hull-House in 1897. A physician, she served on the faculty at the Women's Medical School of Northwestern University and later worked as a pathologist in a research institute. At the settlement, she opened a free clinic for babies—the first in the 19th Ward—and undertook local studies of typhoid, tuberculosis, cocaine addiction, and infant mortality. But she found her true calling when she began studying the diseases that factory workers acquired on the job, especially those related to toxic materials and polluted air. A few European scientists had studied occupational disease; indeed, reading Thomas Oliver's *Dangerous Trades* (1902) helped to inspire Hamilton's interest in the subject. But almost no one had investigated conditions in the United States.

Hamilton began studying the subject on her own and published her first article in 1908. Two years later, she was appointed to direct a nine-month survey of industrial diseases in Illinois. This investigation, which produced pioneering research on lead poisoning, inspired Illinois to pass one of the first occupational disease laws in the country. By the time Hamilton left Hull-House in 1911, she had won national recognition not only as a groundbreaking scientist in the emerging field of industrial medicine but also as an advocate for reforming the conditions that did such harm. Her standing was confirmed in 1919, when she was hired to head the new department of industrial medicine at Harvard Medical School, thus becoming the university's first female faculty member. In 1987, in recognition of her historical contribution, the National Institute of Occupational Safety and Health named one of its principal laboratories the Alice Hamilton Laboratory.

Lathrop, Kelley, and Hamilton were just three of the dozens of men and women (mostly women) who lived at Hull-House in the years between 1889 and 1914. Some, such as Addams' first companion, Ellen Starr, spent most of their adult lives at the settlement; others, such as labor organizer Mary Kenney, were there for only a few months. But at any one time during these years, there were usually about 25 residents living in the main settlement house or in the men's building across the street.

The residents received no salaries for their work at Hull-House; in fact, they had to pay to live there. Addams found wealthy donors to provide "fellowships" for those who required financial assistance or who were needed for full-time assignments at the settlement. But the majority found "day" jobs elsewhere in the city. Of course, most of the neighbors also had daytime jobs, so the liveliest times at Hull-House were evenings and weekends. It was then that the residents generally did their work for the settlement: teaching classes, leading clubs, assisting individual students, organizing the neighbors for political action, collaborating with unions and advocacy groups, undertaking research projects, and helping with the perennial task of "toting" visitors.

What was it like to live at Hull-House? Although the settlement stood out as an oasis of comfort and beauty in the 19th Ward, most of the House residents came from solid middle-class backgrounds, and for them, life on Halsted Street represented no great luxury. The bedrooms were spartan, and residents often had to double up for the night in order to accommodate settlement guests. In addition, bathroom facilities were limited, and for many years, it was necessary to go to the drugstore on the corner to make a telephone call. As for the surroundings, Florence Kelley wrote to a friend that the "filth and overcrowding" in the neighborhood were "worse than I have seen outside of Naples and the East Side of New York,"

The attraction of the settlement for its residents, of course, lay not in its physical characteristics but in its goals and its sense of shared enthusiasm. Alice Hamilton wrote: "To me, life there satisfied every longing, for companionship, for the excitement of new experiences, for constant intellectual stimulation, and for the sense of being caught up in a big movement which enlisted my enthusiastic loyalty." Hamilton and her fellow residents came to Hull-House in the first place because they shared certain strong common interests, and these interests were reinforced and deepened by what Addams called "the fostering soil of community life." The result was a heady combination of comradeship and intellectual ferment that impressed nearly every visitor to Hull-House and changed the lives of many who lived there.

Women were greatly in the majority among Hull-House residents—so much so that Addams herself sometimes referred to the place as "a settlement of women." It is therefore important to note in particular what life at Hull-House meant to its female residents. Most of them had attended college and flourished there. But once they graduated, many had faced the same limited options that had troubled Addams during her first years out of Rockford. Hull-House offered these women a rare opportunity by combining the economic benefits of communal living with an atmosphere that in many ways replicated the companionship and intellectual excitement they had enjoyed at college.

With so many bright and dedicated reformers living together in close quarters, each of them full of ideas and opinions about how best to achieve social justice, there was, as Addams' nephew James observed, "plenty of disputatiousness about the place." Such stresses have torn apart many a communal living arrangement. But Addams managed to keep everyone's eyes on their shared goals, while simultaneously, as her nephew put it, "seeing everything from everybody's point of view." She traveled frequently, and even when she was at the settlement, she did not spend a great deal of time with the residents. Nevertheless, wrote resident Francis Hackett, "The essential fact of Hull-House was the presence of Miss Addams."

Some members of the household found Addams a bit daunting. Madeline Wallin, a volunteer at the settlement, described her as "a bright, restless, strong-minded woman, very original, progressive and executive, but not exactly pleasant for steady companionship. . . . Her incessant activity of mind might prove a trifle wearing." But even Wallin observed on another occasion: "She is really a cosmic individual." Most of the residents admired Addams enormously, and they continually pushed themselves to live up to her expectations. One of them explained: "She never drives anyone to work and indeed is most considerate in that regard. But it is impossible to live with her and not feel to some extent the pressure of work to be done."

Despite Addams' august position, she made an effort to administer the settlement according to the principles of cooperative self-government. She submitted each new project to the Hull-House residents for their approval, and they did sometimes vote down her proposals. Addams also gave the residents greater latitude in choosing their own assignments than was common in other settlements, and she never exerted pressure on those whose activities aroused controversy.

Addams was least collaborative when it came to money matters. During the early years, she resolutely kept the settlement's finances to herself, quietly paying the expenses out of her own income plus the money she raised from local supporters (including major donations from her close companion, Mary Rozet Smith). But as Hull-House kept expanding, covering the costs became more and more difficult. By 1894, with her inheritance virtually gone, Addams had to take out a loan to pay her sister Mary's medical bills. "I probably won't ever be flush again," she wrote a friend. When her sister died shortly thereafter, Addams also assumed responsibility for supporting Mary's two underage children. Meanwhile, Hull-House's deficit was growing larger by the day. Finally, in November 1894, Addams had a "long solemn talk" with the residents, laid out the whole financial picture, admitted what a large part of the expenses she had been paying herself, and promised never again to let matters get so far out of hand. It was agreed that Hull-House must reorganize itself on a more businesslike basis.

Within the next few months, the settlement became a formally incorporated agency—the Hull-House Association— with a seven-person board (including Addams) and more formal accounting procedures. Addams was not pleased about the change; she cherished institutional fluidity and undoubtedly enjoyed the independence that had come from funding so much of the program on her own. But she recognized that circumstances had changed and that she would have to change with them.

In fact, the adjustment cannot have been too difficult. Philosopher John Dewey, an early board member, jokingly explained that the trustees really had only one job, which was to tell Addams: "You are all right! Go ahead." Go ahead she did, and as Hull-House continued to grow, paying its bills represented a perpetual challenge. Nevertheless, the participation of the board did help to stabilize the settlement's finances, and it provided Addams with valuable support. The settlement could not have existed without Addams' personal vision, but it took the dedicated collaboration of board members, House residents, and hundreds of volunteers to make her vision a reality.

Spearheading a Movement

When we stand back a bit from Hull-House and consider the settlement house as an abstract idea, it becomes clear that this concept represented one of the most innovative approaches to collaboration that emerged during the late 19th century. Addams' own vague aspirations for a useful life did not coalesce into a definite plan until she learned about Toynbee Hall in London. The settlement idea appealed to other Americans too. In fact, two settlements also inspired by Toynbee Hall were already operating in New York City before Hull-House began, although Addams only heard about them after her own plans were well under way. More settlements were established within the next few years—some inspired by Toynbee Hall itself and some by the American pioneers in New York and Chicago. By 1892, there were about 15 settlements nationwide.

It was at that point—just three years after Hull-House opened its doors—that Addams had her first opportunity to meet some of her fellow settlement workers from other cities. The occasion was a conference on social reform held in Plymouth, Massachusetts. The settlement workers represented just one small group among the conference participants, but they were united by a sense of optimism and conviction that Addams found deeply moving. Many years later, she wrote: "I doubt if anywhere on the continent that summer could have been found a group of people more genuinely interested in social development or more sincerely convinced that they had found a clue by which the conditions in crowded cities might be understood and the agencies for social betterment developed."

Addams gave two speeches at the conference. In the first, entitled "The Subjective Necessity for Social Settlements," she explained why young college graduates of her generation (especially women) were attracted to settlement work. The three principal reasons, she said, were their desire "to extend democracy beyond its political expression," their wish to share their cultural knowledge with people who lacked access to such resources, and the emergence of a new more humanitarian approach to Christianity, which they wanted to express in their own lives. In Addams' second speech, "The Objective Necessity for a Social Settlement," she approached the topic from the other direction, describing the social problems that the settlements were intended to address. Using Chicago's 19th Ward as an example, she explained the many difficulties her immigrant neighbors faced in their daily lives and reviewed some of the ways that Hull-House was trying to work with them to make conditions better.

Addams' two speeches made a great impression at the conference, and they reached an even wider audience when they were published in *Forum* magazine shortly afterward. The importance of Hull-House in the settlement movement was further certified when—in connection with the Chicago World's Fair in 1893—Addams organized the country's first National Conference of Settlements and convened it at Hull-House. From then on, she was generally recognized as the movement's most respected and influential voice. Lillian Wald, founder of Henry Street Settlement, spoke for many of her colleagues when she wrote to Addams: "We want to be good, and like children look up to you for guidance."

Inspired by such pioneers as Hull-House and Henry Street, the American settlement movement expanded rapidly during the Progressive Era, reaching a total of 74 settlements in 1897, 200 in 1905, and 400 in 1911. Most residents in these settlements were drawn from the upper reaches of the middle class. Nearly all of them had been to college, and a remarkable 50 percent had also had graduate training. The majority were in their mid-20s. Unlike Addams and Wald, most residents moved on after only a few years. But many of them chose careers in related fields and remained dedicated reformers the rest of their lives.

By the late 1890s, America's settlement houses had developed into lively and useful institutions. Few of them had the scope of Hull-House, and some were a good deal more condescending to their immigrant neighbors. But nearly all of them provided their communities with valuable arts, education, and recreation programs. Given the strength of local residents' other loyalties, it was rare for a settlement to become the single dominant institution in an urban neighborhood. Nevertheless, the settlement was often the only local institution in a given community that welcomed people of all nationalities and religions. And to the individuals who found their way there, the settlements provided helpful—and sometimes life-changing—opportunities.

Besides providing services within their own institutions, many of the more enterprising settlement workers became leading advocates for reform in their cities, their states, and sometimes at the national level—collaborating with other groups to lobby for new legislation and working tirelessly to educate the American public about the need for social action. The vigor with which they pursued this task of "creating and informing public opinion," as Lillian Wald put it, is suggested by the fact that during these years—according to one study—a mere 14 settlement leaders managed to produce a total of 45 books on urban problems and the need for social reform.

Addams herself found many of her staunchest allies in this activist wing of the settlement movement. For example, she formed a lifelong friendship with Lillian Wald and worked closely with her on a number of initiatives, including the national fight to end child labor and the six-year campaign to get the U.S. Children's Bureau established. She also collaborated with Mary Simkhovitch, founder of Greenwich House in New York City; Robert Woods of South End House in Boston; Mary McDowell, who directed the University of Chicago's settlement near the Stockyards; and Graham Taylor, who led the Social Gospel–influenced Chicago Commons. In addition, when Hull-House residents moved to other cities, they often joined other settlements, thus further extending Addams' network of friends and colleagues in the movement.

In 1888, a young Jane Addams had visited Toynbee Hall and wondered whether its approach could be transplanted to her own home ground. Less than a decade later, Hull-House was flourishing, and the American settlement movement was expanding across the country. This movement would form an important part of Addams' collaborative life for many years to come.

The University Connection

Besides collaborating with other reformers, many American settlement houses built cooperative relationships with nearby colleges or universities. Hull-House's own academic connection began when the University of Chicago opened its doors in 1892. One of the first professors to pay a call at the settlement was John Dewey. Just turned 35, Dewey had come to the city to join the university's Philosophy Department. Much impressed with Hull-House, he took up residence there until his family joined him, and he visited often in the years that followed.

Dewey's involvement with the settlement included delivering lectures there, serving on the board, and—most importantly—maintaining a running dialogue with Addams that lasted for years and profoundly shaped both their work. Highlighting their shared concerns, Dewey devoted one chapter of his book *Schools of To-Morrow* (1915) to discussing "The School as a Social Settlement." His daughter observed: "Dewey's faith in democracy as a guiding force in education took on both a sharper and deeper meaning because of Hull-House and Jane Addams."

Historians have long noted areas of similarity in the thoughts of Dewey and Addams—most notably in their pragmatic stress on the interplay between ideas and experience and the importance of incorporating real-life experience into the educational process. Because Dewey was a well-recognized leader of the pragmatist movement, while Addams was a settlement worker—and perhaps also because he was a man and she was a woman—many have assumed that he generated all the ideas and she merely interpreted and applied them. However, recent historians have shown that a number of the ideas attributed solely to Dewey either originated with Addams or emerged in an untraceable way from their ongoing conversations.

After Addams' death, her friend Mary Simkhovitch observed: "Jane Addams was an intellectual woman, but I don't think we think enough about that, perhaps because she was so natural." Addams' unassuming manner probably did play a part in people's tendency to underestimate her intellect. So did her gender and her professional base in a settlement house. But she was widely read, fluent in five languages, and a probing thinker about the problems of her day. Dewey, for one, always acknowledged the importance of Addams' influence in his intellectual life, and he gave his daughter the name Jane in affectionate tribute to their long friendship.

Besides bringing John Dewey into her life, the University of Chicago provided Addams with another group of collaborators when it established the first sociology department in the nation. The Chicago sociologists—including Albion Small, Charles Zeublin, Charles Henderson, and W.I. Thomas—were convinced that one way to prove the intellectual heft of their new discipline was to show that their work could actually improve social conditions. Because many of these men had progressive inclinations anyway, that approach had a natural appeal to them. They soon found their way to Hull-House, which was already evolving into a kind of ongoing seminar on urban conditions. Visitors from around the city and around the world encountered each other there—sharing new ideas, discussing the latest books and studies, and comparing notes on their own experiences.

In addition, Hull-House maintained an active research program of its own, including studies of the licensing of midwives, infant mortality among foreign-born families, children's reading, childhood tuberculosis, cocaine sales to young people, the causes and prevention of truancy, the social significance of saloons, and the problems faced by new immigrants.

One of the most distinguished pieces of sociological research undertaken by the settlement was a book entitled *Hull-House Maps and Papers*, published in 1895. The idea for this volume grew out of Florence Kelley's recent survey of labor conditions in the 19th Ward. Expanding on those findings, she collaborated with Addams and other Hull-House residents to produce a book of essays that documented neighborhood life from different perspectives. The book included essays on sweatshops, child labor, the county welfare system, the importance of art in workers' lives, the labor movement, and the experience of three different immigrant groups in the neighborhood.

Hull-House Maps and Papers was inspired by *Life and Labour of the People*, a multivolume report by Charles Booth that was creating a sensation in British reform circles when Addams visited England in 1888. Booth's work provided a detailed description of life among London's poor, illustrated with maps that showed the clustering of problems in different neighborhoods. Inspired by Booth's example, Kelley arranged for *Hull-House Maps and Papers* to include eight hand-colored maps. Some documented—house by house—the prevailing wage levels in the neighborhood; others delineated residential patterns among 14 different nationalities. The completed book did not sell particularly well, but it introduced "social mapping" as a tool in American sociology and is widely cited today as a pioneering work of social research. It helped prepare the ground for many subsequent social surveys, most notably the multivolume *Pittsburgh Survey* (1907–1909), directed by Addams' friend Paul Kellogg.

Impressed by projects such as *Hull-House Maps and Papers* and attracted by the lively atmosphere at the settlement, sociologists from the University of Chicago began spending considerable time there—studying the neighborhood, giving guest lectures, and exchanging ideas with Addams about the methods and challenges of urban social research. At one point, there was even some talk of offering Addams a part-time job on the Chicago faculty. But just as Addams declined suggestions that Hull-House itself should be taken under the university's wing, she also declined a more formal relationship for herself.

Addams recognized that however progressive the Chicago sociologists might be as individuals, their priorities were not the same as those of Hull-House. The settlement residents, she said, were living in the 19th Ward "not as students, but as citizens, and their methods of work must differ from that of an institution established elsewhere." They looked on the ward as their home rather than as a research site, and although they continually sought to understand it better, they put a higher value on addressing community problems than on acquiring abstract knowledge.

One way to appreciate the distinctiveness of the settlement approach is to consider how *Hull-House Maps and Papers* differed from conventional academic research of the time. First, there was the breadth of its subject matter. Long before multidisciplinary collaboration had become common in academic circles, this book wove together insights from economics, sociology, anthropology, political science, education, and what would today be called cultural studies.

The authorship was also different from that of an academic report. Whereas the vast majority of university professors in 1895 were men, 8 of the 10 authors of *Hull-House Maps and Papers* were women. Only 3 of the 10 authors had graduate degrees, and only 6 had even graduated from college. As for the authors' occupations, the team consisted of two ethnic community leaders, several settlement workers, a minister turned political scientist, a recent college graduate, and a labor leader. Few universities would have judged such a group qualified to undertake so ambitious a project.

The third characteristic that distinguished *Hull-House Maps and Papers* from an academic report was its clear intention to move its readers to action. Even the technical note annotating the maps takes an activist tone, suggesting that the intrusiveness of the survey questions on which the maps are based "would be unendurable and unpardonable were it not for the conviction that the public conscience when roused must demand better surroundings for . . . the long-suffering citizens of the commonwealth." The essay on "Wage-Earning Children" ends with an explicit call for child labor legislation. An analysis of household budgets among garment workers concludes that their wages are too low to cover their cost of living. And Julia Lathrop's description of inadequate county welfare services ends with this stern admonition: "There is no mal-administration so strong that it can persist in the face of public knowledge and attention. The public now has and will have exactly such institutions as it demands." Addams and her fellow residents valued doing social research. But the justification for their work lay not in its intellectual elegance but in its capacity to inspire social change.

Many of the sociologists who first came to Hull-House from the University of Chicago believed that they could fulfill their professional priorities while still incorporating their own progressive goals. And for a time, they did. But gradually, the political climate—both in the field of sociology and in the university—grew more conservative. By the time World War I began in 1914, social activists had come to be seen in academic circles as less professionally respectable than those who maintained a scholarly neutrality on social issues. As this trend intensified, most of the sociologists turned their attention to more theoretical work—sometimes voluntarily; sometimes under pressure. Meanwhile, activist social research was relegated to less prestigious circles outside the university.

Elements of the Hull-House approach lived on—generally unacknowledged—in the emerging "Chicago school of sociology." For example, there was the Chicago school's continuing emphasis on the city, its interest in social mapping, and its stress on immigration as a factor in urban life. In addition, studies by the Chicago school tended to echo Addams' own relatively dark view of what life was like in a community such as the 19th Ward. Unlike later sociologists—who often found evidence of considerable vitality in such neighborhoods—both Addams and the Chicago sociologists of her era tended to stress the social and economic problems they saw there.

But if this tendency represented a point of similarity between their two perspectives, the differences were also profound. Where the sociologists concentrated on theorizing about the problems they observed, Addams saw these problems as human situations that required sympathy and action. Thus, discrete features of the settlement's approach to research remained visible in the sociology profession, but the passion for social justice that informed and unified the work at Hull-House was increasingly downplayed.

Addams moved on in her life, enjoying the academic connections that remained to her and building new alliances to replace the ones she had lost. She had benefitted from collaborating with the university men—from their intellectual companionship, their knowledge, and the resources at their command. But even in the best of times, their priorities were not her priorities. Social research was important to her, but it was only one step among many toward the larger goal of social reform.

Building Alliances

To Addams, research had a valuable role to play in the process of working for social change. But after the facts were gathered and analyzed, they needed to be put to use. And this is where advocacy came in—working with other social progressives to address the problems of American society.

Reaching out for new allies, Addams gradually strengthened her relationship with the social work profession. She and her settlement comrades had initially kept their distance from the field of social work because they associated it with the judgmental attitude of the traditional "charity visitor." But during the early years of the 20th century, social workers grew increasingly involved in broader aspects of progressive reform. As this change took hold, the premier social work organization—the National Conference on Charities and Correction—developed into a lively arena for collaboration between social workers and settlement residents. The growing activism of the social work profession was affirmed in 1909, when Addams was elected the first female president of the National Conference.

Meanwhile, businessmen were also growing more open to the need for social reform, especially after the devastating depression of 1893–1894. As unemployment and destitution soared, it grew hard for even the flintiest conservative to insist that the poor had no one but themselves to blame for their problems. Business progressives were certainly not seeking the profound social and economic changes that an activist like Florence Kelley had in mind. But they knew that if social peace was to be preserved, there had to be some dialogue between workers and employers, some recognition of the problems faced by the unemployed, and some sense of common membership in the larger society.

The founding of the Civic Federation is a vivid example of the way that reformers and businessmen sometimes worked together for progressive goals. In the fall of 1893, just as the famous World's Columbian Exposition in Chicago was entering its final weeks, a British reform journalist named William T. Stead came to town. Arriving when he did, he had a chance to see both the glittering "White City" at the fairgrounds and the terrible poverty in other parts of Chicago, where the depression had already begun taking its toll. Stead spent a month exploring the situation, working briefly as a laborer, and spending considerable time at Hull-House. Then he convened a mass meeting with the provocative title, "If Christ Came to Chicago."

Addressing a packed house, Stead thundered out that Christ would be appalled if He could see the suffering of Chicago's poor. He then went on to excoriate the city's prosperous residents for allowing such conditions to exist and urged his listeners to form an alliance that would mount a crusade against the city's problems. Out of this meeting came the Civic Federation of Chicago, which soon evolved into the National Civic Federation. This organization functioned for many years as a cross-class alliance, primarily led by businessmen but governed by a council that—unusually for the time—included clergymen, labor leaders, and both male and female reformers.

Addams participated in many of the federation's early activities, serving on its board and supporting its extensive programs for the unemployed. She joined the federation's unsuccessful effort to arbitrate the bitter Pullman Strike in 1894, and she also played an active role in its campaign to elect reform candidates to city office in the late 1890s. She had a broader view of Chicago's needs than the federation leadership, and she would not have been satisfied with this group as her only organizational affiliation. But she recognized the federation's strengths and worked cooperatively with it during the years when its goals were closely aligned with her own.

The settlement movement, the National Conference of Charities and Correction, and the Civic Federation were only a few of the scores of progressive organizations that Addams worked with during these years. She also participated in the National Child Labor Committee, the Women's Trade Union League, the Playground Association of America, the National Association for the Advancement of Colored People, the General Federation of Women's Clubs, the Chicago Urban League, the National Society for the Promotion of Industrial Education, the National American Woman Suffrage Association, and the American Association for Labor Legislation.

Among the groups that Addams joined, a considerable number elected her to leadership positions. In part, this was simply because of the aura of her name, which had become widely associated with high principles and good works. But she also had a particular gift for building consensus within an organization while simultaneously pressing it to move boldly forward. Theologian Walter Rauschenbusch wrote to Addams: "You are one of the invaluable people who combine velocity and stability."

Besides joining so many organizations herself, Addams encouraged Hull-House residents to collaborate with Chicago reformers on dozens of projects. These initiatives often began with research and then moved on to lobbying for action on the problems that had been uncovered. For example, the housing survey on which Hull-House collaborated with the Chicago School of Civics and Philanthropy set the stage for an all-out campaign in which dozens of reform groups worked to get a new city tenement code passed. Similarly, findings from Kelley's research on working conditions in the 19th Ward helped prepare the ground for the massive lobbying effort by settlement workers, labor unions, women's clubs, and civic organizations that helped push through the state's first Factory Inspection Act.

By 1900, Addams' achievements were known nationwide. Accounts in the press often portrayed her as a kind of urban saint, accomplishing miracles with a mystic wave of her hand. She was indeed a remarkable individual, but her greatest achievements were nearly all collaborations, not solo turns. Looking back on his Hull-House years, historian Francis Hackett recalled how often he would hear Addams call out to one of the residents passing by her chair at dinner, "Mr. Hooker! You can help us. What do you think . . . ?'" This, said Hackett, was what made life at Hull-House so profoundly satisfying. "Her attitude was 'you can help,' and because she elicited goodwill in a common cause, that cause preoccupied the residents." This was one of Addams' great gifts: her capacity to transmute an assortment of less-than-perfect individuals into an effective and even inspired team of collaborators.

Addams sought always to foster in others the feeling that she herself valued most: "the consciousness of participation and well-being which comes to the individual when he is able to see himself in connection and cooperation with the whole." Living in an era when enthusiasm for reform was at its height, she was able to share with hundreds of other progressives the satisfaction of achieving together what no one of them could have accomplished by themselves.

By the time Addams reached her mid-30s, her experience at Hull-House had confirmed in her mind several key precepts that would guide her the rest of her life: the need to bridge the divisions of class and ethnicity that separated American society, the importance of bringing democratic principles to life in daily experience, and the value of collaborative effort. In Part 2, we will look at how Addams applied these precepts during the period from 1895 to 1914—the years of her own greatest influence as an American reformer. The first three chapters explore Addams' work with particular groups— women, children, and the labor movement—while the fourth describes how, in 1912, she and other progressives launched an ambitious campaign to elect a president of the United States.

Working for Progressive Reform

Part of the Hull-House complex, Chicago. (Bettmann/CORBIS)

5

Focusing on Women

One night in 1905, Jane Addams was waiting for the elevator after a late committee meeting in a downtown office building. Looking around, she saw that the woman scrubbing the floor nearby was one of her neighbors. "As she straightened up to greet me," Addams recalled, "she seemed so wet from her feet up to her chin that I hastily inquired the cause. Her reply was that she left home at five o'clock every night and had no opportunity for six hours to nurse her baby." At home, no doubt, her child was weeping with hunger. Downtown, this woman labored on at her job while "her mother's milk mingled with the very water with which she scrubbed the floors."

In Addams' account of this incident, we can feel both her empathy for the scrubwoman's troubles and her indignation that any mother should be forced to choose between her obligations to her child and the need to earn money for her family. Throughout Addams' career, we find these continual reminders of her abiding concern for the lives of women. Factory girls, clubwomen, housemaids, college graduates— Addams seemed to feel connected to them all. She sympathized with their problems and admired their achievements. She was also convinced that they deserved a larger voice in American life.

Rethinking Women's Sphere of Action

Jane Addams grew up in an era that romanticized the idea of woman as a protected species. This idea was a relatively recent phenomenon in American society—the product of important changes in the economic role of women. In colonial times, most economic production was carried out by individual families, and all but the wealthiest wives generally helped to produce whatever the family sold to others as well as the things the family consumed itself, such as food, candles, soap, fabric, and clothing. However, during the 19th century, with the expansion of commerce and the growth of manufacturing, it became possible for families to buy many of the things they used to produce themselves, making the housewife's role as a producer far less important.

Meanwhile, the American middle class was expanding dramatically. Even as early as 1860, when Addams was born, growing numbers of men had begun earning enough as merchants or master carpenters or even well-paid clerks to support their families without any assistance from their wives. And by that time, it had also become more common for men's offices and workshops to be located away from their homes, which further separated women from their husbands' economic lives.

As these changes took hold, the home began to assume an almost religious significance in popular culture, giving rise to what has been called the "cult of domesticity." No longer a vital unit of the economy, the home was now seen as a haven from the marketplace—an oasis to which the husband could retreat for rest and comfort after his daily exertions. Presiding over this haven was his loving and gracious wife. Although she benefitted from her husband's economic activity, she remained separate from its actual practice—kept pure and idealistic by her isolation from the gritty realities of the outside world. This exalted arrangement remained out of reach, of course, for many American women. Nevertheless, the ideal it represented shaped the behavior and aspirations of millions of families.

The differentiation of gender roles prescribed by the cult of domesticity was often expressed in terms of social geography as a distinction between the public and private spheres of life. According to this doctrine, the public sphere was male territory—the place where men engaged in politics, business, and war. Wives reigned over the private sphere, nurturing their children, supervising their servants, maintaining their houses, and ministering to their husbands. From time to time, they might venture forth for shopping or perhaps some charity work, but the private sphere was their base, their arena of special competence, and, above all, their island of protection against the harshness and corruption of the sphere inhabited by men.

Despite the widespread influence of the doctrine of separate spheres, alternative visions were also being discussed in Addams' time. Advocates of women's rights had long maintained that women should be active in both the private and the public spheres. However, these advocates differed among themselves about why women deserved a public role. Some, such as Charlotte Perkins Gilman stressed the fundamental equality of men and women. Others, such as Catharine Beecher, maintained that women should be heard because they were not like men and had their own perspective to contribute. This latter view is often described today as "social feminism" or "difference feminism," although those terms were not used during the Progressive Era; even the word *feminism* only came into common use in the United States after about 1910.

Addams herself could be called a social or difference feminist because she tended to stress the two genders' distinct roles rather than their equality. But in her mind, the fact that the sexes were different only strengthened the argument for giving women a significant voice in public life. As she said: "A woman should fill a woman's place in the world, not a man's place. There are women's talents and women's energies, as there are men's talents and men's energies. To statesmanship she can contribute sympathy and understanding, to business the feminine instinct for cooperation rather than competition."

But even though Addams had a good deal in common with the difference feminists, she did not necessarily agree with them about what it was that made women's contribution to society so important. Many difference feminists maintained that women were, by their very nature, purer than men and would therefore elevate the moral tone of public life. Addams had her doubts on this point. After all, she pointed out, "we have not wrecked railroads, nor corrupted legislature, nor done many unholy things that men have done; but then we must remember that we have not had the chance."

To Addams, it was all a question of history. For tens of thousands of years, she said, women had focused primarily on caring for their families, especially their children. This occupation—so different from hunting or warfare—had inevitably shaped female priorities and influenced the way they saw the world. Women's voices should be heard not because justice required it and not because of women's innate purity but simply because incorporating the lessons they had learned from their distinctive life experiences would produce a better outcome for society. Starting from the female response to individual cases such as a mother scrubbing the floor, and rising to issues as monumental as war and peace, women had something unique to contribute to society, and everyone would benefit if they were allowed to make that contribution.

Addams had enormous respect for motherhood; she once called it "the highest gift which life can offer to a woman." But she never suggested that it was a woman's only significant function. Rather, she maintained that women should try to strike a balance between the "family claim" and the "social claim." She recognized that family responsibilities were the basic starting point for most women's lives. But she was convinced that if women wished their lives to be satisfying and useful, they needed to build outward from there—seeing themselves not only as wives and mothers but also as citizens of the larger society.

It may seem strange that we should be hearing so much about the maternal role from Addams, who was herself unmarried and who spent so much of her career living and working with other single women. But Addams felt that she and her unmarried colleagues were also participants in woman's millennial tradition of nurturing the human race. As professionals, these women—far more than their male colleagues—devoted their careers to working directly with mothers and children, focusing on such family issues as health and welfare. As for their personal lives, they had succeeded in carving out a space for their own careers, but most of them also continued throughout their lives to respond to the needs of parents and siblings. Taking into account both their professional and their personal lives, Addams and her unmarried colleagues could reasonably be included within her mythic vision of Woman, standing "with her hand upon the magnetic chain of humanity."

Myths and legends about women's roles always had a special appeal to Addams—particularly those that associated females with food, healing, and the perpetuation of life. New scientific findings reinforced her ideas, most notably a book by Otis T. Mason, a leading anthropologist, entitled *Women's Share in Primitive Culture*. Far from describing women as the cosseted homemakers prescribed by the cult of domesticity, Mason portrayed them as a major force in human history. According to him, it was women, concerned about their children's welfare, who made the first experiments with agriculture and who persuaded their tribes to give up nomadism and live in settled societies.

Mason's specific conclusions have not stood the test of time, but as metaphors, they spurred Addams' imagination, suggesting how women's maternal role could be connected to their membership in the larger society. Women should not have to choose between motherhood and public lives, she concluded. They had something to contribute to the world around them precisely because of their maternal experience. Caring for their families had given them special insight into many of the problems facing society as a whole. In fact, she observed, "a city is in many respects a great business corporation, but in other respects it is enlarged housekeeping." For women to undertake this kind of "municipal housekeeping"—as it was often called— would allow them to use their skills in a wider sphere and benefit society at the same time.

Addams did not see women's public participation as a diversion from their family obligations. For tens of thousands of years, she said, women had been able to protect the health and welfare of their families through their own individual actions. But in the industrial era, "women's old traditional work has been slowly but inevitably slipping out of the household." Caring for one's family now required paying attention to the quality of city water, the safety of store-bought food, and the regularity of municipal garbage collection. Children received their education in local schools, not at their mother's knee; milk came from commercial dairies, not the family cow; and safe housing depended on landlords and city inspectors and tenement laws. "In short," wrote Addams, "if woman would keep on with her old business of caring for her house and rearing her children, she will have to have some conscience in regard to public affairs. . . . Women are pushed outside of the home in order that they may preserve the home."

Addams was only one of many female progressives who made this argument. For example, reform journalist Rheta Childe Dorr put it this way: "Woman's place is in the Home, but Home is not contained within the four walls of an individual home. Home is the community." This approach—justifying women's public role by connecting it to their traditional responsibilities as wives and mothers—is sometimes called "progressive maternalism." In our own time, many critics have shown the limitations of such thinking. They argue that, no matter how expansively some maternalists like Addams saw municipal housekeeping, the practice of categorizing women primarily as family caregivers tended to justify a more restricted role for them—encouraging men to delegate to the female sex a narrowly defined set of "women's issues" (such as child welfare) while themselves maintaining control over the rest of public life. This is a legitimate critique, and it is given added force by the ways in which maternalist arguments actually have been used over the years to keep women in a subordinated role.

Did the maternalists of Addams' era really think of women only as mothers? Or were they simply offering this interpretation because, at the time, it seemed the most acceptable way of promoting women's entry into the public sphere? Some maternalists probably fit neatly into one or the other of these two categories, but

Addams herself—like many of her contemporaries—seems truly to have had a foot in each camp. On the one hand, she did believe that women's historic role as nurturer gave them a unique and valuable perspective on life; on the other, she was well-aware that in Progressive Era America, stressing that fact was the most effective way of arguing for an expansion of women's public role.

Again and again, Addams' maternalist rhetoric allowed her to wrap a far-reaching argument in unassuming clothes. So, while at one level she was urging women to engage in public activity simply to protect their own families' interests, she was simultaneously conveying her larger message: that each family's interests were entwined with those of the whole community. To illustrate, she told the story of an elderly widow, a longtime resident of the 19th Ward—who for many years held herself aloof from the Italians moving in around her. Resisting any connection with the neighborhood, she raised her two daughters in proud isolation and sent them east to college. Then, one summer, tragedy struck: Her eldest daughter, home for vacation, died in a typhoid epidemic that swept the ward, spread by faulty plumbing. This sad event made clear that the woman was just as vulnerable to the problems of her neighborhood as the immigrant families she had turned her back on. To Addams, the story vividly illustrated "the futility of the individual conscience which would isolate a family from the rest of the community and its interests."

Addams believed that in the interdependent modern world, women could not possibly stay isolated within their separate domestic cocoons. Rich or poor, they needed society's help in order to fulfill their responsibilities to their families. And in turn, society needed women's help in order to fulfill its responsibilities to its citizens.

Women and Their Obligations

One of Jane Addams' great strengths was her ability to conceive ambitious visions for the future while never losing sight of practical realities. So, in the case of women, even while she called for a dramatic expansion of their role as public citizens, she also gave sympathetic attention to the demands they were already facing in their daily lives. Obviously, scrubwomen carried burdens that society matrons did not. But as Addams widened her female acquaintanceship into different classes and ethnic groups, she came to feel that there were women in every walk of life who were struggling to fulfill their different—and sometimes conflicting—family obligations.

When it came to the experience of immigrant mothers, Addams' most intensive education began the day that three Italian women came to the door demanding to see the Devil Baby. As Addams recounted in her book *The Long Road of Women's Memory* (1916), these women had heard that a monstrous infant had been born in the neighborhood—complete with pointed ears, cloven hoofs, and a tail—and that the child had been brought to Hull-House. The settlement workers insisted there was no such baby on the premises, but this made little dent in the women's insistence, and over the next six weeks, many more people came looking for the baby. (The visitors included one redoubtable old woman who escaped from the poorhouse for the occasion and whose disappointment at not finding the Devil Baby in residence at Hull-House seemed to be quite overshadowed by her delight at having made the expedition.)

Addams soon learned that the ancient legend of the Devil Baby was familiar to nearly all her neighbors, although each ethnic group had its own variation of the story. The basic plot was always the same: A man committed some kind of wicked deed and was punished for his sins when his pregnant wife gave birth to a Devil Baby. Addams was particularly struck with how much this story seemed to mean to her female neighbors. She realized that many of their old certainties had been swept away in the move from their home villages to a huge industrial city. In such unfamiliar territory, the story of the Devil Baby seemed to function for them as an "instrument in the business of living"—valuable to them "because of its taming effects upon recalcitrant husbands and fathers." In fact, the deferential tones of the men who came seeking the Devil Baby at Hull-House during this time made Addams think that the women might be right; perhaps the legend did still "act as a restraining influence in the sphere of marital conduct."

After a few weeks, Addams no longer talked with every visitor who came looking for the Devil Baby, but she always went to the door when she heard the "high eager voices of old women." She found herself spending hours with them, listening to life stories they had never shared with her until the intensity of the Devil Baby incident somehow opened the floodgates. Addams came to recognize that in perpetuating and embellishing the legend, these hard-pressed women had done more than simply devise a strategy for managing the men in their lives; they had created "a literature of their own." This dark tale—offering dramatic proof that sin led directly to punishment—clearly helped soothe their spirits and restore their "shaken confidence as to the righteousness of the universe."

Yet if Addams admired the old women's capacity to ease their sorrows by means of their own homegrown art, she was also profoundly moved by their tragic lives. The women rarely complained about their lot. They seemed to take their losses and disappointments as simple facts of life, and they expressed nothing but love for the neglectful children and brutal husbands who peopled their stories. But Addams came away from the Devil Baby experience with a deep appreciation for the inherent sadness of many immigrant women's lives.

The Devil Baby incident was hardly the only time that Addams was reminded of immigrant women's troubles. As she went about the neighborhood, she continually encountered worried mothers trying to care adequately for their children while also working to get the money to feed them. Some of these women's husbands had died or deserted them, some perpetually drank up their wages, and some were unemployed or earned too little to support their families. But whatever the reasons, the neighborhood was full of women who were struggling to fulfill their family obligations—torn like Addams' scrubwoman friend between their roles as mother and breadwinner.

When Addams turned her attention to married women of her own class, she saw people living in far more comfortable circumstances. But considering their privileged status, Addams was struck by how limited their lives seemed to be. With their husbands supporting them, their children in school, and their servants doing the housework, these women often seemed hard-pressed to fill their time productively.

To Addams, this represented a loss for society, but it was also a tragedy for the women themselves. "Nothing so deadens the sympathies and shrivels the power of enjoyment," she wrote, as losing out on "opportunities for helpfulness." She compared the experience to the feeling one gets arriving in a strange city. Everyone else seems busy and connected, while the traveler stands looking on, with nothing to contribute. Clearly, many of these women felt they owed it to their families to remain at home, occupying themselves with the minutiae of homemaking. But Addams believed that they should broaden their horizons—both for the sake of their own fulfillment and for the sake of the world around them.

As a start, Addams suggested that women in comfortable circumstances might take a fresh look at their relationship to their own domestic servants. In millions of American households, she pointed out, "there is still one alien, one who is neither loved nor loving." With great sympathy, Addams described the social isolation of the live-in maid, cut off from both the companionship of working with other people her own age and the comfort of going home at night to her family. She urged women of her own class to make reasonable demands on the women who worked for them and to recognize their needs as individuals, including the fact that they had obligations to their own families. She pointed to recent data showing that more than half of all the female workers in the United States were servants. In other words, she said, if the women who employed these servants chose, they had it in their power to improve conditions for a significant segment of the country's working women.

Addams also urged middle-class women to look beyond their own doorsteps and add their energies to the rising tide of Progressive Era reform. Reiterating her point about the family claim and the social claim, she argued that the modern wife "must supplement her family conscience by a social and industrial conscience." As an example, she pointed out that "our grandmothers" used to take personal responsibility for the well-being of the young women who worked beside them in the home. Now that so many of the old household tasks were being performed in factories, middle-class matrons should feel equal concern for the young women who worked there. "What might not happen," Addams asked, "if women realized that the ancient family affection . . . might now be socialized and brought to bear on the current industrial organization?"

Thus, by encouraging women of her own class to redefine their obligations, Addams sought to inspire them with a larger view of their own potential. Broaden your idea of what a woman in your position can and should accomplish, said Addams, and you can enrich your own life, meet your family's needs more fully, and at the same time improve the lives of other Americans—including the many women less fortunate than you who are struggling to care for their own families just as you care for yours.

Moving into the Public Sphere

When Addams called on stay-at-home wives to enter public life, she was inviting them to join a wave of social activism among American women that had begun early in the 19th century and was particularly vigorous during the Progressive Era. From its very beginning, this movement had two distinct strands. One—involving women's cultural, religious, and charitable activities—was generally well-accepted. The other—which involved campaigning for specific public policies—had always sparked more controversy.

A notable example of the more controversial kind of female advocacy was women's participation in the fight to abolish slavery during the years before the Civil War. A generation of women gained organizational experience and a new sense of their own capacities from this campaign, setting the stage for America's first Women's Rights Convention in 1848 and helping to inspire the long campaign for women's suffrage. Nevertheless, female abolitionists were often bitterly criticized for their "unwomanly" behavior, and many suffragists endured similar attacks.

This history reminds us again why Addams—as well as many other female progressives—chose to stress the link between taking an interest in civic affairs and taking care of one's family. They were well-aware that old gender distinctions still lingered in the air and that, as nonvoters, women who involved themselves in political debate could easily be dismissed as intrusive outsiders. Addams herself had had some thoughts along this line during her early years at Hull-House. Since women were not allowed to vote, she asked herself, was it even ethical for them to be exerting pressure on elected representatives? And wasn't the world of politics a dirty environment that women should try to avoid? However, a few years of experience at Hull-House resolved her doubts. She became convinced that, as citizens, women had a legitimate interest in the well-being of their communities and that this well-being could not be achieved without political action.

Addams' growing interest in political involvement was reinforced by the climate of social progressivism around her. By the late 1890s, the old view that confined government's role to waging war and collecting tariffs was starting to give way to broader expectations. And these changes opened the door to female participation, because so many of the problems that social progressives were urging the government to deal with—especially in the crowded industrial cities—seemed particularly relevant to women's traditional concerns, including such issues as public health, safe housing, child labor, and working conditions for women.

Furthermore, while the political atmosphere was growing more amenable to women's participation, women's organizations themselves were becoming increasingly assertive. In particular, the women's club movement emerged as a major base for female activism. Indeed, it grew so rapidly that by 1905, the General Federation of Women's Clubs had an estimated membership of 500,000. Most of the clubs in the federation had started out simply as cultural and recreational organizations, but their interests expanded dramatically during the Progressive Era. Setting the new tone, Sarah Platt Decker announced at her inauguration as federation president: "Ladies, Dante is dead. He has been dead for several centuries, and I think it is time that we dropped the study of his *Inferno* and turned our attention to our own."

Speaking up with new assertiveness, women's clubs began promoting a host of progressive causes, including conservation, better schools, women's suffrage, and the abolition of child labor. In Galveston, clubwomen launched a campaign to improve sanitary conditions in bakeries and grocery stores. In Boston, they inspected public markets, organized public playgrounds, and campaigned for better methods of waste disposal. The Texas Association of Colored Women's Clubs founded an institution for African American boys. And in Philadelphia, members undertook studies of contagion and water filtration. One club member observed: "I have yet to hear of a town that is experiencing a civic awakening that has not had an active women's club."

In pursuing a broader social mission, the club members made skillful use of their resources, which included enthusiasm, money, and great numbers of volunteers. In addition, they had the capacity to lend social respectability to the causes they supported. For example, when the president of the General Federation of Women's Clubs, Ellen Henrotin, spoke out on behalf of the eight-hour day, she commanded the attention of many people who would have paid no heed at all to a labor leader making the same appeal.

Addams valued the capacity of the women's club movement to provide "ever-widening channels through which woman's moral energy may flow." She herself belonged to a number of women's clubs, gave hundreds of speeches to such groups around the country, and was active in the General Federation leadership. What she particularly appreciated about the clubs was the fact that their blend of sociability and respectability induced thousands of privileged women to educate themselves about social conditions and join the fight to improve them.

As proof that club participation could awaken women's consciences, Addams described how, when she was chair of the General Federation's Child Labor Committee, she sent out a questionnaire asking women's clubs around the country to report on their own local child labor situation. One club in Florida submitted data showing that a great number of Cuban children were employed in the local sugar mills. In returning the questionnaire, the club president chided the federation for not having been quicker with its survey; if her club had only known the facts sooner, they could have organized a campaign for legal protection before the legislature adjourned. "Of course," observed Addams, "the children had been working in the sugar mills for years, and had probably gone back and forth under the very eyes of the club women, but the women had never seen them, much less felt any obligation to protect them, until they joined a club, and the club joined a Federation, and the Federation appointed a Child Labor Committee. . . . With their quickened perceptions they then saw the rescue of these familiar children in the light of a social obligation."

Seeking to extend the benefits of club membership to less privileged circles, Hull-House organized its own women's club, bringing together immigrant women from the neighborhood and more prosperous women from other parts of the city. This group met regularly to discuss current events, monitor the activities of the county juvenile court (described in Chapter 6), and organize monthly parties for the neighbors. Years later, a local girl could still recall what a luxury it was for someone like her mother to attend those gatherings— drinking tea that someone else had brewed and eating cake that someone else had baked.

The most distinguished women's club in the city was the Chicago Woman's Club (CWC), which had been established in 1876 in order to let women, in its founder's words, "take up the live issues of this world we live in." Among its many civic activities, the CWC helped launch the clean streets campaign described in Chapter 3, lobbied to obtain more city jobs for women, fought for municipal ownership of the streetcar system, and worked with Hull-House on many other issues, including child labor, juvenile justice, and women's working conditions.

The partnership between the CWC and Hull-House highlights the fact that although most clubwomen were married ladies of leisure, these organizations benefitted greatly from their unmarried members, many of whom made reform their profession. Thanks in part to their own interests and in part to gender discrimination in other occupations, a disproportionate number of career women during the Progressive Era worked in fields related to social welfare. The result was that, just when married women's voluntarism was at its height, it was reinforced by a new generation of bright, educated, and committed professional women.

These women had strayed from the conventional female path by choosing careers over marriage. But devoting their lives to social welfare—still perceived as "women's work"—gave them a reassuring image in the public eye. Of course, not everyone admired their life choices. Former Harvard president Charles Eliot, for one, bitterly criticized progressives for featuring Addams in a large public meeting, arguing that putting such an "old maid" in the limelight gave people the wrong idea about what women should do with their lives. But many Americans considered unmarried female reformers to be even more noble and self-sacrificing than wives and mothers. For example, when a Chicago newspaper asked its readers in 1906, "Who is the best woman in Chicago?" the editors specified that only single women would be considered because "unless a married woman ignores the wishes of her husband it is difficult for her to achieve the same degree of goodness that the unmarried woman does."

Addams topped that popularity poll—being hailed as usual for her self-sacrifice and nobility of character. Besides the type of work she did, her physical appearance no doubt contributed to this idealized image of Chicago's own "Saint Jane." Her simple dark dresses and plain hairstyle made it clear that fashion had no interest for her, while her huge sad eyes and matronly figure appeared reassuringly maternal. Nevertheless, anyone who followed Addams' career closely knew that she could not have achieved what she did without many more worldly qualities, including administrative skill, tireless fundraising, and careful political analysis. As further proof of her worldliness, historian Allen Davis has documented the care with which Addams shaped her own public image—an effort that no doubt reflected her desire to make her mark in the world but at the same time reflected her awareness that her persona as a selfless humanitarian was one of her strongest assets in working for social change.

Like Addams, most female professionals in the Progressive Era were less ethereal and a great deal more interesting than the secular saints described in the popular press. Addams herself provided a more accurate picture of them when she stressed their "pioneer qualities of character" and their "intellectual hunger." Another characteristic that distinguished these women was their ability to combine passionate idealism about their goals with brisk realism about the actual problems they were combating. Addams once described a lunch meeting at which she commented to a fellow settlement worker how amazing it was that they should be eating a hearty meal while discussing foul slaughterhouses. To which the woman replied that if Addams lived near a creek into which the five biggest slaughterhouses in the world poured their waste, "you would be so interested in garbage that you would talk about it at luncheon or any other time."

By the early years of the 20th century, American women were speaking out on public issues with increasing fervor and effectiveness. From leaders of society like Ellen Henrotin to settlement workers like Jane Addams, they were collaborating in numerous ways to demonstrate the breadth of women's understanding and the depth of their commitment to social reform.

Campaigning for the Vote

The more that American women involved themselves in public affairs, the more acutely many of them came to feel that they could never fully achieve their goals without being able to vote. For years, they had confined their political efforts to public advocacy or trying to influence male officeholders behind the scenes. But it was becoming increasingly clear, as Addams later explained, that women without the vote "were as much outside the real life of the world as any set of disfranchised free men could have been in all history."

Opponents of female suffrage insisted that getting the vote would only drag women down into the dirty world of politics. As writer John Boyle O'Reilly observed: "It would be no more deplorable to see an angel harnessed to a machine than to see a woman voting." This was an argument made by women as well as men. Many conservative women proudly wore the red rose of anti-suffrage, and even outspoken reformers, such as educator Catharine Beecher, maintained that women should stay out of the political arena. As for labor organizer Mother Jones, she dismissed all politics as corrupt and irrelevant, insisting: "You don't need a vote to raise hell." But the suffragists disagreed. The frustration of trying to bring about social change from outside the political arena had convinced them of two things: that women needed the vote in order to be credible as reformers and that male reformers needed the support of female voters in order to build a progressive majority.

Addams herself became active in the suffrage movement in 1906. By then, women had been seeking the vote for nearly eighty years—ever since the first Women's Rights Convention in Seneca Falls in 1848. Having devoted most of their energies to working for the abolition of slavery until the Civil War ended in 1865, the women were bitterly disappointed when they were not included in the Fifteenth Amendment that gave freed male slaves the vote. Neither major political party showed any interest in rectifying the situation, and in the anguished debate over whether to keep pressing at the federal level or pursue a state-by-state strategy, the suffrage movement split into two hostile organizations—one led by the relatively moderate suffragist leader Lucy Stone and the other by the more militant Elizabeth Cady Stanton and Susan B. Anthony. Some ground was gained during the 1890s, when four western territories—eager for female settlers—entered the Union with women's suffrage in their constitutions. But not a single additional state approved votes for women between 1897 and 1910.

Despite this discouraging record, the movement took on a new sense of optimism during the early 20th century. By then, the two warring factions had come back together to form the National American Woman Suffrage Association (NAWSA). With their internal battles behind them, the NAWSA leadership concentrated on building a solid base of socially prominent women. They were knocking on a door that was already halfway open; as women of the leisure class had become more active in reform, many of them had become convinced—as Addams had—that they needed the vote in order to achieve their social goals. Meanwhile, a new generation of younger suffragists energized the movement by reaching out to include a broader range of participants, including women from labor unions, colleges, church groups, and ethnic associations. Soon, women's suffrage was being promoted across the country with parades, rallies, and impassioned speeches.

Addams belonged to NAWSA and served as president in 1911. During this period, the individual state campaigns were operating fairly independently, with only loose coordination from the national headquarters. So Addams worked for suffrage in Illinois and also traveled to other states to support their efforts. In addition, she testified before several congressional committees because some suffrage leaders were still hoping to win the vote through federal action.

As Addams traveled around the country making her case, she never endorsed the argument advanced by some leading suffragists—regrettably including both Stanton and Anthony—that women's votes were needed in order to balance the uninformed votes of male immigrants and ex-slaves. Nor—like some of her allies—did she suggest that the vote should only go to educated women. She insisted that people of all kinds had "reservoirs of moral power and civic ability." And she reiterated the fact that working women had an even larger stake in government than other women because they were more vulnerable to the problems that government should be addressing.

Addams' first major effort on behalf of women's suffrage came in 1907, when she joined a long-standing campaign by

Illinois activists to allow women to vote in municipal elections. Working with society leader Ellen Henrotin and settlement worker Mary McDowell, Addams helped organize a coalition of one hundred women's groups that traveled by special train to Springfield to lobby the state legislature, with eight stops along the way for local rallies. Addams wrote later that the whole atmosphere was "so human, so spontaneous, and so direct" that she was convinced women's hour for political recognition had finally arrived. However, her impression was wrong. The state legislature turned the municipal suffrage bill down and continued to do so every year until 1913.

Not until 1920—after World War I had come and gone—would American women finally become full-fledged members of the electorate. Nevertheless, by the time the war began in 1914, 11 states had given women full suffrage, and others had (like Illinois) approved "partial suffrage," allowing women to vote in certain kinds of elections. It was clear that the tide was starting to turn, and Addams had helped to bring that change about. She had joined the campaign later than many of her friends and colleagues, but historian Louise Young maintains that the importance of her contribution during this latter part of the drive for suffrage "can hardly be overstated."

One of Addams' great talents in this kind of public advocacy was her capacity to make a contentious argument in a disarming way. To see this talent at work, one need only read the engaging essay she wrote in 1913 entitled "If Men Were Seeking the Franchise." Addams asks her readers to imagine a society that has somehow evolved, as the family did, in such a way that its chief concern is nurturing children and protecting the vulnerable. "In short," writes Addams, "let us imagine a hypothetical society organized upon the belief that 'there is no wealth but life.'" Suppose, she says, that because women have always excelled in protecting human welfare, they are the leaders of this society. Now imagine that a group of men has come before the female elders, asking for the vote.

Gently reminding her readers of the empty rationalizations so often dispensed to women, Addams draws our attention to the fact that her imaginary female elders do *not* brush the men off by telling them that most members of their sex are not interested in voting or that politics would corrupt them or that they would probably vote just like their mothers. Instead, these wise women—showing a touch of pragmatism—make an assessment based on men's actual behavior. Taking note of men's carelessness around the home and their readiness to put profit over human life, the female elders ask whether men could really be trusted to keep the cities clean and the factories safe for workers. Furthermore, might they not follow the pattern set by other man-ruled societies and spend more money on prisons and police than on religion, charity, and education? Most importantly, given their penchant for war, would they not be likely to waste public funds on armaments, forgetting that "the real object of the State is to nurture and protect life?"

Addams does not tell us the lady elders' final decision, but the direction of their thinking is clear, and it represents a compelling case for preventing men from monopolizing public affairs. Several larger points also emerge in the course of this essay. Addams reminds us indirectly that no nation is well-served when its government focuses only on increasing military power and financial wealth. And she makes clear that the more a government focuses on the well-being of its people, the more important it is for women to participate in it.

At the most obvious level, this essay is addressed to men because at the time Addams was writing, they controlled virtually all political power. But she is also speaking to women, reminding them of their own highest values and suggesting what society might look like if they could learn to care for their fellow citizens as generously as they have always cared for their families.

6

Nourishing the Spirit of Youth

Of all the social issues addressed during the Progressive Era, few attracted more sustained attention than the needs of children. Thus, for example, when Lewis Hine photographed tenement workshops and southern textile mills, when Judge Ben Lindsey campaigned for changes in juvenile justice, when women's clubs lobbied for parks and playgrounds, and when Lillian Wald went house to house caring for babies on New York City's Lower East Side, their combined efforts continually reinforced the idea that the well-being of the nation depended on the well-being of its children.

Why this emphasis on children? Part of the reason was political. "I think it is unquestionably true," said one reformer, "that if a person wishes to do any constructive social work in a community, the confidence of the people . . . can best be secured by beginning with work for children." But the progressives' interest in children involved much more than just political strategy. They were convinced that changing a person's early environment could change their lives. They recognized that most poor adults had already suffered so many years of deprivation and hard work that by now it would be hard to alter the direction of their lives. But the younger generation was a different matter. Looking at the dark side, Theodore Roosevelt warned that if urban children were neglected, society would undoubtedly "have to pay a terrible penalty of financial burden and social degradation in the future." On the positive side, journalist Jacob Riis observed: "Nothing is now better understood than that in the rescue of children is the key to the problem of city poverty."

Addams shared her fellow progressives' concern for children of all ages. She was proud of the Hull-House kindergarten, and she delighted in watching grade-schoolers at the settlement develop new skills and confidence. But it was adolescents who spoke most directly to her heart. She empathized with their troubles, rejoiced in their zest for life, and regarded their youthful awkwardness with sympathetic understanding. Among all her books, her favorite was the one she wrote about this age-group: *The Spirit of Youth and the City Streets* (1909).

The idea that the ages between about 12 and 18 constitute a specific stage of life emerged gradually during the 19th century, and by the time of the Progressive Era, social scientists were giving close attention to the role that the teenage years play in the transition from childhood to maturity. Seeking a term to describe this in-between period, psychologist G. Stanley Hall coined the word *adolescence* in 1904. He argued that these years represent a critical and often stressful stage in the development of the personality, during which patterns of behavior and thought are established that can shape an individual's whole adult life.

Addams was familiar with Hall's work, and the views she expressed in *The Spirit of Youth* about the place of adolescence in individual development were similar to his. Passages in her book also recapitulated the progressive argument that caring for the younger generation is in society's best interest because today's adolescents are tomorrow's parents and workers and citizens. But Addams added something new to the discussion when she insisted that young people are important to society not only because of what they may accomplish in the future but because of what their energy and "iridescent dreams" contribute to the world every single day.

Addams acknowledged that young people do not always express their aspirations as clearly as they might, but she maintained that instead of scoffing at their idealism, adults should help them channel their bright visions into constructive action. Imagine, she said, that someone is walking down the street calling out, "I am the spirit of Youth! With me, all things are possible." How should the older generation respond? "We may either smother the divine fire of youth or we may feed it. We may either stand stupidly staring as it sinks into . . . the intermittent blaze of folly or we may tend it into a lambent flame with power to make clean and bright our dingy city streets."

What was true for young people in general was especially true for the children of immigrants. Addams observed that they seemed to be even more idealistic than native-born adolescents. Unfortunately, given the circumstances of their lives, their chances for cruel disillusionment were also greater. One of Addams' primary goals throughout her career was to sustain the idealism of these second-generation immigrants and to help as many of them as possible to build happy and productive lives.

A Generation on Its Own

Addams believed that young immigrants needed considerable support as they navigated the challenges of urban life. But she observed that immigrant parents often found it hard to provide that help because they themselves were so new to America. Picture a mother distraught over a son who has stayed out too late or not come home at all. Her anguish is all the greater because, with her limited knowledge of English and of the surrounding city, she does not even know how to look for him. "Who cannot recall at least one of these desperate mothers," wrote Addams, "overworked and harried through a long day, . . . followed by a night of foreboding and misgiving because the very children for whom her life is sacrificed are slowly slipping away from her control and affection?"

It has often been noted that immigrants' children tend to learn the ways of the new society more quickly than their parents. Addams was among the first social observers to point out that this generational imbalance could be a strain on relations within the immigrant family. For example, she noticed that many of her neighbors were at such a loss in the city that they used their children "not only as interpreters of the language, but as buffers between them and Chicago." This role reversal, she said, often resulted "in a certain almost pathetic dependence of the family upon the child."

Having to mediate in this way left many immigrant children feeling burdened and even ashamed. They winced at their parents' halting English and foreign clothes, critically comparing them to the images of "real" Americans that they gleaned from their classmates, the city streets, and the popular press. Addams did her best at Hull-House to teach respect for all cultures, but it was an uphill struggle when young people's own experience showed them every day that what counted in Chicago was being a true-blue American. Seeking to achieve that magical status, many immigrant children concluded that their parents could be of little help to them; they would have to manage on their own.

This sense of independence was often reinforced by the fact that most young immigrants had paying jobs—doing factory work, shining shoes, selling newspapers, or running errands for stores and offices. Indeed, given the unpredictability of adults' employment, it was not uncommon for children's wages to represent a significant part of their families' income, especially during periods of economic downturn. One can easily imagine the difficulty of trying to discipline a 14-year-old son or daughter on whose earnings the whole family depends. Moreover, even in cases where children's wages were not needed for their families' support, the fact that young people could earn their own spending money gave them a level of autonomy that would have been unthinkable in the Old World.

Addams knew that disputes over children's wages precipitated many a family fight, accentuating the growing gulf between the generations. The pain that immigrant parents felt over these strained relationships was brought home to her one night when Hull-House produced a play on the topic, written by an Italian man in the neighborhood. Seeing tears in the eyes of many audience members, Addams hoped that the play had helped to free each one of them from "a sense of isolation and an injured belief that his children were the worst of all."

Addams sympathized with her neighbors' distress, but she was convinced that if they clung to what she called "Old World" methods of parenting—based on coercion and an expectation of traditional obedience—they would only make their situation worse. Instead, they would have to rely on "sympathy and adaptability," appreciating their children's eagerness for experience and helping them find constructive ways of expressing it. She recognized how difficult this was, but she was convinced that it had to be done. For, however painful the present standoff was for the older generation, she believed that it was even worse for their children. At odds with the adults who loved and cared most about them, these young people were trying to grapple alone—at a very vulnerable age—with all the complications of modern urban life.

Coming of Age in an Immigrant Neighborhood

When we talk about low-income urban adolescents during the Progressive Era, it is important to remember that we are almost always talking about workers, not students. This fact struck Addams and her fellow reformers with particular force because in their own middle-class world, the idea of the sheltered child had by then established itself as a powerful ideal. The prevailing cult of domesticity that sought to seclude women from the hurly-burly of the marketplace also applied to their children, placing a strong emphasis on the purity and innocence of childhood.

Rather than expecting their offspring to help the family make its living, as earlier generations had done, urban middle-class parents of the Progressive Era concentrated on what they owed their children: full-time maternal nurturing, education, and financial support well past their teens. Thus, as sociologist Viviana Zelizer has observed, the American child had evolved over the course of the 19th century from an economically useful member of the household to an "economically worthless, emotionally priceless child."

This exalted version of childhood and youth was, of course, an ideal that many American families could not afford to put into practice. But the contrast between ideal and reality was particularly sharp in poor immigrant neighborhoods like the 19th Ward, where nearly all adolescents were engaged in full-time wage labor. Addams was forcefully reminded of this fact at the first Hull-House Christmas party in 1889. When she passed around a dish of candy, several neighborhood girls told her they could not stand the sight of it because they spent 14 hours a day wrapping candy in a local factory. Addams was shocked that children so young should associate this innocent treat with hard work instead of pleasure. But in the years that followed, her education was painfully expanded. From watching tiny children laboring beside their mothers in tenement workshops to comforting the parents of boys killed in factory accidents, she was confronted over and over with the impact of early work on the lives of young people.

During the same years that Addams was discovering the evils of child labor in the 19th Ward, many other progressives were having their own similar experiences. As a result, the effort to eliminate child labor became one of the dominant crusades of the Progressive Era, inspiring years of effort by women's clubs, settlement workers, civic groups, and labor unions all over the country. Addams herself wrote and spoke frequently on the subject, and as she developed her argument, she emerged as one of the campaign's most eloquent advocates.

One common defense of child labor was the claim that going to work early helped to build young people's character. In response, Addams simply asked people to use their own eyes. Look at the working children in your own city, she would say. Notice how gray their skin is; you can spot it even when they are playing in the street. Look at their expressions, shadowed with an air of "premature anxiety and sense of responsibility." She observed that if we encountered conditions like these in a foreign country, we would call them pathetic. But because we see them around us every day, we have come to accept them as part of the urban landscape.

Starting work too soon, said Addams, damaged not only young people's bodies but also their minds and spirits. She quoted a British study indicating that at the age of 21, after seven years of factory employment, young workers had smaller vocabularies, narrower interests, and lower intelligence scores than they had had at the age of 14. No wonder, said Addams. The monotony of their work killed all spontaneity of thought, while the long hours and lack of public recreation facilities made it difficult for them to restore their spirits after work was over. A few years of this kind of life and "the joy of youth is well nigh extinguished." Watch the young people heading home from work, she said; they trudge along as listlessly as people twice their age.

When defenders of child labor argued that parents had every right to send their children to work if they chose to, Addams responded by showing what the system cost society as a whole. For example, she said, we might praise a boy who quit school so he could support his widowed mother. But we must recognize that his entering the workforce so young will involve a social as well as a personal cost—that it will "lower wages, add an illiterate member to the community, and arrest the development of a capable workingman." In terms of the national economy, she said, forcing young minds and bodies to adapt too early to the harsh industrial routine was a sure way to produce a dispirited and unproductive workforce.

Besides pointing to the physical and emotional damage caused by child labor, Addams also made an economic case against it. Think of the wasted public investment, she said. We pour tax dollars into educating the nation's children, but as soon as they leave school, we forget about them. Instead of continuing to nurture this national asset we have created, we give employers a free hand with it, allowing them to deaden and diminish it in any way they choose. Thus, we squander the chance of developing the educated and motivated workforce that our economy needs, and we quench "the divine fire of youth" that our society needs.

One important way to improve young immigrants' working lives, Addams believed, was to give them a better education. Keeping children in school was, in fact, a continuing theme throughout the Progressive Era, although the motivations behind this effort varied widely. On the more punitive side, a Chicago school board report in 1897 explained that truancy laws made it possible "to arrest all these little beggars, loafers and vagabonds that infest our city, take them off the streets and put them in schools where they are compelled to learn moral principles." On the other hand, many reformers supported compulsory attendance laws as a weapon against child labor. As for Addams, she shared the desire to end child labor, but she also had a grander vision of what education could do for young people if it were truly tailored to their needs.

At the time she was writing, the pattern of instruction in most American schools was quite regimented, relying almost entirely on textbook readings, memorization, and rote recitation. Addams did not think this style of instruction was particularly well-suited to children of any social group, and she believed it was especially inappropriate for immigrant children, who were sometimes shaky in their English and came from families who were not well-equipped to broaden their education at home.

In considering how public schools might serve their immigrant students better, Addams was strongly influenced by her years of dialogue with philosopher/educator John Dewey. In books such as *The School and Society* (1900), Dewey argued that students needed to be active participants in their education rather than simply receptacles for cut-and-dried facts dispensed by a teacher. Reading and writing were important, but students also needed to learn by exploring the world around them. And, most importantly, they needed to think of their education—and of life itself—as a continual process of active learning, rather than a series of mechanical steps, each one justified only because it prepared you for the next. "I believe," wrote Dewey, "that education is a process of living and not a preparation for living."

The kind of approach Dewey and Addams favored—often called "progressive education"—had so far only been used with privileged children in such places as Dewey's Lab School at the University of Chicago. But Addams believed that progressive education had even more to offer immigrant children. In particular, stressing the needs and capacities of individual children could help them transcend what she called a "superficial standard of Americanism"—one that devalued their own backgrounds. They should, of course, be helped to learn what they needed to know about contemporary society, but they could also be encouraged to take pride in their own cultural traditions and thus in their families and in themselves. "You must not take away," said Addams in summation, "you must add."

Progressive education often included courses in manual arts as a way of giving children hands-on experience with the real world. Addams supported such programs, but she felt that much more was needed, especially for students who were likely to spend their whole lives as industrial workers. She therefore called for an expansion of vocational education so students could qualify for better jobs when they finished school. Toward that end, she helped to found the National Society for the Promotion of Industrial Education in 1906; this group in turn helped win passage in 1917 of a landmark federal law that provided funding for vocational training.

The campaign for vocational education has sometimes been criticized as a self-interested effort to turn working-class children into obedient factory employees instead of encouraging them to set higher goals for themselves. Some proponents of vocational education did have limited expectations for working class children, and others were simply pursuing their own economic interests. But it would be wrong to include Addams among these people, given the totality of her efforts for immigrant children and the breadth of the educational program she was advocating for them.

One evidence of Addams' more humanitarian approach was her continuing insistence that each worker should be trained to be, as she said, "a conscious member of society, having some notion of his social and industrial value." She hated the idea that once young people left school, so many of them simply turned themselves into automata at work and then made up for it at night with "hours of lurid and unprofitable pleasure." To prevent this dehumanizing routine, she urged that vocational education should include courses that helped students understand how industrial jobs fit into the overall economy and into the whole history of human craftsmanship. This was an aspect of workers' education that Addams had introduced in a small way at Hull-House and she was eager to see it applied more broadly.

However, she was never able to get it accepted as an integral part of the nation's approach to vocational training.

Addams suffered further disappointments when she was named to the Chicago Board of Education in 1905. Assigned to chair the committee that oversaw teacher promotions and salaries, she found the issues so bitterly contested that she was unable to accomplish anything at all—except, as it turned out, to antagonize everyone. Addams insisted that she herself played "a most inglorious part in this unnecessary conflict." She described dealing one year with a majority that struck her as "exasperatingly conservative" and the next year with a group who seemed "frustratingly radical." Trying to strike a middle path, Addams found herself "of course highly unsatisfactory to both." When the next mayor dismissed most of her former allies and Addams chose not to resign in protest, she came in for still more condemnation. "What a dreadful backward step has been taken because of St. Jane," raged one acquaintance.

Given Addams' flair for coalition-building and organizational politics, it is a little surprising to see her fail so dismally in this particular arena. Perhaps the skills that worked so effectively in voluntary organizations were not as well-suited to the more abrasive and exposed world of public agencies. Or perhaps the kind of bridge-building at which she excelled was simply out of the question during a period of such extreme polarization. Whatever the reasons, Addams was unable during her brief term on the Board to achieve any of the educational changes she had hoped for. Nevertheless, in her private capacity, she continued for the rest of her life to try to help young immigrants make the transition from school to work and from childhood to maturity.

The Temptations of the City

As urban adolescents made that passage from childhood to maturity, what kinds of dangers did they face? Addams thought that without really meaning to, they could drift into behavior that would get them into serious trouble. Indeed, when she first began thinking about the book that became *The Spirit of Youth and the City Streets*, she considered calling it *Juvenile*

Delinquency and Public Morality. The judgmental tone of that title hardly does justice to the sympathy with which she approached her subject, but Addams' concern about juvenile delinquency did haunt nearly every page of the book—not so much because she feared the damage that delinquents would do to society but rather because of her conviction that wrong steps taken in adolescence could prove irreversible in later life.

In choosing to write about juvenile delinquency, Addams was addressing a social problem that was attracting growing public concern. Most working-class urban adolescents during this period had jobs that removed them from the oversight of their families throughout the workday, and many also spent their leisure hours on their own. "Never before in civilization," wrote Addams, "have such numbers of young girls been suddenly released from the protection of the home and permitted to walk unattended upon city streets and to work under alien roofs. . . . Never before have such numbers of young men earned money independently of the family life, and felt themselves free to spend it as they choose."

The concerns Addams expressed were felt by many progressives. Look at the urban scene through their eyes, and you see a whole generation of young people cut loose from the traditional social anchors—dismissive of their parents, exploited by their employers, minimally prepared for life by their schooling, full of adolescent desires, walking the anonymous city streets, ripe for trouble. Addams understood why the sight of these young people made her fellow reformers uneasy; sometimes, it worried her too. But many of the most sympathetic passages in *The Spirit of Youth* were the ones in which she sought to explain the innocent hunger for fun and excitement that she believed drove these youthful pleasure-seekers.

For example, Addams said that we may be put off by the brassy voice of the strutting shopgirl as she parades her cheap finery down the street. "And yet through the huge hat, with its wilderness of bedraggled feathers, the girl announces to the world that she is here. She demands attention to the fact of her existence, she states that she is ready to live, to take her place in the world." Every generation, said Addams, longs for "reassurance as to the value and charm of life." If young people cannot find this reassurance in positive forms, they will reach for it in other ways. The teenage gambler, the petty thief, the girl of easy virtue—nearly all these young people get into trouble in the first place, she suggested, simply out of "a love for pleasure, 'gone wrong.'"

Addams' views on what constituted proper social behavior sound quite strict—even prudish—in terms of today's standards, although they were not unusual for her time. She not only opposed drinking and gambling and extramarital sex; she also worried that young people devoted too much time to roller-coaster rides and dance halls and the movies. It is in this respect that Addams come closest to resembling the Progressive Era reformers who campaigned against behaviors such as gambling, prostitution, drinking, and pornography. Because these moral crusaders tended to target settings that primarily served the working class, they were accused by their critics at the time—and by many historians today—of trying to impose their own behavioral preferences on people whose lifestyles were different from their own. It is a legitimate point, and at least some of the progressives who specialized in these crusades can fairly be faulted on those grounds.

As for Addams, her warnings about the dangers of drinking and early sex and even roller-coaster rides do sometimes seem to echo the preachings of the moral crusaders. Nevertheless, it is important to remember that she did not focus on young people's potential sinfulness or criminality but on their vulnerability to bad influences and bad choices. For example, her stand against alcohol was based on her conviction that young people were more likely to drift into trouble when they had had too much to drink. Furthermore, her views were strongly influenced by having lived in a neighborhood where husbands' excessive drinking did indeed impose a terrible toll on many families— both in terms of lost wages and domestic abuse.

Addams also favored sexual abstinence for the young, stressing particularly the dangers young girls faced in the city. She did occasionally acknowledge that during adolescence, girls as well as boys experienced "bodily desires" that were "keen and insistent." But her main concern was to protect young women from unwanted male advances. This view of the relations between the sexes was not uncommon for the time; indeed, many social expectations and customs were based on the assumption that physical desire was an exclusively male characteristic. Like her contemporaries, Addams tended to take it for granted that if a young woman engaged in sexual dalliance, it was because she was too eager for the favors offered in exchange or too naïve or too frightened or too tipsy to say no.

Young women's vulnerability was one of the dominant themes in Addams' book *New Conscience and an Ancient Evil* (1912). The "ancient evil" referred to in the title was prostitution. This topic aroused enormous public interest during the Progressive Era, partly because of general concern over urban vice but more specifically because of dramatic stories about so-called "white slavery rings"—elaborate criminal networks that supposedly operated across state and even national borders to lure young women into prostitution and then profit from their earnings.

Most historians today agree that these allegations were considerably exaggerated. But in a neighborhood like the 19th Ward, Addams had had plenty of opportunities to see prostitutes being badly treated by the men who profited from their work. Responding to these experiences as well as to the lurid stories about the "white-slave traffic," she concluded that prostitution was indeed a form of slavery. She considered its female participants to be victims, not sinners, and in *New Conscience*, she called on her fellow citizens—especially women—to take up this cause just as the abolitionists had rallied against slavery in the 19th century.

Prostitution was, of course, a women's issue to Addams, but more than that, it was a young women's issue. Young women were the most attractive to predators, and they were also the most easily intimidated. Furthermore, one misstep at this early age could, in Addams' view, change a girl's life forever. This concern was undoubtedly somewhat overdramatized, but it was not entirely irrational in an era that placed enormous emphasis on female purity and severely restricted information about birth control. Addams had seen firsthand how cruelly young women could be rejected—even by their own families—if they became pregnant out of wedlock. And she was well-aware of the grim alternatives such women were likely to face when they tried to manage on their own in an unforgiving city.

While sexual entanglement represented the greatest hazard for young urban women, the most common pitfall for young men was crime. Addams observed that boys' first infractions often involved minor episodes of thievery, such as stealing spare lumber to build a fort or a dime-store trinket on a dare or coal for their families. But troubles with the police could escalate, and if things went badly, a young man could ultimately find himself carrying two burdens: the brutalizing experience of prison and the stigma of a criminal record. As with the troubles of wayward girls, what haunted Addams about these situations was the heavy price that an adolescent boy might have to pay for one misguided adventure.

Helping Young People Stay Out of Trouble

Addams believed that virtually all adolescents who got into trouble—male or female—could be helped if they were reached early enough and in a humane enough way. It was this belief that underlay one of the most famous reform initiatives in which Hull-House participated: the first juvenile court in American history.

In 19th century America, each state defined for itself the age at which children could be held criminally responsible for their actions; most states set the age somewhere between seven and twelve. Above that age, young offenders were tried in the same courts as adults and often imprisoned with adults if they were convicted. Many progressives expressed concern about this arrangement; for example, John Peter Altgeld (future governor of Illinois) wrote a book in 1882 arguing that to expose young offenders to the grim world of adult prison caused more crime than it prevented. "Brutal treatment brutalizes," he wrote. Nevertheless, except for some procedural reforms in Massachusetts, the system remained more or less unchanged.

Then, in the early 1890s, a predominantly female coalition led by the Chicago Woman's Club started a campaign to create a separate court for young offenders that would focus on rehabilitation rather than punishment. (Hull-House residents participated in this effort, particularly Julia Lathrop, who helped write the proposed legislation.) After several years of advocacy, the bill was finally approved in 1899, establishing the nation's first juvenile court. The new law allowed the juvenile court judge great latitude in terms of procedure and gave him the option of putting young offenders on probation rather than imprisoning them.

Once the Court legislation passed, the group of women who had worked to get it set up reorganized themselves into a monitoring committee (based at Hull-House) to ensure that the system worked as they had hoped. They immediately recognized one serious drawback: The enabling legislation provided no funding for probation staff or for juvenile detention facilities. Clearly, reforming the trial process would accomplish little if the young defendants who were convicted wound up either jailed with adults or thrown back unsupervised on the street.

It was at this point that Hull-House made its most important contribution to the project, spearheaded by a volunteer at the settlement: Louise DeKoven Bowen. A wealthy and socially prominent woman just a year older than Addams, Bowen was a member of the Hull-House board and the settlement's largest donor. Her strong opinions and imperious manner occasionally caused difficulties, but she was devoted to Addams, and Addams handled her with great diplomacy, soothing her occasional tempers, accommodating her idiosyncrasies, and always making clear how much she valued this "most active and ardent of the Hull-House trustees."

In 1900, when Bowen became chair of the monitoring committee, she took charge of the effort to resolve the court's funding problems. Working with Julia Lathrop, the Chicago Woman's Club, local churchwomen, and other supporters, Bowen raised enough money to staff the entire probation department, and she continued to do so every year for the next six years. Finally, in 1906, Bowen led the campaign that persuaded the county to put all the probation workers on the public payroll and to erect a brand-new court building and detention home on land donated by the city. Hull-House had played only a supporting role in getting the court established, but it was the dominant force in converting it from a limited experiment into a formal juvenile justice system.

Two years after the juvenile court opened in Chicago, a similar court was established in Denver, Colorado, presided over by the well-known progressive Judge Ben Lindsey. Soon, both Chicago and Denver were besieged with requests for information, and by 1925, all but two states in the country had established juvenile courts of their own. Today, more than a century after the reformers achieved their goal, juvenile courts are an integral part of the American judicial system.

The juvenile court places great reliance on the wisdom of the presiding judge, who conducts the proceedings with a relatively free hand and decides the case based on his or her own best judgment. Critics have argued that to give a single individual such control over young people's lives places the judge in an almost parental role, trespassing on the rights of the defendants' own families. Historian Michael McGerr takes the argument even further, maintaining that the juvenile courts are simply one example of the progressives' broader campaign to remake American society in their own middle-class image.

It is true that many of the juvenile court activists worried about the capacity of poor and immigrant parents to see their children through the hazards of urban adolescence. On the other hand, the court plan also reflected the reformers' optimistic conviction that, given a chance, almost every juvenile delinquent had the potential to make a fresh start in life. And to appreciate why the activists believed that reform was needed, it is worth recalling that during the last six months before the juvenile court was established, 145 boys between the ages of 9 and 13 were sent to the Chicago city jail for terms ranging from a few days to nine months. Whatever the flaws of the juvenile court, it replaced a system that was much worse.

Addams herself was convinced that the juvenile court made a valuable contribution by identifying young people when they first got into trouble and trying to help them avoid getting in any deeper. But what could be done to help young people stay out of trouble in the first place? Once Cook County assumed full responsibility for the court, the members of the court-monitoring committee reorganized themselves as the Juvenile Protective Association (JPA). In that capacity, they devoted themselves to what they saw as one key aspect of prevention: providing the city's young people with wholesome forms of recreation. They lobbied against the sale of liquor, drugs, and tobacco to minors; exposed the close alliance between the liquor industry and the more unsavory dance halls; pressured movie theaters to improve the quality of their offerings; and worked to increase the city's supply of social centers, gardens, and bathing beaches.

Addams supported the JPA's activities, especially the effort to give young people more options for their leisure time. She was convinced that the love of play was a vital part of human culture, providing young people with valuable opportunities to express their own individuality, overcome differences of language and religion, deal fairly with one another, and imagine themselves in other settings and other lives. Her quarrel with saloons and dance halls and amusement parks was not that they catered too much to young people's love of play but that the kind of play they offered was too narrow, too materialistic, and too passive.

Addams understood that one could not lure young people away from commercial recreation just by preaching at them. In order to compete for their attention, it was necessary to accept their natural longing for fun and simply give them better ways of expressing it. After all, she said, there were more than 800,000 young people in Chicago—all of them eager for diversion. If public-spirited adults did not address this yearning, then businessmen out for a quick profit surely would.

American progressives in many cities shared Addams' view of the challenge, and like her, they lobbied municipal officials for more public recreation facilities—more parks, more gymnasiums, and more playgrounds. They particularly stressed building playgrounds, partly because they could be constructed on relatively small city lots and partly because the reformers believed, as psychologist Henry S. Curtis put it, that the supervised playground had the potential to be "a school of character and all the social virtues." The growing enthusiasm for playgrounds was reflected in the formation of the Playground Association of America in 1906 (with Curtis and Addams among the founders). By 1908, the *New York Times* estimated that 200 American cities would soon have new "well-organized" playgrounds.

Not all young people welcomed the supervised recreation the reformers valued so highly; for example, one boy complained that playing was much less fun when there were "so many men and women around telling you what to do." But looked at overall, progressives did succeed in dramatically increasing the amount of public recreational space available to urban children, particularly in poor neighborhoods.

Besides lobbying for public parks and playgrounds, reformers themselves sponsored a broad array of recreational activities in churches, settlement houses, and neighborhood centers. Hull-House had its own extensive sports program, with teams and classes as well as Saturday night contests that brought out the whole neighborhood. A Chicago newspaper noted in 1902 that the Hull-House girls' basketball team had not been defeated since its second year and was now "considered invincible." The settlement also maintained a summer camp outside the city at a country estate donated by Louise Bowen.

If there was one thing that brought young people to Hull-House in even larger numbers than athletics, it was the chance to socialize—which, as Addams noted, "all young things crave and which those who have spent long hours in a factory or shop demand as a right." Adolescents participated by the hundreds in parties, dancing classes, and social clubs. The drinks at these gatherings were non-alcoholic, and the level of supervision is suggested by Addams' comment that "certain kinds of dancing" were "strictly prohibited." But if these rules caused some high-livers to stay away, huge numbers of young people came regularly and seem to have had a good time.

Besides sports and socializing, the Hull-House program also included a great variety of educational clubs and classes. The experience of one young woman from the neighborhood, Hilda Polachek, suggests what this array of offerings could mean to an ambitious adolescent. Polachek had already started working when she first visited Hull-House at the age of 14. As a Jew, she was uneasy about going to the settlement, which she knew was run by Protestants. But when friends persuaded her to come with them to the annual Christmas party, she was overwhelmed by the warmth of Addams' welcome and the sight of young people from so many different countries enjoying each other's company. "What greater service can a human being give to her country," wrote Polachek, "than to banish fear from the heart of a child? Jane Addams did that for me. . . . I know that I became a staunch American at that party."

In her autobiography, Polachek describes how starved she was for "the social stimulus of people my own age" after working all day in a garment factory. Hull-House filled that hole in her life, and by the time she was 18, she was spending almost every night there—first in a reading club, then in an art class, then the Shakespeare Club, a dancing club, the gym, and an English composition class, with each step personally encouraged by Addams. One day, when Polachek was in her early 20s, Addams took her breath away by asking her to teach an English class for adults. Later, also at Addams' suggestion, Polachek organized a club specifically for people her own age; the group met every week, alternating between dances and discussion nights.

Meanwhile, even though Polachek had left school after fifth grade, Addams arranged for her to spend one term at the University of Chicago as a "special student." Not only did Addams arrange for free tuition, but she also reimbursed Polachek's family for the wages they lost while she was in school. The courses were a struggle and Polacheck did not pass all of them, but she left the university, she says, with "an everlasting desire to read and study." She adds: "I often wonder what my life would have been like if I did not have that short term in the university made possible by Jane Addams." Polachek never returned to the factory. After a brief spell working at Hull-House, she married and moved to Milwaukee, raised a family, and then devoted the rest of her life to working for a variety of public causes, including unemployment assistance during the Depression, war relief during World War II, and world peace in the 1950s.

Hilda Polachek's story reminds us how important Addams' own personal involvement was in shaping adolescents' experience at Hull-House. "No one will ever know," wrote Polacheck, "how many young people were helped by her wise counsel, how many were kept out of jail, how many were started on careers in the arts, in music, in industry, in science, and above all, in instilling in their hearts a true love of country—a love of service."

The young people who came to the settlement knew very well how low immigrants stood on the Chicago social scale, and this made Addams' interest and faith in them all the more inspiring. "'You can do it. You can do it,'" one girl remembers her telling them. "And we did it, partly because we didn't want to disappoint her." Addams' contributions as a mentor were made all the more compelling because she took such visible pleasure in young people's company. This, says a local woman, is what the Hull-House young people would always remember about Addams: "She loved to be with us."

Throughout the Progressive Era, many reformers dedicated themselves to improving the lives of poor children. Some acted from fear and some from pity. But at their best, they were also motivated, as Addams was, by a conviction that the younger generation represented a genuine asset to American society. Give these young people the support they deserve, said Addams, and they will enrich both our present and our future.

7

Speaking Up for Labor

One day in 1890, Jane Addams invited a factory worker named Mary Kenney to dinner at Hull-House. Kenney was 26 years old—just a little younger than Addams—and like Addams, she had only recently moved to Chicago. But the similarities between the two women ended there. Kenney had been born to Irish immigrants, had left school after the fourth grade, and had been supporting herself and her widowed mother ever since. A bookbinder by trade, she had recently helped to organize her fellow workers into a union—one of the few in Chicago composed entirely of women. Never having heard of Hull-House or Jane Addams, Kenney assumed that the dinner invitation was simply a patronizing effort to entertain the poor, so she decided to say no. But her mother insisted that she give these strangers the benefit of the doubt, so off she went.

It turned out that Kenney had been invited not for an evening's diversion but to meet a group of visiting British labor leaders. This was certainly more worthwhile than she had expected, but Kenney found it hard to talk to such eminent people. She was also stiff with Addams at first. But Addams seemed so genuinely eager to be helpful that the young visitor gradually unbent. Voicing the thought that had struck her the minute she walked in the door, she said how nice it would be if her union could hold its meetings at Hull-House instead of in the dirty room over a saloon where it usually met. Of course they could, said Addams. What else can we do? Well, said

Kenney, there was the matter of distributing fliers around the neighborhood. Addams immediately said she could do that herself; she also offered to pay for printing them. By the end of the evening, Kenney's doubts had receded, and by the end of the week, after Addams had tramped up and downstairs all over the 19th Ward handing out the fliers, Kenney knew she had found an ally. She wrote later: "When I saw there was someone who cared enough to help us and to help us in our way, it was like having a new world opened up."

Over the next few years, Kenney spent a great deal of time at Hull-House. She enrolled in several courses that helped her make up for her limited education. She also worked closely with Addams on a number of projects, joined the settlement staff in campaigning for labor legislation, and even lived at Hull-House for a time. Meanwhile, her growing self-assurance was recognized in 1892, when Samuel Gompers, president of the American Federation of Labor (AFL), appointed her as the federation's first full-time female organizer.

In 1894, just a few years after she first came to Hull-House, Kenney moved to Boston, where she later married journalist John O'Sullivan. She stayed in touch with Addams, however, and starting in 1903, they served together as founding members of the Women's Trade Union League. In the years that followed, Kenney continued to dedicate herself to labor issues—first as a union organizer and later as a factory inspector for the state of Massachusetts.

Kenney always stressed how meeting Jane Addams changed her life. But Addams also benefitted a great deal from meeting Kenney. Addams later recalled that before she came to Hull-House, she felt sympathy for the poor but clung to the idea that somewhere up there, there were wise authorities who would magically banish all society's injustices if they just knew what was happening. Only after she had been at Hull-House for a few years did Addams conclude that one of the best ways to improve conditions for working Chicagoans was to support their own organized efforts to better their lives.

Kenney was not the only person who helped bring Addams to this changed viewpoint. Florence Kelley, in particular—as Addams wrote in later years—"galvanized us all into more intelligent interest in the industrial conditions around us." Addams' economic education was also enhanced by her friendship with Henry Demarest Lloyd, the progressive author of *Wealth Against Commonwealth*, one of the most influential attacks on monopoly capitalism. Lloyd talked with Addams about contemporary issues and introduced her to a wide circle of Chicago's labor leaders, progressive activists, and political radicals. The depression of 1893–1894 also had an effect, forcing her to recognize that it was not enough to minister to her neighbors' spirits if their bodies were broken by hard work and poverty. On top of all this, there was the simple experience of living at Hull-House, which functioned as a kind of nonstop seminar on public issues. In particular, Addams benefitted from the Working People's Social Science Club—not only the lectures and the reading it inspired her to do but also the experience of hearing her working-class neighbors talk so thoughtfully about questions of social and economic justice.

Mary Kenney was an important part of this process. Addams was already interested in labor issues before she met her. But over the next few years, she progressed from generalized feelings of goodwill to a conviction that unions were an important expression of American democracy. Because Addams was always especially responsive to the immediate personal example, Kenney helped to propel this change by describing the conditions of her own life and explaining the vital role that unions played in empowering women like her to address their problems. Historian Allen Davis states: "Mary Kenney, perhaps more than anyone except Florence Kelley, broadened Jane Addams' perspective and made her sympathetic to organized labor."

The Human Cost of Industrialization

When Addams arrived in Chicago in 1889, industrial capitalism was in the midst of the most productive and the most brutal period it had ever known—an era during which businessmen were generally free to produce as much as they possibly could, with virtually no accountability to the public or their workers about how they did it.

This single-minded focus on output was good for the owners' income and good for the nation's status as an industrial power, but it was very hard indeed on the workers who made the output possible. Take the question of occupational injuries. Getting hurt on the job could be a catastrophe for a worker because—with no workers' compensation laws, no sick leave, and minimal health insurance—every day off the job was a day without wages. But the level of risk in the typical industrial workplace was extraordinarily high, with unguarded machinery, intense pressure to work fast, and highly polluted air. National statistics tell the story. Between 1876 and 1910, at least 25,000 workers were killed on the job every year (some authorities put the annual figure as high as 80,000), and nearly half a million workers were injured. In 1908, the *Chicago Tribune* calculated that more people had died in work-related accidents during the previous four years than all the battle deaths on both sides during the four years of the Civil War.

One might think that the businessmen who operated such unsafe workplaces would have been subject to legal action. But few workers could afford to take their employers to court, and those who did rarely won because if either the claimant or his fellow workers could be shown to have been negligent in any way, the employer was almost always exonerated. More generally, the courts operated on the principle that if workers thought certain jobs were dangerous, they were free to turn them down. If they chose to accept them and things turned out badly, they had only themselves to blame. To interfere with this arrangement, the courts insisted, would violate the employer's property rights and the worker's "freedom of contract."

Besides the pro-management tilt of the legal system, one of the most significant factors keeping labor conditions the way they were was the oversupply of workers in most industrial cities. Asked why he had not repaired a broken roof that had caused several injuries, a manager explained, "Men are cheaper than shingles. There's a dozen waiting to fill the place of one that drops out." It was this knowledge that kept millions of employees from quitting or complaining more aggressively about bad working conditions. They knew that there was one thing worse than a dangerous or disagreeable job, and that was no job at all.

Every worker dreaded being jobless because there was no unemployment insurance and few families had enough savings to live for long without wages. But periodic unemployment was a common feature of the industrial economy, it being standard practice for companies to lay off workers whenever business was slack and then hire them back when demand picked up again. Addams saw the human cost of such practices, and she spoke out strongly against the cruelty of maintaining an economic system that depended, as she said, on a mass of hungry unskilled workers "ready to be absorbed or dropped according to the demands of production."

Chicago's West Side, where Hull-House was located, was the center of the city's garment manufacturing. There were relatively few large factories in the area, but the abuses of the industrial labor system were just as visible in the many sweatshops that filled the district. These small factories generally operated under contract to larger firms and tended to run on razor-thin budgets, with the managers' only hope of a profit deriving from the low wages they paid and the ferocious work pace they enforced. Moreover, because the work was seasonal, "sweated" labor involved desperately long hours during the busy season, followed by months of unemployment during the slack period.

Integral to the sweatshop system was the practice of "homework," under which such detailed tasks as sewing on buttons or making artificial flowers were contracted out to workers—usually women and children—to complete in their own tenement apartments. Pay, which was calculated by the piece, was even lower than in the sweatshops, and the seasonal pressures were just as relentless. Even the minimal state controls on child labor did not apply to homework, so thousands of children as young as five or six spent entire days hunched over a kitchen table doing small repetitive tasks over and over and over. Historian Cynthia Daniels describes this system as "a sweatshop in every kitchen."

Many progressives, including Addams, worked hard to improve labor conditions, seeing the campaign as a fundamental part of their larger struggle to build a more just and democratic society. Within the Hull-House community, Addams' colleague

Florence Kelley played a particularly important role in this effort. Soon after she moved to Hull-House in 1891, Kelley was hired by the Illinois Bureau of Labor Statistics to participate in two local research projects—one focused on women's work and the other on sweatshops. Shortly thereafter, she did further research on neighborhood working conditions for the U.S. Bureau of Labor Statistics as part of a national study of four urban slums. Kelley's reports documented terrible working conditions—both in the local sweatshops and among the hundreds of people in the neighborhood who did piecework in their own apartments. The effort to improve these conditions became a primary concern at Hull-House in the years that followed.

Addams may have come to Chicago originally to nurture the spirits of the poor, but by the mid-1890s, she had become keenly aware that better working conditions were an essential part of any program for social reform and that the labor movement had an important role to play in bringing those better conditions to pass.

The Value of Unions

Addams' conversion to the cause of labor was a clear indication of how far she had traveled from the world she grew up in. Communities like her hometown of Cedarville—having benefitted during their early years from unregulated railroad building and industrial development—tended to think that large corporations could do no wrong. "To criticize them," Addams said, "was considered unpatriotic." So, when labor unions— "backed by an occasional strike"—demanded higher wages, many local citizens condemned them for endangering "the best interests of the community." Feelings on this topic ran even higher in Chicago. Indeed, said Addams, after the Haymarket Affair, "it became a patriotic matter to denounce the eight-hour day, higher wages, and collective bargaining as anarchistic plots to destroy American institutions."

But as Addams learned more about labor issues, she became convinced that just as the great corporations of the day were using the power of combination to achieve their goals, so must workers combine forces in order to achieve theirs. For workers to form unions was not just rational, she concluded; it was admirable because it blended values such as solidarity and sacrifice with the practical effort to achieve a better life for working Americans. Defying middle-class assumptions, Addams wrote in 1899: "Probably the labor-unions come nearer to expressing moral striving in politics than any other portion of the community."

As much as Addams admired what the unions stood for, she was not always happy about their practices. In fact, there were a few organizations, such as the Teamsters, which she considered fundamentally corrupt. Most unions had worthier motives, she believed, but even they discriminated against Asians and African Americans. Moreover, their legitimate grievances against their bosses were all too often expressed in polarizing rhetoric, a divisive emphasis on class conflict, and sometimes even violence.

Like many progressives, Addams tried to play down the idea of class conflict, arguing that labor disputes could be best settled by compromise rather than polarization and blame. She expressed the hope that "as the labor movement grows older and riper, it will cease to divide all men so sharply into capitalist and proletarians, into exploiter and exploited." After all, she said, "life teaches us nothing more inevitable than that right and wrong are most confusedly mixed; . . . that right does not dazzle our eyes with its radiant shining, but has to be found by exerting patience, discrimination, and impartiality." Not all workers were angels, she pointed out, and not all bosses were devils. In the end, "all sense of injury must fall away and be absorbed in the consciousness of a common brotherhood."

Whatever her doubts about the unions' rhetoric, Addams worked vigorously on their behalf, as did Florence Kelley, Ellen Starr, Mary Kenney, and many other House residents. Alice Hamilton said later: "At Hull-House one got into the labor movement as a matter of course, without realizing how or when." The settlement provided regular meeting space for a number of unions, and everyone collaborated on campaigning for labor legislation. Hull-House residents also joined other progressives in working with unions on many shared projects, including a huge "industrial exhibit" in downtown Chicago showing "the conditions and rewards of labor;" this display drew large crowds throughout its two-week run.

The cause of women workers was especially close to Addams' heart, and some of Hull-House's most significant contributions to labor were made on behalf of women. One of these activities was the Jane Club, a cooperative residence for working women. The idea emerged one day when a group of young women on strike from a local shoe factory were meeting at Hull-House. They agreed that workers who had trouble paying their rent were the most likely to give up on a strike, and they concluded that it would be ideal if they could have a "boarding club" of their own.

With Addams' support and Mary Kenney's leadership, the young women developed a plan for a cooperative residence and then rented two apartments in a nearby building. Hull-House bought the furniture and paid the first month's rent; after that, the Jane Club was on its own. The project was an immediate success, and at the end of the third year, the 50-member club took over all six apartments in the building. The Jane Club is believed to have been the first working women's residential club in the United States, and it inspired many more—both in Chicago and elsewhere.

The Jane Club was exactly the kind of labor project Addams liked best because it fostered worker solidarity without demonizing management. Many union leaders, of course, took a far more militant stand, but Addams hoped that over time, she and her colleagues could help to soften the movement's harsher impulses and nourish its more peaceable ones. As she wrote Leo Tolstoy: "Our stand at Hull-House has always been to seize upon the highest moral efforts we could find in the labor movement or elsewhere, and help them forward."

Union leaders sometimes expressed doubts about whether they could trust well-born supporters such as the group at Hull-House. But the settlement workers' middle-class background did give them extra credibility when it came to educating the public about labor issues. In carrying out this responsibility,

Addams freely acknowledged that union activities sometimes appeared to be "uncouth and unruly manifestations of social effort." But she insisted that when labor and management were in conflict, the public should not simply assume that all the good was on management's side. Sometimes, Addams observed, we discover that "the good of yesterday is opposed to the good of today, and that which may appear as a choice between virtue and vice is really but a choice between virtue and virtue." Making clear that labor, not management, represented "the good of today," Addams urged her listeners to recognize "the noble purposes of trades-unions and the desirability of the ends which they seek."

The Problem of Strikes

In all Addams' dealings with the labor movement, she struggled to balance her sympathy for the workers with her lifelong preference for compromise rather than confrontation. Nothing strained that balance more sorely than the many strikes that convulsed Chicago during the 1890s and early 1900s.

Few American employers at the time accepted unions as legitimate representatives of their workers. The result was that, although labor unions were often highly effective in giving their members a sense of collective identity, they were rarely allowed to fulfill what today we would consider one of their most important roles: serving as an orderly channel for bringing workers' concerns to management's attention. Most major industrialists, of course, maintained that this function was quite unnecessary. They insisted that they knew their own workers very well and needed no instruction from "outsiders" on how to deal with them. In fact, however, in most large companies, there was a tremendous gulf between top managers and their largely immigrant employees. And the intermediate supervisors—the factory foremen and sweatshop operators—generally felt little obligation to pass the workers' concerns up the ladder to company management.

As a result, instead of being systematically addressed, workers' dissatisfactions tended to fester until they exploded in strikes. Between 1880 and 1900, there were 23,000 strikes in the

United States—some of them involving hundreds of thousands of workers. Many grew so violent that it took state militias to restore order. Hundreds of people died in these confrontations, and many more were injured—most of them workers.

Chicago had its own share of these lacerating labor conflicts—most notably, the Pullman Strike of 1894. The company owner, George Pullman, had made his fortune by designing the first comfortable sleeping car and then marketing his Pullman Sleepers to virtually every American railroad line. Seeking to insulate his workers from radical influences, he established his company in a brand-new model town that he built (and named for himself) 20 miles from Chicago. Pullman won national praise for his town, drawing visitors from around the world to admire the sturdy brick houses he rented to his workmen as well as the town's free school, well-stocked public library, and attractive parks. But the seeds of his future problems could be seen in the high-handed way Pullman administered his town. Among other things, he permitted no bars, no independent newspapers, and no town meetings, and he insisted on the company's right to inspect workers' houses to be sure they were kept clean. Progressive economist Richard Ely observed that the power of German autocrat Otto von Bismarck was "utterly insignificant when compared with the ruling authority of the Pullman Palace Car Company in Pullman."

Pullman's paternal benevolence waned during the depression of 1893–1894. Facing a precipitous drop in company sales, he slashed wages by 25 percent. When the workers learned that their rents would remain just as high despite the wage cut, they asked to meet with Pullman, but he refused to see them. Some of the employees had recently joined Eugene V. Debs' American Railroad Union (ARU), and many more now signed up. In May 1894, the Pullman workers declared a strike, whereupon the ARU launched a national boycott in support, announcing that its members would refuse to handle any train that had a Pullman car attached. When the companies refused to detach the cars, 125,000 railroad workers walked out, virtually closing down 11 major lines. Meanwhile, public opinion in Chicago divided sharply over the strike. Working-class people generally supported it, while more prosperous Chicagoans strongly opposed it. Addams heard one well-bred acquaintance state flatly that all strikers should be shot.

Despite the rising tensions, many progressives still hoped to find some middle ground between the warring camps of capital and labor. Taking the lead, the Chicago Civic Federation organized a committee of distinguished citizens, including Addams, who offered themselves as neutral arbitrators. For days, the group rushed back and forth between strikers and management in a desperate effort to make peace. Talking with the workers, Addams was struck by their faith in Pullman and their certainty that he would respond as soon as he understood their grievances. On the other hand, it was clear from the committee's talks with Pullman that he was not prepared to give an inch. Addams had met Pullman socially and had always respected his philanthropic activities, but on the issue of the strike, she found him absolutely intransigent.

In late June, just as matters reached a crisis, Addams was called away to the deathbed of her sister Mary. As a result, she missed the next tense chapters of the strike: the decision by U.S. Attorney General Richard Olney (a railroad lawyer for 35 years) to obtain a federal court injunction against the strike on the grounds that it was interfering with the U.S. mails; the jailing of Debs and other union officials when they refused to call off the strike; and several episodes of massive property damage. Finally, over the strenuous objection of Governor John Peter Altgeld, federal troops were sent into the city, ostensibly to protect the mails. By late July, when Addams returned to Chicago after Mary's death, there were thousands of soldiers camped out downtown and a sorry tally of recent violence around the city. Thirteen people had been killed and many more wounded, and property worth hundreds of thousands of dollars had been damaged. Never before, Addams said, had she witnessed such a "distinct cleavage of society."

The strike was broken soon afterward, and Debs was sent to prison, but Addams continued to brood over her experiences during "all those dark days." As she so often did, she organized her thoughts by developing them into a speech. Then, after delivering it several times in Chicago, she reworked it into an essay entitled "A Modern Lear." In both the speech and the essay, she compared George Pullman to Shakespeare's King Lear; like Lear, she suggested, Pullman had assumed he could maintain total control over his domain and had felt betrayed when his "subjects" asserted their independence.

"A Modern Lear" was built around Addams' familiar argument that when circumstances change, ideas and practices also have to change. In the case of labor relations, Addams observed that over the past century, industrial production had evolved into a "vast social operation," while the arrangements for industrial management had remained stubbornly individualistic, even autocratic. Taking George Pullman as an example, Addams acknowledged his beneficence to his workers but noted that he had constructed his model town strictly according to his own idea of what his workers needed. His idea of ethics, she maintained, was based on the individualistic virtues of an earlier time. That was how he had built his town and that was how he ran his company. But his employees had been shaped by the more socialized environment of the modern factory, which required people to work together. As a result, they had embraced a newer, more inclusive view of life. "Outside the ken of philanthropists the proletariat had learned to say, in many languages, that 'the injury of one is the concern of all.'"

It was the workers, Addams argued, not the company president, who truly grasped the social ethics—the mutuality—required in a modern democracy. Pullman might, like King Lear, rail against his thankless subordinates, but his obduracy during the strike only showed how out of touch he was with his times. It was not enough that he had been true to the values of the world he grew up in. "A task is laid upon each generation to enlarge their application, to ennoble their conception, and, above all, to apply and adapt them to the peculiar problems presented to it for solution." This Pullman had failed to do. And his failure, more than anything else, had caused the "industrial tragedy" that followed.

Some labor supporters who heard Addams' speech felt that she was being too kind to George Pullman; Eugene V. Debs, for one, called it "just another attempt to put out a fire with rose-water." But in a city still pulsing with class resentment, it was more controversial than Debs acknowledged for Addams to offer middle-class audiences any criticism at all of Pullman, let alone to praise the strikers as exemplars of modern social ethics. Just how controversial her argument was became clear when four magazines in a row refused to publish the essay based on the speech. So, she put it aside until she judged that the atmosphere had cooled off sufficiently. "A Modern Lear" was finally published in 1912—18 years after the strike.

In the years that followed the Pullman Strike, Addams continued to be guided by the lessons she had absorbed from it. On the one hand, having seen how a major strike could aggravate existing social tensions and cause new ones to develop, she continued to believe that such confrontations should be avoided if at all possible. Any collective action by workers, she said, had within it an element of "ethical fellowship," but a strike was a particularly "wasteful and negative demonstration" of that fellowship. Moreover, during a period of labor conflict, each side tended to retreat to "the method of warfare," making it harder than ever to arrive at a satisfactory resolution. Major strikes like Pullman also tended to draw in the general public, turning the event into a kind of gruesome spectator sport, with the entire city population "divided into cheering sides." For all these reasons, Addams regarded strikes as regrettable occurrences.

On the other hand, reflecting on her experience in 1894 gave Addams new respect for the way that participating in a strike— even an unsuccessful one—could build solidarity among a group of workers. As she observed: "The transient aspect of the strike is the anger and opposition against the employer, and too often the chagrin of failure. The permanent is the binding together of the strikers in the ties of association and brotherhood, and the attainment of a more democratic relation to the employer."

Hull-House could help the cause of labor, Addams believed, by pushing for prompt arbitration of each strike rather than letting the prolonged struggle heighten animosities on both sides. But she also believed that the settlement had an obligation to sustain the workers while the arbitration process was proceeding. For this reason, she often presided at meetings organized to raise money for striking workers—even while she was pursuing arbitration to bring the strike to an end. She also often made personal visits to the employers involved to speak as eloquently as she could for their workers' concerns.

By thus seeking to maintain dialogue with both sides, Addams frequently managed to leave everyone unsatisfied. For example, when she helped to settle a major garment-workers strike in 1910, neither labor nor management chose her to represent them on the board that was established to arbitrate future disputes; each side thought she was too partial to the other. But whatever the participants' doubts, Addams gave her primary allegiance to the labor movement, because she was convinced that it was a vital instrument of American democracy.

The Fight for Government Action

Despite her commitment to labor unions, Addams agreed with many other social progressives that labor conditions in the United States could not be fundamentally reformed unless government also did its part. Here, the progressives believed, was another example of the need to adjust old institutions to fit new circumstances. At the time the U.S. Constitution was written, it had seemed sufficient to define government's responsibilities purely in political terms and assume that the economy would take care of itself. But the industrial revolution had transformed society and now the country could not maintain its democratic ideals without taking economic relationships into account. Americans were beginning to understand that industrial conditions had civic implications, said Addams, and as their own sense of ethical obligation broadened, "each advance in ethics must be made fast by a corresponding advance in politics and legal enactment."

To start with, the government should take more responsibility for keeping labor strikes peaceful. As matters stood, striking unions were generally expected to maintain order entirely on their own—which they were not really equipped to do, especially since their members were often the victims rather than the instigators of violence. "The public shirks its duty," said Addams, and then "blames the union men for the disaster." Furthermore, when city or state forces did intervene, they frequently seemed concerned only with protecting strikebreakers and company property. Peaceful protest was a constitutional right, said Addams, and the government had an obligation to protect everyone involved, including the strikers.

Going deeper into the causes of labor conflict, Addams concluded that many strikes should not even be necessary because they arose out of dissatisfaction with working conditions that should be illegal in the first place. She recognized that Americans had always been reluctant to limit the way that private entrepreneurs ran their businesses. But she thought no employer should be free to impose conditions so harsh that they made ordinary civilized life impossible for the workers. "As the very existence of the State depends upon the character of its citizens, therefore, if certain industrial conditions are forcing the workers below the standard of decency, it becomes possible to deduce the right of State regulation."

Addams was convinced that workers had a right to expect a certain minimum standard of living. And the most harmonious way to meet that expectation was to give it "quiet and orderly expression in legislative enactment." It was therefore essential, she said, for government to enforce existing labor laws more vigorously, to interpret them more broadly, and to pass new legislation that further expanded the scope of its obligation to its citizens. "For unless the growing conscience is successfully embodied in legal enactment," observed Addams, "men lose the habit of turning to the law for guidance and redress."

Of all the areas in which labor legislation was needed, none meant more to Addams than the protection of working women and children. Shortly after she arrived in Chicago, a cross-class coalition known as the Illinois Women's Alliance had worked with labor unions to get a child labor law passed. But it had included no mechanism for enforcement, and Florence Kelley's research in local sweatshops a few years later made it clear that women and children were still being subjected to terrible working conditions.

In 1893, the state legislature appointed a commission of enquiry to investigate Florence Kelley's findings. Such commissions have often been used to give controversial reports a quiet burial. But Addams, Kelley, and their colleagues at Hull-House welcomed the commission members to the ward so enthusiastically, gave them such extensive tours, and besieged them with so much advice and information that their final report emerged as a clarion call for legislative action.

As soon as the commission submitted its report, Addams and her Hull-House colleagues set to work with a large coalition of progressives and labor unions to get a state law passed that would truly protect working women and children. For several months, Addams made speeches on behalf of the proposed legislation almost every night of the week, addressing women's clubs, unions, mothers' groups, and anyone else who would listen. She also appealed to working-class parents, urging them to forego their children's earnings so their children could get a better start in life. She urged prosperous women to make common cause with poorer women. And she testified in detail at legislative hearings—in such detail, in fact, that a Chicago newspaper reporter wrote in mock horror: "What can be done with a 'reformer' of this kind? She knows her own business and if she tries to reform somebody else's business she sets to work and studies it until she knows more about it than he does."

The Illinois Workshop and Factory Act, as passed in 1893, made it illegal to employ children under 14 in factories and set an 8-hour day and a 48-hour week for women and children. It also established a Department of Factory Inspection, with significant enforcement powers. This law made Illinois a national leader in labor legislation; Addams' friend Henry Demarest Lloyd called it "the best anti-sweatshop law on the books of any civilized community." And as a sign of the state's commitment to the Factory Act, Governor John Peter Altgeld appointed Kelley to run the new Factory Inspection Department.

Unfortunately, the reformers' victory lasted only two years. In 1895, in *Ritchie v. Illinois*, the Illinois Supreme Court ruled that it was unconstitutional to limit women's working hours because it violated their right to dispose of their labor as they chose. Reflecting on this defeat, Addams concluded that perhaps the Factory Act had been too far ahead of its time. Sometimes, she thought, it was possible to push through legislation by perfectly legitimate means yet have it fail if it "was not preceded by full discussion and understanding." Clearly, much more would have to be done to educate the public—and the courts—about the importance of protective legislation.

The need for reformers to carry on the campaign for protective legislation became all the more urgent in the late 1890s, when the American Federation of Labor more or less removed itself from the fight. Just like Addams, the AFL president Samuel Gompers had been reflecting on the lessons of the Pullman Strike. But his perspective was different—and so were his conclusions. As Gompers saw it, the labor movement had spent the last 20 years promoting a grand vision of reform designed to undo all the injustices of industrial capitalism. This vision had energized the nationwide railroad strike of 1877, the massive demonstrations for the eight-hour day in 1886, the Pullman Strike of 1894, and hundreds of other uprisings in between.

And what had the workers got for their 20 years of struggle? Violence, government-sponsored repression, reversals in court, and a succession of lost strikes. Looking at this dismal record, Gompers concluded that it was time to call a truce. Industrial capitalism was here to stay, and labor should simply concentrate on cutting the best deal it could for itself. Gompers had been leaning in this direction for some time, but the loss of the Pullman Strike was to him the final confirmation. From now on, the labor movement should confine itself to what he called "pure and simple unionism." No more fiery speeches about social reform, no more mass organizing of vulnerable groups like unskilled workers and women, and no more trying to fulfill wage and hour demands through legislation—just stable unions of skilled craftsmen negotiating in a businesslike way with their employers.

Gompers' policy ruled out two activities that Addams and her fellow activists believed were absolutely essential for improving the lives of female workers: organizing them into unions and seeking protective legislation for them. Progressive groups in various American cities had been pursuing these goals, but—especially with the AFL out of the picture—a broader organization was needed. Accordingly, in 1903, Mary Kenney O'Sullivan and reformer William English Walling spearheaded the formation of the Women's Trade Union League—an organization in which working-class and leisure-class women would join forces to enroll working women in unions. (The WTUL was modeled on a British organization of the same name.)

Because most AFL unions did not accept female members, the WTUL board agreed to focus primarily on building new women's unions, which hopefully would become AFL affiliates. Once Samuel Gompers signed off on the idea, they established WTUL branches in three cities (New York, Boston, and Chicago), each based in a local settlement house. In the years that followed, relations between the WTUL's working-class and middle-class members did not always go smoothly, but the organization weathered its problems and established itself as an important voice on behalf of women's labor, especially after the formidable Margaret Dreier Robins assumed the presidency in 1907. By 1911, the WTUL had 11 branches around the country.

Unfortunately, the WTUL made little headway in persuading male union leaders in the various industries to help or even make room for their efforts. Largely because of this opposition, the WTUL never managed to draw as many women into unions as it had hoped. But it did provide invaluable support to working women during a number of major strikes—most notably the huge garment workers' strikes that swept New York, Philadelphia, and Chicago in 1909–1910. In addition, the WTUL worked with many other women's groups to mobilize support for a variety of social reforms, and it played a leadership role in virtually every coalition dealing with women's working conditions.

Addams committed herself to the WTUL from the start. She attended the founding meeting, served as vice president, and provided office space at Hull-House for the Chicago branch of the league. In addition, three women's unions were organized on the Hull-House premises. These activities reflected Addams' specific concern for the needs of female workers as well as her general dedication to the cause of labor.

Inevitably, Hull-House's identification with labor antagonized a number of its donors. Indeed, Addams observed, "When Labor is in disgrace we are always regarded as belonging to it and share the opprobrium." One businessman scolded the settlement for straying from its fundamental mission of caring for the poor; he then made the reason for his dissatisfaction crystal clear by complaining that Hull-House had in fact supported a strike against his own factory. "I believe you have gone far afield from your original purpose," he wrote, "and have done a vast amount of harm." Another donor warned that Addams was becoming "too socialistic in her tendencies." Even when contributions were offered, Addams' commitment to labor sometimes forced her to refuse them, as when she declined a $20,000 donation for the Jane Club because the would-be donor was notorious for underpaying the women who worked in his factory.

Given Addams' passion for seeing both sides of every fight, it is significant that she aligned herself so wholeheartedly with labor. She regretted the more conservative turn of the AFL leadership, and she recognized that identifying herself with labor sometimes meant being associated with episodes of inflammatory speech or even violence. Nevertheless, she said, in the struggle between management and labor, it was the labor movement that stressed "the sympathetic and the human" aspect of economic life. And it was the labor movement, she was certain, that—for all its flaws—represented the path of social progress.

8

Taking Progressivism
to the Nation

Over the past six chapters, we have traced Jane Addams' experiences and achievements during the first great stage of her career: from the opening of Hull-House in 1889 until 1912. By the end of this period, Addams had built the settlement into one of the most famous social welfare institutions in America, and she had also achieved tremendous personal recognition. She habitually headed national popularity polls, she was given numerous honorary degrees, and she even had a chrysanthemum named after her. A Philadelphia editorial writer asserted: "She is one of the ten greatest citizens of this republic. She is, moreover, probably the most widely beloved of her sex in all the world." A magazine called her "the only saint America has ever produced."

No doubt the honors that Addams was accumulating would have made her happy no matter what else was happening in her life. But in fact, everything seemed to be going well for her in the years just before World War I. Hull-House was a stable and flourishing organization, her personal relationship with Mary Rozet Smith gave her warm emotional support, and she had established a huge network of progressive colleagues with whom she enjoyed working.

Besides taking pleasure in what she had already built, Addams was filled with hope for the future. Starting about

1900, all the myriad progressive initiatives that had been developing independently around the country had begun to coalesce and interact. Urban reformers had discovered that if they joined forces, they could pass laws at the state level; state groups were forming national associations; and organizations with different interests were finding more and more ways to make common cause. By 1912, progressives were even talking about nominating their own candidate for president.

For anyone who cherished the "the joy of association" as Addams did, the sense of moving forward buoyed by a wave of like-minded people was both reassuring and exhilarating. Perhaps it is no wonder that, much later in her life, Addams looked back with sharp nostalgia to those last few years before World War I—a period during which, she said, there was "a veritable zeal for social reform throughout the United States." In many respects, these were the happiest years of her life.

Things Fall into Place

Addams' family obligations had diminished considerably by 1912. Her sister Mary and her stepbrothers Harry and George had all died, and her brother Weber had become so mentally ill that there was little she could do to help him. As for Mary's children, they had all reached their 30s, so Addams could enjoy their company without the same sense of responsibility for them that she had felt when they were younger. Her relations with her sister Alice had been quite strained, but after Alice's husband died in 1905, she reached out to Addams, and the two women remained on reasonably amicable terms until Alice's death in 1915.

The even more damaged relationship between Addams and her stepmother was also mended during these years. Anna had never really forgiven her stepdaughter for building a life of her own in Chicago instead of remaining in Cedarville as Anna's companion—or perhaps as George's wife. For years, Addams' letters to her stepmother went unanswered and her visits home were so poisoned by recriminations that she began staying elsewhere when she was in Cedarville, limiting herself to brief—often difficult—courtesy visits. But as Anna approached her 80th birthday in the early 1900s, some of the fire seemed to go out of her old resentments, and she gradually re-established friendlier contact with Addams. They remained in touch until Anna's death a decade later.

The center of Addams' emotional existence by 1912 was, of course, not her family but Mary Rozet Smith. The two women did not live together; Smith had a house in another part of Chicago. But she and Addams took extended trips together, and from time to time, when Addams was sick or overtired, Smith would sweep her away to her own house for a few weeks until she felt stronger. In addition, in 1904, Smith bought a house on Mount Desert Island in Maine, where the two women spent at least part of every summer for nearly 30 years.

Smith's sizable income helped her to ease Addams' life in many ways. Besides paying for all their joint travels, she frequently bought her friend personal items that Addams herself could never quite remember to shop for. More importantly, Smith played a significant role in keeping Hull-House on an even keel financially. She did this not only with periodic major donations, such as her gift of the Children's Building, but also with many small cash contributions. Addams' nephew James Linn says that it was Smith's "constant overcoming of deficits here and there, small but apparently insurmountable that literally kept the work going."

Throughout these years, Addams' first close companion, Ellen Starr, was still living at Hull-House. (She remained there until ill health forced her to move elsewhere in the 1920s.) There had always been something dramatic about Starr, and that quality seemed to sharpen with age. She taught art at the settlement with passion and verve, picketed fearlessly for striking labor unions, and showed a taste for religious intensity that led her from youthful searching to Episcopalianism to, in her later years, Roman Catholicism. Starr had been the perfect companion when the young Addams had needed someone who would challenge her assumptions and stimulate her thinking. But the more demanding Addams' public life became, the more she needed a private relationship that would give her peace and stability. And peace and stability were never Ellen Starr's specialty.

Toward the end of her life, Starr wrote Addams a poignant note saying that she had been rereading their old letters and realized she could never have lived up to Addams' expectations. She insisted that she had "always, at any rate for a good many years, been grateful that Mary came to supply what you needed." She was also very glad, she said, that she had never been jealous of Mary "in any vulgar or ignoble way" because that would have been unfair to someone "so humble, so self-deprecating." One can read Starr's pain between the lines and empathize with her sense of loss. And yet, one can still recognize that, in the long run, what she said about Smith's greater suitability for Addams was probably true.

Mary Smith was no clinging vine. She belonged to a number of local and national reform organizations and was especially active in efforts to improve life for African Americans. But from the early 1890s on, her overriding concern was Addams' well-being. "That was her career," writes Addams' nephew, "that was her philosophy." Addams and Smith both used the word "marriage" to describe their relationship, and whether or not it was a marriage in the physical sense, it was surely one in the emotional sense. The comfort of this partnership was a crucial element in Addams' happiness during the early 1900s.

However, private happiness alone was never enough for Addams. If we are to understand what the prewar years meant to her, we must bear in mind the great professional satisfaction they brought her—not only the honors mentioned above but also the pleasure of seeing Hull-House flourish. Although the period of constant expansion ended around 1912, the settlement remained vital and influential—actively serving its neighborhood and continually finding new causes to champion. Hilda Polachek, who started coming to Hull-House in 1900, observed that Addams spent less time there as the years went by. But she was still the settlement's central figure, said Polacheck, and "her presence was always felt, whether she was there in person or in spirit."

During these years, Addams was also reaching a growing audience with her writing and lecturing. Between 1906 and 1912, she produced more than 70 speeches and essays. Much of this material was then reworked into four books: *Newer Ideals of Peace* (1906), which is discussed in the next chapter; *The*

Spirit of Youth and the City Streets (1909), a call for adults to understand and support the aspirations of adolescents; her memoir, *Twenty Years at Hull-House* (1910); and *A New Conscience and an Ancient Evil* (1912), about the need to save young women from the miseries of prostitution.

The third of these books, *Twenty Years at Hull-House*, was by far the most successful. In writing it, Addams wove together two compelling narratives. The first was the story of her own path from rural girlhood, through youthful uncertainties, to her fulfilling career as a settlement leader and social reformer. The second was the story of how Hull-House itself evolved from a small-scale experiment to a thriving institution that exemplified Addams' dream of "socializing democracy."

Addams explained in the preface to *Twenty Years* that she had written the book, in part, to head off two biographies that she feared would make the settlement movement appear "all too smooth and charming." Of course, her own version of the facts was also smoothed and shaped, causing historian Victoria Brown to describe it as a "rich but slippery source of information on her life." (Both Brown and Allen Davis have documented the many ways in which Addams adjusted the facts of her life to highlight the points she was making.) Nevertheless, the book's vivid combination of anecdotes, autobiography, and social commentary found an enthusiastic audience, inspired generations of social workers and reformers, and has attracted readers ever since its publication. *Twenty Years at Hull-House* has never been out of print since the day it first appeared.

All in all, by 1912, Addams had reason to look around her with considerable satisfaction. She had several well-regarded books on the market, her relationships with her sister and stepmother had improved, and Hull-House was doing well. Besides that, she had considerable personal renown and a loving partnership with Mary Rozet Smith. But there was something more. Progressivism was evolving into a national movement, and a great age of American reform seemed on the brink of being born.

Going National

One of the hallmarks of these peak years of American progressivism was the emergence of national organizations that reinforced and expanded the efforts that were already going on in local communities. The breadth and diversity of the movement had always been one of its strengths, but by the early 20th century, the progressives were becoming convinced that scattered reforms in different cities and different states were not going to be enough to achieve their goals. As Addams' friend Henry Demarest Lloyd observed: "We need . . . to do everywhere what someone is doing somewhere."

Among the many national reform groups founded during these years were the following, in all of which Addams participated: the Women's Trade Union League (1903), the National Child Labor Committee (1904), the American Association for Labor Legislation (1905), the National Society for the Promotion of Industrial Education (1906), the Playground Association of America (1906), the National Association for the Advancement of Colored People (1909), and the National Federation of Settlements (1911). We can appreciate the significance of this trend toward national coordination if we look more closely at two particularly important initiatives, one private and one public: the National Consumers League and the U.S. Children's Bureau.

The first of these efforts—the National Consumers League— began as a response to the bad working conditions endured by female store clerks. With the growth of urban commerce in the late 19th century, the number of women working in stores increased dramatically. Their pay was generally low, their hours were long, and sexual harassment was common. Here were thousands of exploited women under the very noses of their middle-class customers. In response, prosperous women in several cities organized consumers' leagues so they could pressure the stores where they shopped to improve the lives of the women who worked there.

Like the female patriots of the revolutionary era who organized boycotts of British fabric, like the abolitionists who refused to use cotton or sugar produced by slave labor, and like the college students today who have used similar tactics to combat exploitation in Third World garment factories, the consumers' league members of the Progressive Era were determined to use their purchasing power to bring about social change. They began by drawing up a list of standard working conditions that all stores should provide. Wanting to avoid the unpleasant tone of a blacklist, they instead published "White Lists" of stores that met their standards and urged the public to do their shopping there. White List stores were then given labels so they could publicize their compliance. So successful was this system that some leagues had to go to court to prevent noncomplying stores from displaying fake compliance labels.

In 1898, the various local leagues came together to form the National Consumers League (NCL). Hull-House resident Florence Kelley—who had been looking for satisfying work since being ousted from her job as Illinois' Chief Factory Inspector—moved to New York City to become the first NCL director. Kelley brought her characteristic intensity to the new job as well as her strong sense of moral purpose. "Consumers are entitled to a clear conscience if they act as conscientious people," she said. "They can, if they will, enforce a claim to have all that they buy free from the taint of cruelty."

Under Kelley's leadership, the NCL moved from monitoring conditions in stores to campaigning for better conditions in the factories where the goods were produced. By 1904, the NCL had 64 affiliated leagues in 20 states. Besides helping to coordinate women's advocacy for the Pure Food and Drugs Act in 1906, it played a leadership role in the campaigns to abolish child labor, to improve factory conditions for women, and to eliminate the sweatshops that so notoriously exploited women and children.

One of the NCL's most notable achievements was its role in the famous court case of *Muller v. Oregon*. Once Illinois had passed its pioneering 1893 Factory Act regulating women's and children's labor, a number of other states had followed suit. But, as in Illinois, state courts generally struck down the sections that limited women's hours of work on the grounds that legislators had no right to interfere with a woman's "freedom of contract." The Oregon hours-limitation clause was similar to those rejected in other states, but when the first test case came to trial in Oregon, the courts upheld the law. So, in 1907, the convicted employer—a laundry owner named Curt Muller—took his case to the U.S. Supreme Court.

Illustrating the value of the national network that the National Consumers League had established, Kelley first got word of the *Muller* case from the organization's Oregon branch. She then talked the matter over with the NCL director of research: Josephine Goldmark. The two women agreed that if the Supreme Court could be persuaded to uphold Oregon's hours-limitation law, it would set a precedent that would affect labor legislation all over the country. To argue the case, they recruited Goldmark's brother-in-law, Louis Brandeis, a lawyer who had taken so many public interest cases that he was known as the "People's Attorney."

Looking at the existing precedents, Brandeis recognized that it was useless to defend the hours-limitation clause simply on the basis of social justice. As recently as the *Lochner* case (1904), the Supreme Court had ruled that because there was no evidence that working long hours did any harm, legal restrictions were "mere meddlesome interference with the rights of the individual." Brandeis therefore asked Kelley and Goldmark to gather as much statistical evidence as they could to prove that long hours were harmful, especially to women. In a virtuoso piece of social research, the two women prepared a 100-page report meticulously documenting this claim, based on hundreds of American and international studies produced by unions, physicians, factory inspectors, economists, and social workers. Brandeis then broke new ground in American jurisprudence by submitting the full report as his brief, introduced with just a few pages of legal argument.

The "Brandeis Brief" achieved its goal. The Supreme Court voted unanimously to uphold *Muller*, confirming the government's right to limit female workers' hours. However, the decision leaned more heavily on women's unique needs than the three reformers had hoped. Kelley, Goldmark, and Brandeis did believe that workplace arrangements should take into account women's physical differences from men, including their responsibility for child-bearing, and they stressed this point in their argument because they thought the court would find it persuasive. But like many social progressives, they had hoped for an outcome that would pave the way to improving conditions for all workers. Instead, the court's decision focused entirely on women's physical vulnerability and on the state's vital interest in protecting their capacity to bear and raise children.

The decision in *Muller v. Oregon* left two legacies. On the negative side, requiring special arrangements for female workers made some employers more reluctant to hire them, and it also tended to undermine women's claims to equal treatment by stressing their physical weakness and implying that their only significant role in society was as mothers. But the *Muller* decision also had positive effects. It gave legal recognition to the undeniable difficulties faced by many working women, and it affirmed for the first time—however narrowly—the right of the government to set some limitations on what an employer could require of his workers. It also demonstrated the power of a national example to energize local reform. Within 10 years of the Muller decision, 39 states passed laws limiting women's work hours.

The National Consumers League played an important role in Progressive Era reform not only through its high-level policy work (as in the *Muller* case) but also through its mobilization of middle-class women on behalf of working women and children, and its effective partnership with labor groups and other reformers for a variety of progressive causes. Underlining both the opportunity and the obligation underlying the NCL approach, Kelley declared: "To live means to buy, to buy means to have power, to have power means to have responsibility." Thus, in an era when the concept of "consumer" was already starting to be associated with a single-minded focus on one's own needs and desires, the NCL provided a compelling alternative vision, demonstrating that women could instead use their roles as consumers to improve the world they lived in.

The U.S. Children's Bureau is another example of a national program launched during the Progressive Era that acted as a catalyst for action. Once again, Florence Kelley played an important role, but in this case, her ally was Lillian Wald, director of the Henry Street Settlement. (Kelley lived at the settlement once she moved to New York.) According to legend, the idea for the bureau was born one morning in 1903 when Kelley and Wald were going through the settlement mail. Two letters that day told poignant stories of children in distress. Then, in the daily paper, the women saw that the U.S. Secretary of Agriculture was about to travel south to examine the effect of boll weevils on the cotton crop. Wald exclaimed: "If the Government can have a department to take such an interest in what is happening to the Nation's cotton crop, why can't it have a bureau to look after the Nation's crop of children?" The two women agreed that the answer was to establish a Children's Bureau within the federal government.

To give their idea the right send-off, Wald persuaded Jane Addams and Edward T. Devine, director of the Charity Organization Society, to go with her to talk about it with President Theodore Roosevelt. Once the president gave the plan his blessing, they launched a massive campaign for public support. While Addams rallied the formidable circle of Chicago reformers, Wald and Kelley reached out to progressive organizations around the country. Many of these groups—such as the National Conference on Charities and Correction, the National Congress of Mothers, and the General Federation of Women's Clubs—had affiliates in every state, and these groups in turn spread the word to their own members. Wald and Kelley also worked with Samuel Lindsay, director of the National Child Labor Committee, to draft the necessary legislation.

Even with all this effort—and even though the proposal called only for a small fact-finding agency—passage did not come easily; the bill was defeated every year between 1906 and 1911. At last, however, in 1912, the bill passed both houses of Congress and was signed into law by Roosevelt's successor, President William Howard Taft.

Both Wald and Addams were invited to apply for the position of Bureau chief, but they each declined. Instead, they immediately started lobbying to have Hull-House resident Julia Lathrop appointed. The question arose: Should they also nominate a man in case the president was unwilling to choose a woman? "It does seem a pity not to have a woman—and a very able one," Addams wrote Wald. "Let's try hard for a woman first." The influential men who led the National Child Labor Committee were persuaded to support Lathrop's candidacy, and President Taft agreed to the appointment. Thus, Lathrop became the first woman in American history to head a federal agency.

Comparing the bureau's modest funding (only $25,000) to Lathrop's outsize talent, Wald later observed: "The first budget was small, but the first appointment was large." Lathrop's aspirations for the bureau were also large—well beyond its fact-finding mandate. But she knew she would need to start cautiously because the bureau had plenty of critics: southerners who worried about federal encroachment on states' rights, employers fearing pressure on child labor, Catholics wary of government intrusion into family life, and budget hawks opposed to any expansion of the federal government. Taking this into consideration, Lathrop began by undertaking two projects she knew would appeal to a broad public: lowering infant mortality rates and teaching parents about child health.

The bureau began its work on infant mortality by gathering the incomplete statistics then available and using them to estimate the rate of infant deaths in the country. When the findings suggested that the American rate (132 deaths per 1,000 live births) was worse than that of at least half a dozen other countries, including Scotland and Bulgaria, Lathrop commissioned the nation's first investigation into the reasons for infant mortality. Refuting the traditional tendency to blame defective genes and indifferent parenting, the study made clear that poverty was one of the most decisive factors. On the basis of this finding, the bureau developed a number of programs in later years designed to give poor children and infants better access to medical care.

Even before those efforts came to fruition, however, Lathrop recognized that the country could not monitor its progress in reducing infant mortality unless the states did a better job of gathering birth data. At the time, only eight states in the country met the federal standard of registering at least 90 percent of all births. Reaching out to women's clubs around the country, Lathrop built an army of volunteer investigators who went house to house to identify new babies, checked the names against official birth records, and publicized the discrepancies, which were usually enormous. The volunteers then moved on to lobbying for improvement—pressing for new laws, tighter enforcement, and better medical compliance so all births would be recorded. More than 3,000 women participated in the effort, and by the end of World War I, the campaign had added 15 states to the list of those that met federal reporting standards. By 1929, all but two states in the country were in full compliance.

When it came to health teaching, Lathrop had the bureau compile accurate but readable information about child health and then disseminate it to American mothers through demonstrations, exhibits, press releases, mailings, and a series of hugely popular pamphlets. One of these pamphlets—*Infant Care* (1914)—sold 63,000 copies in just 6 months and 1.5 million in the next 7 years. Bureau staff also provided information to state and local welfare agencies and corresponded with thousands of individual mothers. In addition, the bureau developed a lively interactive relationship with women's clubs around the country, sending them lecturers, suggesting projects they might undertake, inviting their ideas, and urging them to lobby their state and federal representatives on child-related issues.

Within just a few years, the Children's Bureau had become, according to historian Molly Ladd-Taylor, the most important child health organization in the country. As such, it functioned at the hub of a vast network of women's organizations around the country. The political clout of this network was demonstrated as early as 1913, when Lathrop submitted a budget for the coming year that would raise the bureau's budget from $25,000 to $164,000 and its staff from 15 to 76. When the House Appropriations Committee said no, Lathrop turned to her key supporters: Kelley, Wald, and Addams. They promptly contacted every group they knew, and these organizations in turn rallied their own members. Wires and letters poured into Congress, and when Lathrop's budget came to a vote, the House approved the full amount she had requested: 276 to 47.

For nearly a decade thereafter, the bureau maintained its commanding position in the forefront of progressive reform.

When the national temper turned more conservative during the 1920s, the bureau came under brutal attack. It revived to play a significant role in drafting the child-welfare sections of the Social Security Act in 1935 and then saw its role steadily diminish in the years that followed. It is thus the bureau's first decade (1912–1921) that remains its most memorable.

Even during its best years, the agency did not achieve everything Lathrop, Kelley, and Wald had hoped for. Nor did it ever challenge the traditional assumption that husbands should support their families while their wives stayed home with the children; in fact, Lathrop and most of her staff shared that maternalist view. But the bureau did act as a powerful center for information and advocacy, mobilizing the energies of thousands of female professionals and middle-class volunteers and providing hundreds of thousands of mothers with clear and reliable information about their children's health.

Launching the Progressive Party

The countrywide impact of a single court decision like *Muller* and the remarkable achievements of a tiny government agency like the Children's Bureau only confirmed in many progressives' minds the importance of federal action in furthering social reform. On the legislative side, a single federal law passed by the U.S. Congress could establish a national standard that otherwise would have to be negotiated separately in state after state. The progressives did not abandon their interest in action at the state and local levels, but they were convinced that if the country was to move forward, the federal government would also have to expand its role. In his influential book *The Promise of American Life* (1911), Herbert Croly spoke for many progressives when he wrote: "The problem belongs to the American national democracy, and its solution must be attempted chiefly by means of official national action."

By the early 20th century, the federal government had already moved toward a more activist stance in the regulation of large monopolies. But when it came to national action on socioeconomic issues such as working conditions and public health, the reformers had made little headway. What the progressives were seeking—just as they had done at the city and state levels—was for the federal government to fundamentally rethink its relationship to its citizens, accepting responsibility not only for protecting them in wartime but also for ensuring their health and well-being every day.

The progressives knew they could not achieve this kind of transformation unless they created a national political climate that would support such a change. And to do that, they recognized that they would have to mount a level of public education and outreach far broader than anything they had contemplated in the past.

While the reformers were thus considering how to move progressivism into the national political arena, the party to which most of them belonged—the Republican Party—was also thinking about the national implications of progressivism. Still seen as the party of Lincoln, the Republicans had won nearly every presidential election since the Civil War. But the ferment of the times had emboldened a group of younger Republican congressmen to start agitating against the conservative policies of their own party leaders, including the president: William Howard Taft.

In 1909, these insurgents found a leader: Senator Robert LaFollette. As governor of Wisconsin. "Fighting Bob" LaFollette had won national attention with his "Wisconsin Idea"—an ambitious program of social and economic reform, grounded in research at the well-regarded state university. Once LaFollette arrived in the Senate, he emerged as one of the most outspoken of the rebels. And in October 1911, a convention of insurgents from 30 states—calling themselves the National Republican League—nominated LaFollette to challenge the incumbent president for the party nomination in 1912. Unfortunately, the mercurial LaFollette proved to be an erratic campaigner. When he delivered a rambling, almost incoherent speech in February, the event highlighted his somewhat unstable temperament and more or less destroyed his candidacy.

But as LaFollette's chances diminished, another candidate stepped forward, announcing "My hat is in the ring." At 52, Theodore Roosevelt was already an ex-President (the youngest in American history), a hero of the Spanish-American War, a former governor of New York, a world traveler, the author of half a dozen books, and winner of the Nobel Peace Prize. But as his children observed, Roosevelt wanted to be "the bride at every wedding and the corpse at every funeral." Nothing he did after leaving the White House in 1909 assuaged his hunger for activity and attention, and as his restlessness mounted, so did his dissatisfaction with his successor, President Taft.

Back in the fall of 1911, Roosevelt had refused to support LaFollette's insurgent candidacy, maintaining that the president could not be beaten. But LaFollette's withdrawal left an opening. And the enthusiastic audiences Roosevelt encountered in his various speaking tours—as well as some primary victories—suggested that perhaps after all he could muster enough delegates to defeat Taft at the Republican convention in June.

As it turned out, President Taft was unbeatable. His delegate count was only slightly larger than Roosevelt's, but he had a firm grip on the party machinery—particularly the Credentials Committee, which reviewed the 252 contested seats at the convention and gave 238 of them to Taft. Roosevelt could not even muster full support from the insurgent wing because the embittered LaFollette refused to release his delegates. So, turning his back on the Republicans, Roosevelt summoned his followers to join him in forming a new Progressive Party. Out they marched, with his climactic speech ringing in their ears: "We fight in honorable fashion for the good of mankind; fearless of the future, unheeding of our individual fates, with unflinching ears and undimmed eyes. . . . We stand at Armageddon and we battle for the Lord."

Two months later, the Progressive Party held its own convention in Chicago. Harking back in later years to those "halcyon days in the Coliseum," Addams described how thrilling it had been to feel "that a new kind of political party was being launched which should redress the wrongs of the humblest citizen, not through the coercion of the master group in the state but through their enlightened cooperation." Dispassionate observers noted that there were not many of the humblest citizens actually present at the convention nor many leading Republicans either. But the reformers were there in force, and they were ecstatic.

The part of the proceedings that moved Addams most deeply was the writing of the party platform. The committee began by holding hearings at which all delegates and all Chicago residents were welcome to speak; this, a reporter observed, was "a new thing in platform-making." Once the actual writing began, Addams was thrilled to see how, "by night and by day, through much enthusiastic discussion, the platform seemed to be coming nearer to our hearts' desire." In this atmosphere, she said, "it did not seem in the least strange that reticent men and women should speak aloud of their religious and social beliefs, confident that they would be understood."

When it came time to draft the social and industrial planks of the platform, the committee chose to base them on a report recently completed by the Occupational Standards Committee of the National Conference of Charities and Correction (NCCC). This committee had been established by Addams in 1909, early in her term as NCCC president. After two years of research and consultation, the committee members (including Florence Kelley and Alice Hamilton) had concluded that if progressives wished to match the pace of other nations' social legislation, they must "place these questions before the entire country as a coherent political program." The committee's final report—entitled "Social Standards for Industry"—offered a list of essential legislation that included, among other things, a minimum wage, an eight-hour day, a six-day week, better housing codes, workers' compensation, health insurance, and the prohibition of child labor.

The social workers from the NCCC had presented these recommendations to the platform committee of the Republican convention back in June, but the Republicans showed no interest at all. (Addams got a similar brush-off when she addressed the committee on the subject of women's suffrage.) But after Roosevelt bolted the Republican convention, the social workers visited him at his home on Long Island and got a much warmer reception. Some of their ideas found their way into his keynote speech at the Progressive convention in August, and their list of social standards was incorporated into the party platform almost word for word.

Not everything in the platform matched Addams' ideas as closely as the social and industrial planks. For example, she "swallowed hard" when the committee approved a plank calling for the construction of two battleships a year. She gamely explained later that she had had to face the necessity of choosing from among her principles "those that might be advocated at the moment, and of forcing others to wait for a more propitious season." Her opposition to the battleships could be pursued another day, she decided. For now, the fact that the Progressive Party was stalwart in the cause of labor made "the more intimate appeal."

Addams faced another test of her loyalty over the question of whether the convention should seat a group of African American delegates from the South who had been excluded from their states' segregated selection process. Addams urged that the delegates be admitted; she also worked to get a racial equality plank included in the platform. But Roosevelt was determined not to alienate southern white voters, and neither proposal was approved. Some of Addams' friends criticized her sternly for not having fought harder on the matter. Sophonisba Breckinridge angrily observed: "It seemed as though she could not do anything that was in the nature of an exercise of compulsion or control." Addams agonized over these attacks and later tried to explain her decision in an essay published in *Crisis*, the magazine of the National Association for the Advancement of Colored People. But to her critics, the incident was just one more example of Addams' willingness to compromise on matters of principle.

When the Progressive Party platform was finally complete, it did seem to justify all the compromises along the way. Besides the social and industrial planks adopted from the NCCC, it called for a host of other reforms, including votes for women, a federal income tax, a national health service, electoral reforms like primaries and the direct election of senators, the expansion of the national parks, a limit on campaign contributions, the registration of lobbyists, and a national highway system. The section on business regulation began with these words: "We demand that the test of true prosperity shall be the benefits conferred thereby on all the citizens."

Not everyone appreciated the document's vast sweep; political insider Amos Pinchot thought it was too long and too idealistic, apparently determined to cover "everything from the shorter catechism to how to build a birch-bark canoe." But to Addams and to many of her longtime associates, the platform was a dream come true. The night it was announced, she told a reporter: "The Progressive Platform contains all the things I have been fighting for, for more than a decade."

The convention concluded with the nomination of Roosevelt for president. Addams and Judge Ben Lindsey of Denver were chosen to make the seconding speeches. Addams' address drew considerable attention—in part because she was a woman and in part because of her celebrity. The *Literary Digest* (with a wry nod to Roosevelt's capacity to dominate any room he entered) called her "easily the most conspicuous figure present, save, of course, one."

Addams was hardly a Roosevelt disciple. She was rather wary of his foreign policy, and she found his buoyant self-involvement a little comical. But he had been quite open to her reform suggestions during his earlier years in the White House and had established a reasonably progressive record on social issues—even coming out belatedly for women's suffrage. In any case, as she pointed out in her nominating speech, Roosevelt was "one of the few men in our public life who has been responsive to the social appeal." Moreover, she was well-aware of what his popularity could do to publicize the progressive agenda. Addams made her priorities almost tactlessly clear when she observed during the campaign: "It is the platform we women care about, the platform which embodies so much that we desire. But with a platform there must be candidates, and we are very glad to have so distinguished a man to lead our cause."

Given America's winner-take-all method for tabulating the states' electoral votes, Addams knew that a third-party candidate like Roosevelt had little chance of winning the presidency. But she believed that the Progressive Party campaign could give voice to "the action and passion of the times" and make social reform "a political issue of national dimensions." Even if the party could not win the presidency that year, it could educate the public and send representatives to Congress and the state legislatures who were publicly committed to pushing reform. Over time, this could influence the Republican Party to become more progressive or perhaps it could precipitate such a dramatic realignment that the Progressive Party itself could win a future election.

And so, the campaign began. At last, as Addams said, the progressives' ideals for America would be thrown "into the life of the nation itself for corroboration." During the next 10 weeks, Addams served on the party's national committee and published four magazine articles as well as six syndicated newspaper columns explaining the Progressives' goals. She also made many speeches—in Boston, New York City, and on an extended tour through the Midwest. Women's groups gave her a particularly warm reception, and many organized Jane Addams Choruses to promote the Progressive cause in song. In fact, so enthusiastic were the crowds that Addams sometimes lost sight of her initial realism about the probable outcome.

Realism reasserted itself on the day after the election. When the votes were counted, Democratic candidate Woodrow Wilson had won the presidency with 42 percent of the vote, compared to 27 percent for Roosevelt and 23 percent for Taft. Essentially, Roosevelt had split the Republican vote with Taft while failing to win away enough Democrats to weaken Wilson. Part of the problem in attracting Democratic votes was the fact that Wilson himself had established a reasonably progressive record as governor of New Jersey. Indeed, another way of looking at the election results is to note that together, the two progressive candidates—Wilson and Roosevelt—won nearly 70 percent of the vote. And even separately, each of the two progressives did better than the more conservative President Taft.

Addams was not dissatisfied with the outcome. She felt that the campaign had educated the public just as intended and that the Progressive Party's respectable showing would help to keep the issue of reform alive in President Wilson's mind. But it soon became clear that the Progressive Party itself would not be playing an active role in the process. Relatively few Progressives had been elected to Congress and to state legislatures, depriving the party of the foothold in federal and state law-making that had been anticipated. In addition, Roosevelt's interest in the party soon waned. One of Addams' colleagues wrote to another: "The Colonel has become suspicious of the whole social worker crowd except Jane Addams and he is afraid of her, and we must depend on her to save the situation."

Addams could not, of course, "save the situation," and by the following year, she too had moved on to other activities. But watching Woodrow Wilson's first term—during which a number of items from the Progressive Party platform were put into law—she felt sure that the campaign had been worthwhile. Perhaps it was inevitable, she wrote, that "new parties ultimately write the platforms for all parties; that a cause which a new party has the courage to espouse is later taken up by political organizations to whom direct appeal has previously proved fruitless."

1912 had not ended precisely as Addams had hoped, but even if the Progressive Party was no longer very active, the progressive movement was full of life. Perhaps presidential politics was not the right arena, but the campaign had reaffirmed her conviction that collaborative effort was the key to social progress. Looking hopefully toward the future, she wrote in late 1912: "There is a tremendous advantage in numbers when it comes to enthusiasm, good-will and humanitarian zeal, and if we could only direct the moral energy of which this country possesses so much into the same channels at the same time, there is almost nothing we could not accomplish."

Broader Horizons

Jane Addams (right) holding a peace sign in 1915. (University of Illinois
at Chicago's University Library. Jane Addams Memorial Collection)

9

Trying to Stop a War

The fact that Theodore Roosevelt lost the election of 1912 was a disappointment for Jane Addams, but it did not diminish her hopes for the future. Woodrow Wilson was also a reform-minded president, even if he was not the one she had campaigned for. And the huge network of advocacy organizations that had emerged in recent years was as active as ever. Thus, as late as the summer of 1914, Addams continued to believe that the Progressive Era would last for many more years.

However, 400 miles away, events were unfolding that would transform Addams' life—slowing the pace of reform, refocusing her own interests, and subjecting her to a level of hostility she had never faced before. The changes began with a burst of gunfire.

On June 28, 1914, the Archduke Franz Ferdinand, heir to the throne of the Austro-Hungarian Empire, was shot and killed, along with his wife, in the provincial capital of Sarajevo. The murderer, a young Serbian nationalist, was part of a movement that was demanding self-determination for the empire's large Slavic population. Within a month of the shootings, the Austrian emperor declared war on nearby Serbia, which he blamed for the assassinations.

Under other circumstances, the matter might have remained a dispute between neighbors. But over the previous 20 years, an intricate structure of alliances and commitments had grown up among the great European powers, requiring each one to go to war if its partner was attacked. One by one, the dominoes fell, and by August 1914, every major European country had been drawn into the conflict—Russia to defend Serbia, France to defend Russia, and Germany to defend Austria-Hungary. Finally, when Germany attacked France through neutral Belgium, Britain went to war to prevent Germany's domination of western Europe. World War I had begun.

Thinking About Militarism

Over the course of the next year, Jane Addams emerged as a major figure in the international effort to stop the war. This might seem like an unexpected progression for a Chicago settlement worker—even a famous one. But in fact, Addams had been writing and lecturing for nearly 15 years about how militarism obstructed social progress.

Addams first spoke out on the subject in 1898, at the time of the Spanish-American War. After defeating the crumbling Spanish Empire in just four months, the United States seized Spain's former colonies (Puerto Rico, Guam, and the Philippines) and imposed tight restrictions on the nominally independent new government of Cuba. Soon afterward, the United States found itself putting down a rebellion among some of its new subjects. The Filipinos, who had fought bravely beside the Americans to expel the Spaniards, were enraged to learn that they had simply exchanged one master for another. The Philippine-American War that followed lasted more than a decade, involved great brutality on both sides, and killed hundreds of thousands of Filipinos as well as more than 4,000 U.S. soldiers.

To Addams and to many reformers like her, these events represented a betrayal of everything the United States stood for. How could a country with America's particular history be playing the villain in another country's fight for independence? And, more generally, how could America square its democratic values with the coercion involved in being an imperial power?

The first organized opposition to the country's new role emerged in October 1898, with the formation of the Boston Anti-Imperialist League. Addams—who attended the organizing conference—found the experience unsettling; it was the first time in her life that she had ever participated in a direct challenge to national policy. For years, she had admired Count Leo Tolstoy's willingness to act on his pacifist convictions. Now her own convictions were being tested. She wrote to her sister: "I will have to become more of a Tolstoyan or less of one right off." She chose to become more of one, and six months later, she gave the keynote speech at the founding meeting of the national Anti-Imperialist League. She continued to participate until the organization split into factions over whom to support in the presidential election of 1900.

Brief though her involvement was, Addams' work with the league started her thinking about how militarism related to her own goals for society. As she brooded on this issue, she crystallized her ideas by presenting a number of speeches on the topic and teaching a summer course at the University of Wisconsin. Finally, she combined and reworked all this material into a book entitled *Newer Ideals of Peace* (1906).

The core idea in this book is that militarism is not just a wartime issue; it can be recognized whenever people seek to achieve their goals through coercion rather than cooperation. In developing this argument, Addams presented her discussion of war and peace in a series of chapters dealing with urban government, immigration, labor laws, trade unions, child labor, and women's involvement in public life. In each case, Addams showed the destructive effect of relying on the abuse of power to solve human problems; for example, she pointed to urban bosses whose bribe-taking disenfranchised the voters, to employers who ruled by intimidation, and to unions who resorted to their own forms of coercion. In each case, she called for a "newer" approach based on human understanding and mutual obligation.

What did these various aspects of American experience have to do with war? Addams argued that the more accustomed a society became to using coercion in daily life, the more inclined it would be to use force in solving international disputes. The way to prevent war, she argued, was not to engage in last-minute protests as the troops were lining up on the field but to change the way people related to each other all the time. Developing habits of cooperation and empathy could prevent destructive conflict at every level of human experience—from the factory floor to international relations. Peace, she said, was not just the absence of war but "a rising tide of moral feeling" that would ultimately make war impossible.

Addams believed that fighting was not an inborn human characteristic but a relic of past conditions. No doubt it had been appropriate in some earlier era, but it made no sense in modern life. People therefore needed to do the logical thing in the face of changing conditions: change their behavior. After all, she observed, we might not object to a boy's defending himself on the way to school, but we would be very sorry to see him bullying people as a gangster when he grew up. Similarly, we could appreciate war's historical significance while recognizing that different behavior was called for today.

To Addams, the first step away from militarism had already occurred in the prehistoric past, when "primitive man, by the very necessities of his hard struggle for life, came at last to identify his own existence with that of his tribe." Over time, people's circles of concern had widened as they learned to express their "genius for goodness" in larger groups. They found ways to live together in relative peace in cities and eventually developed feelings of patriotism that bound whole nations together. In the future, Addams thought, this kind of human connectedness could develop even further—to the point where people felt equally connected to the citizens of other nations. "We may then give up war," she wrote, "because we shall find it as difficult to make war upon a nation at the other side of the globe as upon our next-door neighbor."

It is important to notice that Addams rarely offered religious reasons for abandoning war. Although she referred occasionally to her father's Quaker tendencies, he himself was no pacifist; as a state legislator during the Civil War, he had supported every war measure that was proposed and helped raise a regiment to fight with the Union Army. However, what John Addams did instill in his daughter was a vision of human solidarity that—especially as she matured—meant much more to her than organized religion.

This, then, was the primary reason that Addams opposed militarism and war. She believed that humanity's most fundamental task was to build a just and caring society. Peace made that work possible, while war not only impeded it but pushed mankind backward toward the barbarous past. Isolated reforms might be achieved in time of war, but the values of sympathy and understanding that were essential for sustained progress were fostered by peace, not war.

As the years went by, Addams alternated between periods of hope and periods of discouragement. She recognized the signs of growing militarism at home and abroad, but she also took eager note of each indication that people were learning to resolve their differences by peaceful means. Then, in the summer of 1914, came the gunfire at Sarajevo. The message was clear: The time for gradual progress toward peace had run out.

Organizing a Campaign for Peace

Europeans' ideas about what the war might mean to them were conditioned by the fact that between 1812 and 1914, not a single war in western Europe had lasted more than a year. So, when World War I began, most of the people caught up in it expected it to follow a similar pattern; in August, the German Kaiser assured his departing troops that they would be home "before the leaves have fallen from the trees."

The American public took a darker view. Right from the start, they were shocked by the huge casualties, troubled about the potential economic costs, and worried that the United States might be drawn into the fighting. Addams said later that the outbreak of war engulfed her and her pacifist friends with a "sense of desolation, of suicide, of anachronism." As public concern mounted, antiwar demonstrations were held in a number of cities. In one of the earliest protests, held in New York City just a few weeks after the war began, 1,500 women dressed in black marched up Fifth Avenue to the sound of muffled drums.

Addams did what she could to rally public support for a peaceful settlement of the war: she wrote an article for the *Ladies' Home Journal*, gave a number of speeches, and agreed to chair one of the first antiwar organizations formed: the Henry Street Group, so named because it met at the Henry Street settlement in New York City. But she and her pacifist friends were gripped by a sense of their own powerlessness and impatient with the established peace organizations, such as the American Peace Society and the Universal Peace Union, which seemed slow to react to the crisis.

In September 1914, the antiwar movement got a jolt of new energy when a flamboyant pacifist named Rosika Schwimmer sailed in from England. A native of Hungary, she had been working in London as press secretary for the International Woman Suffrage Alliance. Schwimmer had concluded that the way to end the war was to convene a Council of Neutral Nations to mediate between the opposing sides. She had come to the United States to present President Wilson with a petition signed by thousands of European women, calling on him to lead the mediation effort. Suffragist leader Carrie Chapman Catt, whom Schwimmer had met in Europe, arranged for her to see the president; he was courteous but noncommittal. Schwimmer then embarked on a cross-country speaking tour, focusing particularly on women's groups.

Soon afterward, another charismatic pacifist arrived from England. Born Emmeline Pethick, she was such a devout feminist that she had persuaded her husband, Ernest Lawrence, that they should both take the same last name: Pethick-Lawrence. Like Schwimmer, Pethick-Lawrence set out on the lecture circuit, making an even more explicitly feminist cause for peace. Current events made clear, she said, that men could no longer be trusted to run the world. With war raging on the Continent, "the failure of male statecraft in Europe is complete." It was now up to women to save the world, and the first essential step was to declare "a women's war against war."

Pethick-Lawrence got a particularly enthusiastic reception in New York City, where radical feminists in the peace movement were exasperated over the inaction of the (male-led) mainstream peace societies. It was time, they said, for women to form their own peace group. Looking for the most respectable sponsors possible, they persuaded Addams and

Carrie Chapman Catt to issue the call for a women's peace meeting. It convened in January 1915 in Washington, D.C., with about 75 women in attendance, representing organizations ranging from the Women's Christian Temperance Union to the Women's Committee of the Socialist Party.

Addams served as chair and keynote speaker for the proceedings, which had two notable outcomes: the formation of a Women's Peace Party (with Addams as chair) and the adoption of an 11-plank Peace Platform. Endorsing Rosika Schwimmer's call for neutral mediation, the Peace Platform recommended a new mediation mechanism that had been devised by a Wisconsin college professor, Julia Grace Wales. The Wales Plan called for "continuous mediation," meaning that the mediators would sit in continuous session, offering proposals and responding to the belligerents' counterproposals until a settlement was reached.

Besides neutral mediation, the Peace Platform called for just and merciful peace terms, and it presented a vision of postwar international relations that clearly influenced President Wilson's famous Fourteen Points speech three years later. The 11 planks included freedom of the seas, arms limitation, reduction of trade barriers, and the establishment of a Concert of Nations to maintain the peace. Historian Thomas J. Knock calls this document "the most comprehensive manifesto on internationalism advanced by any American organization throughout the entire war."

The formation of the Women's Peace Party was a milestone in Addams' life. She had been speaking for years about the evils of militarism and war, but her main strategy for ending these evils had simply been to encourage moral and social reform. The outbreak of World War I changed everything. The ongoing slaughter in Europe made the campaign for peace more urgent, the idea of neutral mediation provided a concrete program to work for, and the new emphasis on women's role in the peace process spoke directly to her heart. Energized by the new circumstances, Addams threw herself into the work of the Women's Peace Party.

Over the months that followed the Washington meeting, the Peace Party worked tirelessly on its own and with other organizations, such as the American Union Against Militarism, to publicize the need to end the war. Meanwhile, the party's membership mushroomed, rising from 500 in 1915 to more than 25,000 in early 1917. Addams later recalled a bit wistfully that at that time, "it was still comparatively easy to get people together in the name of Peace." So acceptable was opposition to the war, in fact, that one of the most popular songs of 1915 was "I Didn't Raise My Boy to Be a Soldier."

Reaching out to allies around the world, 42 members of the Women's Peace Party set sail in April 1915 to attend an International Congress of Women that was being convened by European suffragists at The Hague in the Netherlands. Besides Addams, the American group included a considerable number of her friends and associates, including Alice Hamilton, Sophonisba Breckinridge, Grace Abbott, Lillian Wald, Julia Wales, and Emily Balch.

Congress participants were required to accept two platform planks in advance: commitment to the peaceful resolution of international disputes and women's suffrage. There was also one procedural requirement: So as to avoid getting bogged down in mutual recriminations, the congress would not discuss how the war had begun but only how to end it. Balking at this rule, the French stayed away. But more than 1,000 women from 12 different countries did attend, including representatives from Austria, Germany, Great Britain, and Belgium.

Many participants from belligerent countries had had to brave sharp criticism at home from people who thought that attending the congress amounted to fraternizing with the enemy. For example, the British delegates were caricatured in the London press as "Pro-Hun Peacettes." But the buoyant sense of common purpose at the congress was affirmed on the very first day, when the two Belgian delegates made a point of shaking hands with the representatives from Germany before sitting beside them on the platform. Emily Balch described the prevailing mood as one of "passionate human sympathy, not inconsistent with patriotism, but transcending it."

Addams was elected to preside over the congress, partly because she was so well-known and partly because of America's importance among the neutrals. One can imagine the limitless opportunities for antagonism and resentment in a gathering such as this, as well as the din of a huge hall packed with passionate delegates and watchful police, and the challenge of conducting the proceedings without microphones in three different languages. But Addams steered the group harmoniously through four days of sensitive discussions and the adoption of 20 different resolutions. In her final remarks, she observed: "We have been able to preserve good-will and good fellowship, we have considered in perfect harmony and straight-forwardness the most difficult propositions, and we part better friends than we met."

At the close of the congress, the group adopted a set of resolutions that included many elements from the American women's Peace Platform: a Council of Neutral Nations to undertake continuous mediation and a set of internationalist goals to preserve the peace once the war ended. In addition, the resolutions included a call for women to play a larger role in public affairs—at the peace conference, in national governments, and in international organizations. The women at The Hague were convinced that simply by working together so well, they had provided a vivid contrast to the way men were running the world. The best hope for peace in the future was to manage public affairs along these constructive lines.

The most audacious step taken by the congress was the decision—initially proposed by Rosika Schwimmer—to send a group of "envoys" to meet with the heads of every major European government—belligerent and neutral—as well as President Wilson. Addams was one of the five women elected for the task. The envoys' primary mission was to assess each government's interest in the possibility of ending the war through neutral mediation. Would the neutral countries be willing to participate? How would the belligerent countries respond if mediation were offered?

Addams and a Dutch participant, Arletta Jacobs, took responsibility for visiting most of the belligerent governments, while the three other envoys traveled to Russia and to each of the European neutrals. Over the next eight weeks, Addams and Jacobs visited London, Berlin, Vienna, Budapest, Paris, and Le Havre (home of the Belgian government in exile). For Addams—now in her mid-50s—the travel under wartime conditions was hard, the burden of responsibility heavy, and the value of their efforts uncertain. "At moments it seems worthwhile," she wrote to Ellen Starr, "and again it fades into nothing."

Addams' doubts notwithstanding, what strikes a contemporary reader is how many high-level officials she and Jacobs were able to see and how warmly they were received. The intolerable cost of war seemed plain to everyone; in fact, throughout this period, the fighting was producing more than 3,000 casualties a day. No belligerent country was willing to be the first to sue for peace, but each of them expressed interest in mediation. "What are the neutrals waiting for?" asked one leader. Skeptics in Washington later insisted that these officials were simply brushing off their lady visitors with empty pleasantries. But Addams' own account of these visits (in *Women at the Hague*, a book she co-authored with Alice Hamilton and Emily Balch) suggests a level of interest in the possibility of mediation that would seem to have been worth exploring.

While Addams and Jacobs were getting positive responses from the belligerents, the envoys visiting the neutrals were encountering more resistance. Most neutral leaders seemed to be afraid that endorsing mediation would antagonize one or another of the countries currently at war. Four governments indicated that they might consider participating if some other country got the process started, but not one was willing to launch it themselves. Thus, once again, the spotlight turned to President Wilson, who seemed to be the only neutral leader with the clout to bring the rest onboard.

When Addams returned home from her travels in July 1915, she received a mixed welcome. Some Americans praised her efforts to end the war, some thought them noble but misguided, and some assailed them as near-treason. Theodore Roosevelt, for one, maintained that the only effect of the women's gathering at The Hague had been "to advance the cause of international cowardice."

Addams herself had one overriding concern: to get Wilson to commit himself to the mediation plan. Her strenuous months in Europe had revived kidney and bladder problems she had had in the past, initiating a period of poor health that would plague her for the next several years. She was acutely ill during the fall of 1915, but even, so she made the long trip to Washington six times to talk with Wilson. Many other peace advocates also met with him and with Wilson's aide, Col. Edward House, and the Secretary of State, Robert Lansing.

Wilson was courteous, even friendly to Addams, telling her more than once that he had been studying the Women's Peace Party platform. Behind the scenes, however, House and Lansing were advising the president to keep his distance. They were convinced that America would ultimately have to enter the war on the side of Britain and France, and they told Wilson that any involvement in the mediation effort (which they were sure would fail) would only diminish his influence. The meetings dragged on, but by November 1915, when Wilson made a major speech about the need for military preparedness, it seemed clear that he was not going to participate in mediation, even if some other country got the process started. Social Gospel leader Washington Gladden spoke for many anxious pacifists when he warned: "It appears probable that our nation is going to be sucked into the maelstrom; and plunged into a conflict with a people with whom we have no legitimate quarrel."

Wilson's disinterest in mediation meant there would be no conference of official representatives from the neutral governments. But some peace advocates, including Addams, had long thought that a group of distinguished private citizens from neutral countries could do the job just as well. Plans were soon underway to organize this type of conference in Stockholm, Sweden. Unfortunately, the project was immediately overshadowed by industrialist Henry Ford's insistence on chartering a large ship to transport a flock of Americans to the proceedings. The "Peace Ship" soon became a media joke, complete with a raffish cast of characters assembled for the voyage, Ford's reckless promise to "have the boys home by Christmas," and minimal attention to the serious deliberations that were already going on among the delegates in Sweden.

While all this was happening, Addams was continuing to struggle with very poor health. She later described the period from fall 1915 to fall 1918 as "three years of semi-invalidism" filled with "weeks of feverish discomfort." The Peace Ship contretemps did little to improve her condition. She was particularly disturbed to see the voyage widely described as her personal project. She had opposed the idea from the first, privately directing Arletta Jacobs, vice president of the International Congress of Women, to make certain that their organization remained separate from "the Ford enterprise."

Addams did reluctantly agree to travel on the Peace Ship because of its association with the neutrals' work in Sweden. But in December, she came down with pneumonia, which made the trip impossible for her. She collapsed at a meeting of the Women's Peace Party in January and, accompanied by Mary Smith, spent most of the winter convalescing in California. Then, when they returned to Chicago in April, she was diagnosed with tuberculosis of the kidney and had to have one kidney removed.

Despite her ill health, Addams continued to speak and write about issues of peace and war. In the fall of 1916, she also made the difficult decision to support Wilson for re-election. On the domestic front, he had taken a number of progressive steps, including winning passage of income tax legislation and an eight-hour day for railroad workers, elevating Louis Brandeis to the Supreme Court, and naming John Mitchell, former head of the United Mine Workers, as Secretary of Labor. Wilson had also begun calling for a League to Prevent War, which suggested greater willingness to involve himself in international peace efforts. Moreover, his opponent, Charles Evans Hughes, seemed even less open to antiwar arguments than Wilson was. Persuading herself that Wilson was moving in the right direction and that popular pressure would push him the rest of the way, Addams campaigned for him that fall. He won a narrow victory, bolstered by his ringing campaign slogan: "He kept us out of war."

In January 1917, in a speech calling for "Peace Without Victory," Wilson urged that the war be ended on just terms before either side annihilated the other. This was music to Addams' ears, but it was the last good news of the year. Not long afterward, Germany began unrestricted submarine warfare, in response to which the United States broke off diplomatic relations. As the tension mounted, Addams helped to organize demonstrations in front of the White House and a blitz of letter-writing. Peace advocates held rallies in a number of cities, and the American Union Against Militarism took out full-page ads in major newspapers across the country.

In March, a huge peace meeting in New York chose a delegation, headed by Addams, to visit the president one last time. Wilson explained to his visitors that he had to enter the war so as to have influence at the peace conference. Addams later recalled: "I hotly and no doubt unfairly asked myself whether any man had the right to rate his moral leadership so high that he could consider the sacrifice of the lives of thousands of his young countrymen a necessity." The delegates, she said, left the meeting "in deep dejection." On April 6, 1917, the United States entered the war. "The world," said Wilson, "must be made safe for democracy."

A Pacifist in Wartime America

Except for the summer of 1881, when her father died, the spring of 1917 was probably the worst time in Addams' life. Although the war had troubled her deeply ever since it began, she had been buoyed by the excitement of participating in a huge movement pursuing two compelling—and, she believed, attainable—goals: to end the war through neutral mediation and to keep the United States out of the fighting. Now both campaigns had failed. She was still a pacifist, but her country was at war.

Addams knew very well the cost of being at odds with the American public on military matters. Back in July 1915, when she first returned from visiting the European capitals, she gave a speech at Carnegie Hall in New York City. Her basic message was that there were people all over Europe who would welcome a mediated peace. She made her fatal error when she said that in several countries, the soldiers had to be given stimulants before they could bring themselves to use their bayonets. Her point was that these young men were too humane to gouge the life out of another human being. What her critics heard was a slur on the courage of the men at the Front. A storm of criticism erupted; the press, which had always treated her with kid gloves, turned on her, and on one occasion, she was booed by an audience for the first time in her life.

Addams had received public scoldings before, but the attacks on her speech at Carnegie Hall were much harsher. Furthermore—perhaps because of her poor health—she seemed less able this time to understand why her opponents might feel as they did and to move on to the next event. Convinced that she was being willfully misrepresented by the press and brooding on the injustice of it, she noted darkly that the pacifist in wartime "finds it possible to travel from the mire of self-pity straight to the barren hills of self-righteousness and to hate himself equally in both places."

Some people held this incident against Addams for years; she herself had trouble forgetting it. But for most Americans, the furor died down within a few weeks, and Addams regained her place as a revered social reformer. She continued to be in demand as an author and speaker, and even people who did not share her views on the war seemed generally to admire her commitment to peace. It is a measure of Addams' continued high standing that in 1916, both presidential candidates sought her endorsement, and the Democratic Party made a point of announcing in October that she had decided to back Wilson.

But as soon as America entered the war in April 1917, public tolerance for dissent plummeted to zero. Earlier that spring, President Wilson had observed to a reporter: "Once lead these people to war . . . and they'll soon forget there ever was such a thing as tolerance." His prediction proved all too accurate. Vigilantism swept the country, focusing particularly on radicals and people of German birth. Meanwhile, new state and federal laws against "sedition" were used to put hundreds of people in jail simply for speaking against the draft. Chicago was no exception; poet Edgar Lee Masters, who was living there at the time, described "an orgy of hate and hypocrisy, of cruelty and revenge." The Women's Peace Party office in Chicago suffered continual harassment: Addams reported that mail on the party's front steps was spat on and the door "was often befouled in hideous ways."

Given Addams' history, it is somewhat surprising that she chose to hold out against this tide. Time and again in the past, she had alienated her more doctrinaire friends by her willingness to compromise. Rosika Schwimmer, the feisty European pacifist, was so suspicious of Addams' flexibility that she called her "slippery Jane." Addams herself noted the unfamiliarity of her new position, observing that until the war, "my temperament and habit had always kept me rather in the middle of the road; in politics as well as in social reform I had been for 'the best possible." Yet here she was, standing with the militant minority. She was not driven by ideology like the socialists nor by religion like the Quakers. But she believed fervently that war exacerbated international problems rather than solving them and that human progress could only occur under conditions of peace. And she was convinced that at least some people had to be willing to say so.

The great majority of progressives chose a different course, although for a variety of different reasons. Establishment internationalists like Elihu Root and Nicholas Murray Butler had long advocated creating structures that would preserve world peace, but they had taken little part in the effort to stop the war because they had decided early on that an Allied victory was necessary before international peace could be achieved.

Even people who had been in the forefront of the campaign to stop the war generally fell into line as soon as the United States entered the conflict. Some were simply avoiding the ferocity directed at anyone who spoke out in protest. For example, Carrie Chapman Catt was concerned that publicly identifying herself with pacifism would undermine support for her first priority: women's suffrage. Even the redoubtable Julia Lathrop kept her opposition to the war quiet so as not to arouse antagonism to the Children's Bureau. Other former peace advocates, such as Paul Kellogg, persuaded themselves that certain social reforms might be passed more easily in wartime. In addition, there were some true converts, such as Washington Gladden, who optimistically echoed President Wilson's assurances, stating: "There are to be no more wars. . . . This is the last war."

Whatever their reasons, the outcome was that Addams endured anguished splits with many of her closest friends and colleagues. Settlement worker Mary Simkhovitch, a friend of many years' standing, wrote that those who loved and respected Addams deeply regretted "that we cannot think or act in unison with her." Addams' longtime comrade John Dewey broke with her over the war, as did Hull-House's hugely generous donor, Louise Bowen.

Neither Simkhovitch nor Dewey nor Bowen turned their political differences with Addams into personal enmity, but there were many who did, including some members of her own family. Social workers with whom she had collaborated for decades stopped writing to her. The Chicago Woman's Club— an institution that had been close to Addams' heart for 25 years—notified her that her peace committee was no longer welcome to meet there.

Besides suffering these private losses, Addams also lost public standing. Even during the worst of the controversy over her Carnegie Hall speech in 1915, most critics had confined themselves to suggesting that she was a good woman who was meddling in affairs she did not understand. But the tone in 1917 was far more virulent. A typical newspaper editorial called her "a silly, vain, impertinent old maid." Her mail was filled with vicious personal attacks, and when she tried to explain her position in a speech entitled "A Pacifist in Wartime," newspapers around the country dismissed her remarks as "pro-German twaddle" and "seditious balderdash."

All through these difficult years, Addams' friend Alice Hamilton—who had by now built a distinguished career in occupational medicine—devoted herself with special care to sustaining Addams' spirits. Although Hamilton had left Hull-House in 1911, she and Addams had remained in touch, and after America entered the war in 1917, their friendship grew closer still because both of them remained committed pacifists. Throughout Addams' years of ostracism and her many months of ill health, Hamilton provided her with continuing support—both as a devoted friend and as a physician. In gratitude, Addams dedicated one of her very last books to Hamilton, "whose wisdom and courage have never failed, when we have walked together so many times in the very borderland between life and death."

No one understood better than Hamilton what the war years meant to Addams. She said that Addams "had two conflicting traits which sometimes brought her great unhappiness: she was very dependent on a sense of warm comradeship and harmony with the mass of her fellow men, but at the same time her clear sighted integrity made it impossible for her to keep in step with the crowd in many a crisis." Hamilton observed that many reformers she had known seemed to take a kind of virtuous pleasure in feeling that they were being martyred for a just cause. But, said Hamilton, "this was never true of Jane." Driven by her conscience, Addams maintained her stand against the mass of her fellow citizens because she felt she must. But in doing so, she paid a terrible price in what Hamilton described as "spiritual loneliness."

One of Addams' most disarming qualities had always been her willingness to give her opponents the benefit of the doubt—to think that perhaps they were right and she was wrong. Even when she took controversial stands, they often involved not defending a particular viewpoint but instead defending the right of all people to believe what they chose. This open-mindedness had been an asset in the past, but it was poor equipment for a lonely dissenter. Throughout the war years, she was tortured by the idea that she was being arrogant—even undemocratic—to put her own opinions above those of other Americans. "In the hours of doubt and self-mistrust," she wrote, "the question again and again arises, has the individual or a very small group, the right to stand out against millions of his fellow countrymen?"

Addams did find "a certain healing of the spirit" in her work with other pacifists in groups such as the Women's Peace Party and the Fellowship of Reconciliation. But however restorative it was for Addams to commune with these other outcasts, she was haunted by "moments when one longed desperately for reconciliation with one's friends and fellow citizens." She wrote to a friend, "I feel as if a few of us were clinging together in a surging sea."

Being a pariah meant losing not only private friends and public respect but also the chance to do useful work. By the summer of 1917, Addams was receiving far fewer invitations to speak, and magazines had entirely stopped asking for her articles. She submitted an essay based on her "Pacifist in Wartime" speech to her longtime friend, *Survey* editor Paul Kellogg, who for years had welcomed anything she submitted. He told her the article was too controversial and refused to print it. Most of the remaining Women's Peace Party members were encountering similar rebuffs. Many were forced to resign from social organizations they had served for years, including some they themselves had founded.

In this dark time, Herbert Hoover's food conservation campaign came as a blessed deliverance to Addams. She and Hoover had become acquainted during the early years of the war when he was in Europe organizing food relief for the Allies. In 1918, he returned to the United States to promote the same cause in the newly created position of U.S. Food Administrator and immediately recruited a flock of speakers, including Addams, to travel the country explaining the urgency of the Allies' need and calling on Americans to conserve their food and produce more of it.

Addams rejoiced that here at last was something useful that she and her pacifist friends could do. She predicted—correctly, as it turned out—that "if we were not too conspicuous we might be permitted to work without challenge." She developed a standard speech, entitled "The World's Food Supply—America's Obligation," and criss-crossed the country throughout 1918, speaking to national and state groups as well as to schools and women's clubs. She found the work rewarding—both because of the program's immediate value and because, in her mind, it was connected to a much grander theme: the elemental human impulse to feed the hungry.

In her book about her wartime experiences, entitled *Peace and Bread*, Addams wrote: "It seemed to me that millions of American women might be caught up into a great world purpose, that of conservation of life." At the same time, she took it as a hopeful sign that the Allied countries had subordinated their national differences and commercial motives in a collaborative drive to feed their people. Perhaps this effort could lead to other forms of international organization, giving pacifists something positive to work for instead of simply opposing war.

The one aspect of the American food relief program that troubled Addams was its single-minded focus on the needs of the Allies. After all, it was well-known that women and children were also going hungry in Germany and Austria. Accordingly, Addams constantly reminded her audiences that withholding food from mothers and children should not be regarded as a weapon of war. It is a mark of Addams' courage that, having just won back some small measure of public respectability, she was willing to risk it again so soon by speaking out on behalf of humanity across enemy lines. There were few repercussions, however, and Addams continued to travel for Hoover's program until the war was over.

The end of World War I on November 11, 1918, found Addams feeling tentatively hopeful. The progressive movement seemed to have been floundering ever since America entered the conflict—both because of internal disagreements over the war and because as long as the fighting lasted, there was little public interest in domestic reform. But Addams hoped that progressivism would revive once peace returned. And, in addition, perhaps the example of wartime food relief would inspire new forms of international cooperation.

What about Addams' own prospects? Would her ostracism end with the armistice? At the height of the wartime attacks on her, many critics had stated flatly that her public career was over. In fact, she would continue to lead Hull-House, work for peace, give speeches, and write books and articles for the remaining 17 years of her life. But in one respect, the critics were right: Addams' career as Saint Jane—as an untouchable American heroine—had indeed come to an end.

10

Searching for Hope
in the 1920s

In May 1919, in Zurich, Jane Addams officially opened the second meeting of the International Congress of Women. At the group's first gathering, in 1915, many of these same participants had come together—determined to stop World War I (then only eight months old) before it could do more damage. They had failed, and by the time the armistice was declared in November 1918, at least 20 million people had been killed. Four empires— the German, Austrian, Russian, and Ottoman—had been obliterated, large sections of Belgium and France had been devastated, and millions of soldiers had been exposed to the horrors of trench warfare, including the use of poison gas.

The members of the Women's Congress had spoken out boldly in 1915 about the social, physical, and economic dangers of an extended war. Their warnings had turned out to be correct and even conservative. But rather than being respected for their prescience, they had been vilified as defeatists and traitors. In addition, the European members on both sides of the conflict had suffered physical privations during the war, and many participants had lost family members as well. (Addams herself had lost her beloved oldest nephew, John Linn.) Nevertheless, the predominant mood at the congress was one of optimism. Here they were—just a few months after the armistice—hoping that the principles of international understanding and social justice that they had preached unsuccessfully in 1915 might be more acceptable in 1919.

The congress was an emotional reunion, bringing together delegates from 16 countries. The participants were sorry that the Allies had chosen to convene the official Peace Conference on their own home turf in France (in the town of Versailles); the women believed that meeting on neutral ground would have set a more constructive tone, which is why they held their own gathering in Switzerland. But they knew that President Woodrow Wilson was still determined to achieve the kind of just peace he had outlined in his Fourteen Points speech. They were also convinced that the futility of trying to solve international problems by force had been demonstrated so conclusively during the war that by now, the leaders at Versailles would be ready for a more humane approach.

And so the Women's Congress set to work, hammering out a variety of proposals to foster international peace, including disarmament, social reform, and extending food assistance to the former enemy nations. Addams presided over the proceedings, inviting broad participation but also keeping the pace moving. At one point, according to the minutes, "the president called attention to the short time left for the many who wished to speak, and said that a discussion of the ideal as compared with the practical might lead nowhere." Alice Hamilton, who was attending the congress, wrote to Mary Rozet Smith: "I do long for you to be here to see J.A. in all her glory, happier I am sure than she has been in five whole years."

Midway through the congress, a copy of the completed peace treaty arrived from Versailles. As the women had hoped, it recommended forming a League of Nations to resolve future international disputes. But the actual peace terms dictated by the treaty seemed focused more on retribution than on fostering international understanding. For example, ignoring Wilson's call for "open covenants openly arrived at," the treaty affirmed several secret deals that the Allies had made among themselves during the war. It also required only the defeated nations to disarm, forced the losers to hand over sizable chunks of territory, and held them responsible for paying huge reparations to cover all civilian damage during the war.

Convinced that the resentment engendered by these terms would make war more likely in the future, the congress spent its final week drafting amendments that they proposed adding to the treaty, including a "Women's Charter," which laid out their proposals for expanding women's participation in world affairs. In addition, the group agreed to establish itself as a permanent organization named the Women's International League for Peace and Freedom, with Addams as president. The office would be in Geneva, near the future League of Nations.

Staffing the new office would be Addams' longtime friend and colleague, Emily Balch. A sociology professor at Wellesley College for many years, Balch had helped to organize a settlement house in Boston in 1892, had worked actively with the Women's Trade Union League, and was a founding member of the Women's Peace Party. She had attended the initial International Congress of Women at The Hague in 1915, and as one of the envoys sent by the congress to visit European heads of state, she had collaborated with Addams and Alice Hamilton on their book about that experience: *Women at the Hague* (1915). Balch's continuing opposition to the war, even after the United States entered the hostilities in 1917, had led to her dismissal from Wellesley. From 1919 on, she would devote most of her energies to the Women's International League.

With the league's organizational future agreed on, the Zurich meeting came to a close and Addams led a group of five women to Versailles to present their proposed amendments to the treaty. Wilson being unavailable, she gave the document to his aide. She then traveled to Germany, where she helped the American Friends Service Committee survey conditions among the civilian population and deliver emergency supplies. Having spent the week just before the Zurich meeting searching military cemeteries for her nephew's grave, Addams was now brought face-to-face with what war could do to civilians. The sight of so many suffering women and children stayed with her for years. Surely, she thought, people all over the world would soon come to understand that this must never be allowed to happen again.

In July 1919, Addams sailed home to America, hoping that in the years ahead, the nations of the world could learn to live together in peace, that the United States would resume the buoyant pace of social reform it had maintained before the war, and that she herself would find acceptance again in the eyes of the American public.

The Progressive Era Is Over

"I think the worst is over," a progressive friend had written to Addams in the summer of 1918. As soon as the fighting ended, he said, the country was certain to get back to work on the reform activities that had been interrupted by the war. But his prediction did not come true. In postwar America, the cause of social reform simply did not command the same respect and enthusiasm that it had during the Progressive Era.

It is true that two of the reformers' longtime goals were achieved in the years just after the war: Prohibition in 1919 and women's suffrage in 1920. But these two achievements represented the culmination of decades of earlier activism; few new initiatives were being launched. And even though, as historian Alan Dawley has shown, some progressives—including Addams—continued to speak for change throughout the 1920s, theirs had become a minority position. Calls for progressive reform would continue to percolate through American society, but the period when these ideas held a central place on the national agenda—the Progressive Era—was over.

World events played some part in this retreat from reform. As grand promises like "the war to end all wars" were swallowed up in the grim reality of muddy trenches and poison gas, people had developed a certain skepticism toward lofty rhetoric. More than 100,000 Americans had died in a war that, in retrospect, seemed to have had little to do with the country's own needs. Had all that slaughter really helped to "make the world safe for democracy," as President Wilson had promised? Many people remained unconvinced. And their skepticism soon broadened to cover the whole bygone era when, as one writer sardonically recalled, "we all believed in ideals." What had all that noble aspiration and self-sacrifice produced? Perhaps, many people concluded, it was better to take pleasure in the moment and stop worrying so much about saving the world or even about working for social change at home.

Americans' inclination to focus on their own immediate well-being was reinforced by the nation's prosperity during the 1920s. After a brief depression in 1920–1921, the economy rebounded quickly, spurred on by mass-produced cars, a booming advertising industry, and expanding distribution networks for everything from groceries to movies. In the past, Americans had tended to think of themselves primarily as producers. In the new economy, their role as consumers was just as important.

The expansion of consumerism held little attraction for Addams. Nor did she care for the worldview that seemed to go with it. She later described the 1920s as "a period of political and social sag." However, she did notice that her friends in the 19th Ward were benefitting from the better times. Many of her immigrant neighbors were able to move to larger apartments further out of the city, and some even managed to buy homes of their own. Meanwhile, she observed, their Americanized children were making sure that their families acquired the two necessities of modern American life: a car and a radio.

As old neighbors left the 19th Ward, new ones arrived, including African Americans from the south and some Mexicans. (The African Americans encountered particularly harsh discrimination in Chicago, most notably in the terrible race riot of 1919, during which 38 people were killed, 23 of them black. Although the main center of black settlement in Chicago was some distance from the 19th Ward, one of the black riot victims was murdered just a few blocks from Hull-House.) The staff at Hull-House treated their new African American and Mexican neighbors well, but they never established quite the same rapport with them that they had had with the earlier European immigrants.

The atmosphere among the residents of Hull-House had also changed by the 1920s. The formidable earlier generation—women like Florence Kelley and Julia Lathrop—had all moved on, and many of the newcomers who replaced them seemed more inclined to think of Hull-House as a place for professional training rather than as a spiritual home. Addams herself was away from the settlement a good deal. Now in her 60s, she had periodic health problems, and although she traveled extensively for the Women's International League, she usually conserved her strength when she was in Chicago by staying at Mary Smith's home. But she remained an absolutely central figure at Hull-House—still spending part of each day there when she was in town and still making a huge impression on the young people who congregated there. A woman who grew up in the neighborhood during these years remembers Addams vividly: "She was larger than life. White hair. Black dresses down to the floor. And big, big eyes."

Addams made no move to prepare for a transition in leadership at the settlement, and despite her frequent absences, she continued to have the last word in virtually every major policy decision. Her centrality to the operation was reinforced by the fact that—through her personal contributions and her talent for fundraising—she still generated a sizable share of the money needed each year to balance the perennially stretched budget. The main difference from the prewar years was the fact that there was now a second organization—the Women's International League—that meant almost as much to Addams as Hull-House. She was devoted to the settlement and supported it generously to her dying day. But it was no longer quite so central to her life.

Addams' growing dedication to the cause of world peace was obviously one factor in lessening the intensity of her involvement with Hull-House. Another factor was her cool-eyed recognition that the settlement movement as a whole was no longer the engine of social change that she had envisioned in the 1890s. Now, she wrote, "settlements have become part of the established order of things."

In truth, the overall movement had never been as adventurous as its most distinguished members. For every

Hull-House, every Henry Street, there had always been plenty of settlements that were little more than neighborhood recreation centers. Moreover, by the postwar era, even movement leaders like Hull-House were beginning to suffer from their own success. Many of their earlier initiatives, such as playgrounds, children's art programs, employment offices, and adult education courses, had been taken over by public agencies or the schools. Addams had always supported this kind of transition, assuming that settlements would continue to come up with new programs to replace those they handed over. Lillian Wald had shared Addams' vision, maintaining that one of a settlement's strengths was the fact that, "uncommitted to a fixed program, it can move with the times." But by the 1920s, the settlements were starting to lose that capacity to move with the times. They were still useful neighborhood institutions, but few of them could be called pioneers.

If Addams was saddened by the waning vitality of the settlement movement, she was downright disheartened by trends in the field of social work. To her mind, the field's growing emphasis on professionalism put far too much emphasis on clinical detachment while underrating the "candid and intimate relationships" that she believed gave social work its value and vitality. She was especially concerned about the rising importance of psychiatric social work, which focused almost entirely on clients' own personal adjustment. Adopting such a narrow focus, Addams believed, would leave a host of larger problems unaddressed. Unless the profession rededicated itself to social reform, she said, "we will fail in an essential obligation, in a sense we will be traitors to our original purpose."

Addams' frustration with social workers' declining interest in reform was intensified by her acute awareness of the many important progressive goals that remained unrealized. Of them all, none concerned her more than child labor. She had been involved in this issue for more than 30 years. She had served on the National Child Labor Committee since its founding in 1904 and had worked to get a federal law passed in 1914, only to see it declared unconstitutional two years later. A revised law, passed in 1918, was also struck down by the Supreme

Court. Then, a constitutional amendment prohibiting child labor passed Congress in 1924 but failed to achieve ratification in the states. Addams recognized the formidable opposition to the law—among employers, among states wary of federal intrusion, and among many working-class families. But she was convinced that persistent advocacy and public education on an issue like this was a far more important endeavor for social workers than focusing on the maladjustments of individual poor people.

Some of the progressive goals that had been realized had proved almost as frustrating to Addams as the ones that had not. For example, the troubled history of Prohibition was a painful topic for her. She had never been entirely comfortable with the branch of progressivism that tried to enforce its own standards of morality through legislation, but she had come to believe that prohibiting the sale of liquor in the United States would be a positive change. Unfortunately, Prohibition achieved far less than she had hoped. Overall drinking rates dropped somewhat, but the pervasive presence of bootlegging, speakeasies, and drinking in private homes made clear how little progress had been made in addressing the fundamental problem and how disinclined public officials were to take the matter further.

Addams was reluctant to give up on what she still saw as an admirable experiment. But the lack of genuine public support for the law troubled her. Again and again in the course of her career, she had insisted that pioneering social legislation could not be effectively enforced if it was pushed through before the American people were fully behind it. She suspected that this was the case with Prohibition—that the passage of this law represented not so much a wholehearted embrace of temperance as a desire to control the behavior of the working classes. Perhaps, she concluded, the fatal flaw in the whole effort had been "a certain self-righteousness in the good citizen when he voted for laws which he himself had no intention of obeying."

The achievement in 1920 of another long-sought goal—women's suffrage—brought Addams further disappointment. For decades, she and many other progressives had argued that if women were allowed to vote, they would constitute a "revolutionary force" in American politics—reducing corruption and humanizing public policy. Of course, women had disappointed Addams bitterly when they supported the war. Nevertheless, she remained convinced that, given the vote, women had the potential to transform American society. But even after the suffrage amendment took effect, male party officials continued to find ways to exclude women from full political participation. Moreover, female voters' turnout rates were low, and the women who did vote made electoral choices that were quite similar to men's. Addams did not despair; she observed philosophically that "ideas change less rapidly than events." But, as with Prohibition, it must have been discouraging to see that a change she had believed in so strongly and worked for so long was producing so little immediate benefit.

Addams' perplexity over women's voting choices was part of her larger struggle to understand the whole worldview of the postwar generation. For her and for many of her friends, the process of defining themselves as adults had been closely entwined with the challenge and satisfaction of joining the progressive struggle for social justice. It was therefore hard for her to understand a generation of young people—and particularly of young women—who seemed so concerned with their own happiness and so uninterested in achieving better conditions for others. She confessed that when young people assured her that self-expression was "the next step in social reform," she simply did not know how to respond.

What explained young people's preoccupation with their own personal lives during the 1920s? In part, it reflected the same backlash observed among their parents against what many now viewed as the overblown idealism of the Progressive Era. Other contributing factors were the prosperity of the times and the casual lawbreaking associated with Prohibition. Addams also believed that Sigmund Freud played a part—not directly but through the distorted version of his ideas that permeated popular culture, suggesting that to repress any impulse was unnatural and unhealthy.

Whatever the reasons for young people's single-minded pursuit of happiness, one of the forms it took that made Addams particularly uncomfortable was, as she said, "an astounding emphasis upon sex." She herself had a healthy respect for the power of the sex drive, but she had always stressed the need to sublimate this impulse and channel it into "higher" expressions, such as love and art and service to others. Now young people seemed to be "opposed to all hampering social conventions and even to established reticences." Addams understood that not every flirtation led straight to the bedroom, but she believed that in expressing their sexuality so freely—in their dress, in their conversation, in their dancing—young people were putting themselves at the mercy of "blind impulses" that could easily run away with them.

Besides the personal damage that Addams believed young people could suffer from devoting themselves so heedlessly to their own pleasures, she was sorry to see them abdicate the role that the younger generation had played so often in the past: that of goad and conscience for the rest of society. In fact, in matters of political and social controversy, she was amazed at how passive and even conformist the young people of the 1920s seemed to be. Hearing a young journalist sing the praises of self-expression and individual liberty, she asked him why he did not speak up for the liberty of the Haitians, whose country was currently being occupied by the United States. He clearly saw no connection between his liberty and theirs. "We seemed," she wrote, "to be speaking two different languages." Again and again during these years, Addams must indeed have felt that the language she spoke—based on Victorian virtues and progressive ideals—was of little use in trying to communicate with Jazz Age America.

Red Jane

Addams believed that the political passivity she found so troubling among young people was only a more extreme version of the conformity she observed throughout American society in the 1920s. And although she knew that the pleasure of concentrating on one's own personal concerns had considerable appeal, she believed that there was also another reason why people were staying away from public issues: In postwar America, the cost of speaking out was too high. Addams later observed that in political terms, there was "less scope for self-expression" during the 1920s "than there ever had been before on American soil."

Like many other people, Addams had assumed that the wartime obsession with traitors and spies would end once peace was declared. By 1919, however, new events were stoking Americans' paranoia even higher. For one thing, as soon as wartime wage controls ended, workers all across the country launched a wave of strikes designed to bring their earnings back in line with the cost of living. During this period, more than 350,000 steelworkers walked off the job, a police strike in Boston forced the governor to call in the National Guard, and a general strike in Seattle virtually closed down the city.

Few of these strikes lasted very long or gained a great deal for the participants. But the specter of angry workers on the march shook the nation and helped to justify the systematic repression of organized labor for years thereafter, weakening a sector of society that had been a major force in Progressive Era reform. In addition, the presence of so many immigrants among the strikers reinforced the connection in Americans' minds between labor activism and foreign-born radicals.

A wave of revolutions in Russia and eastern Europe intensified Americans' worries about imported radicalism. Although most of these uprisings were quickly put down, the rise of the Bolshevik-led Soviet Union as the world's first Communist nation sent a chill through the West. Haunted by the idea that communism might sweep the world, Americans began to see a Communist in every striking worker and a Soviet spy in every immigrant. At the height of the so-called Red Scare (1919–1920), U.S. Attorney General A. Mitchell Palmer launched a series of raids on radical individuals and organizations, hitting 33 cities in 23 states within just a few weeks. Thousands of suspects were arrested, and more than 800 were deported.

The Palmer Raids were so extreme that they caused a public backlash, but fear of radicalism remained a powerful force, and the tendency to link all advocacy with subversion continued throughout the 1920s. In this political atmosphere, observed labor attorney Donald Richberg, "To doubt, to question the wisdom of the powers that be, . . . ceased to be an act of virtue, the proof of an aspiring spirit. Such attitudes were 'radical' and 'destructive.'" Noting the same trend, Addams observed, "Any proposed change was suspect, even those efforts that had been considered praiseworthy before the war. To advance new ideas was to be a radical, or even a Bolshevik."

Just to make matters worse, anarchism had a kind of revival in the early 1920s. It was not very organized or widespread, but anarchists were involved—or suspected of being involved—in numerous bombings and assassination attempts, including an explosion on Wall Street in 1920 that killed 38 people. And for every actual act of terrorism, there were a hundred arrests and a thousand suspicions. It was in this poisoned atmosphere that two Italian anarchists named Ferdinando Sacco and Bartolomeo Vanzetti were arrested—and ultimately executed—on the charge of committing a robbery/murder in Massachusetts. Scholars still argue about whether the two men were guilty, but virtually all authorities today agree that the trial was grossly unfair and that a great deal of the prejudice against the defendants was because they were Italians and anarchists. Clearly, it was considered worse to be an anarchist than an Italian, but in fact, the two conditions were so linked in people's minds that one seemed to lead directly to the other.

As can be seen, the topic of immigration wove its way through nearly all American concerns about subversion during this era. Resistance to immigration had been rising in any case, simply because of the enormous numbers of arrivals during the decade before the war. At the same time, "old stock" Americans' ethnic prejudices were fueled by books such as Madison Grant's *The Passing of the Great Race* (1916), which warned that accepting so many immigrants from supposedly inferior racial groups would result in the "mongrelization of Anglo-Saxon blood." Postwar events reinforced these nativist attitudes and set the stage for action.

The result was the passage of two of the most restrictive immigration laws in American history: the Emergency Quota Act of 1921 and the National Origins Act of 1924. Together, these laws set the first-ever cap on the total number of immigrants admitted each year and introduced a system of national quotas that made it extremely difficult for so-called "new immigrants"—Eastern Europeans (many of them Jews) and Italians—to enter the country. Affirming the ethnic bigotry of the era, the chair of the House Immigration Committee congratulated the nation on stemming "the stream of alien blood." He concluded: "The United States is our land. . . . We intend to maintain it so."

Given this political atmosphere, it is not hard to understand why Jane Addams—pacifist, friend of labor, champion of the immigrant, and defender of radicals—should have run into trouble during the 1920s and indeed should have been placed under surveillance by the U.S. Department of Justice. Not only did she disagree with current trends in American politics, but she also spoke out on controversial issues at a time when many of those who agreed with her were holding their tongues. Among other things, she publicly condemned the Sacco-Vanzetti trial, called for more lenient immigration policies, denounced false forms of patriotism that constrained free speech, and helped found the American Civil Liberties Union (ACLU) to protect the rights that were being infringed.

Addams' pacifism caused her even more trouble than her progressivism. As we have seen, her opposition to military action had already gotten her labeled as disloyal during the war, when it was equated with favoring the Germans. Once peace returned and the pacifists began advocating disarmament, their critics accused them of plotting to weaken America against the Communists. Under these circumstances, Addams' position as president of one of the best-known pacifist organizations in the world—the Women's International League for Peace and Freedom—made her a prime target.

The smooth pathway from wartime to peacetime vilification can be seen in the activities of Archibald Stevenson, a prominent New York lawyer. Soon after the armistice, Stevenson published the names of 62 "pro-German" Americans—based, he claimed, on War Department records. Addams' name led the list. Newton Baker, Secretary of War, responded instantly, dismissing Stevenson's allegations and noting in particular that Addams "lends dignity and greatness to any list in which her name appears." Undeterred, Stevenson next helped Clayton R. Lusk, a member of the New York state senate, establish a committee to investigate "seditious activities" in the state. The Lusk Committee produced a four-volume report elaborately documenting imaginary connections between international communism and an array of groups favoring peace, women's rights, and social reform. For the rest of the decade, the Lusk Report was cited repeatedly as evidence that Addams and other pacifists were serving the cause of America's enemies.

Female pacifists also came in for enmity from the federal government, particularly when they interfered with the War Department's plans for the future. Soon after the armistice, the War Department submitted a proposal to Congress to establish a permanent army of nearly 600,000 and to require all young men to have three months of military training. The U.S. branch of the Women's International League joined women's groups across the country in campaigning against the proposal, which Congress turned down in 1920.

Many war-weary Americans had opposed the plan, but Secretary of War John Weeks was convinced that women's groups had masterminded its defeat. Accordingly, he set off on a cross-country lecture tour, attacking them mercilessly. At Weeks' encouragement, other military officers joined the assault. To buttress their charges, they publicized the fictitious "Slackers' Oath"—a pledge not to help one's country in time of war, even in such matters as assisting the Red Cross or making hospital supplies. This oath, the officers insisted, had been formally adopted by the Women's International League. Despite explicit denials from the women involved, the accusation was picked up and recirculated by many conservative groups.

Another count against Addams and many of her progressive allies was their long-standing commitment to increasing the government's involvement in such fields as public health and child welfare. In the overheated climate of the 1920s, this kind of effort was interpreted by many right-wingers as a conspiracy to prepare the way for socialism. The passions this topic aroused were clearly visible in the rise and fall of the pioneering Sheppard-Towner Act, which for the first time in American history allocated federal money to help the states promote maternal and child health. Championed by Lathrop at the U.S. Children's Bureau and strongly supported by women's reform groups across the country, the act was passed in 1921 but aroused such enmity from the American Medical Association and from conservative women's groups, such as the Daughters of the American Revolution (DAR), that it was closed down in 1929.

The association of Addams and her followers with the Sheppard-Towner Act only confirmed the conspiracy-hunters' idea that these women were out to subvert America. As the magazine *Woman Patriot* explained: "Practically all the radicalism started among women in the United States centers about Hull-House, Chicago, and the Children's Bureau, at Washington, with a dynasty of Hull-House graduates in charge of it since its creation." The magazine insisted that, even though these women might not themselves be Communists, the effect of their work was to "build communism with non-communist hands."

The blending of attacks on pacifism and social reform can be seen in the famous "Spider Web Chart," which purported to display graphically the connections among several dozen leading progressive women through their overlapping memberships in various pacifist and reform groups. (Addams belonged to most of these organizations, and in some versions of the chart, her name appeared first on the list of suspect individuals.) The Women's International League was featured, as one might expect. But many less controversial groups, including the Women's Christian Temperance Union, were also listed. No specific allegations were made against most of these organizations, but displaying them all together—with "spider web" lines showing their overlapping memberships—suggested that they were all part of a single conspiracy—an implication that was reinforced by the headline at the top of the document, a quote from the Lusk Committee: "The Socialist-Pacifist Movement in America is an Absolutely Fundamental and Integral Part of International Socialism."

Targeting Addams herself, the DAR issued a "dossier" in 1926 itemizing the evidence of her subversive tendencies. Although most of the long document simply listed her associations with a variety of "suspect" organizations and individuals, it concluded: "All her actions have tended toward the strengthening of the hands of the Communists to make for the success of a Communist war in our country." Ironically, Addams had been made an honorary member of the DAR in 1900. When the organization cancelled her membership in 1926, she observed tartly: "I supposed at the time that it had been for life, but it was apparently only for good behavior."

The majority of Americans did not participate in attacks like these; many probably did not even believe them. But they recognized the power of such accusations to destroy reputations, and they became far more cautious about their own exposure to criticism. For example, groups such as the General Federation of Women's Clubs, whose members had thrown themselves into social advocacy during the Progressive Era, virtually abandoned such activities in the 1920s and began to focus on safer topics, such as promoting home economics. Trying to stiffen the spines of her fellow social workers against this kind of conformity, Addams asked them in a 1924 speech what they would do if someone suggested that curing toothaches was Bolshevist. Would they insist on closing down dentistry? Too often, it seemed, the answer was yes.

Not surprisingly, Americans' fear of involving themselves in controversy had a chilling effect on Addams' own career. Many of her friends remained loyal to her, and some spoke up bravely in her defense. But she received few speech invitations, and the mass-circulation magazines that had done so much to broaden her audience before the war cut her off almost entirely. As for her books, after producing five between 1907 and 1916, she published only one between 1918 and 1928—*Peace and Bread In Time of War* (1922), about her experiences with the peace movement and the food conservation campaign. Meanwhile, her friends ran into immovable opposition when they tried to have her elected president of the National Conference of Social Work on the occasion of its 50th birthday. And efforts by Emily Balch and other friends almost every year during the 1920s to have her considered for the Nobel Peace Prize all went down to defeat.

Maude Royden, a British suffragist, later observed that when she first came to the United States in 1912, she discovered that one could not even refer to Addams without being interrupted by prolonged applause. When Royden visited again in 1923, she was stunned to see "how complete was the eclipse of her fame." By then, any mention Addams' name was met with stony silence. What a staggering change, said Royden. "What she must have suffered!"

Trying to Shape the Peace

If Jane Addams had had only the beleaguered world of American reform to occupy her, she might have found the 1920s truly unbearable. Fortunately, however, the Women's International League for Peace and Freedom (WILPF) provided another outlet for her energies and aspirations. Her association with the league certainly complicated her life in the United States, but in international circles, Addams' role as WILPF president brought her respect, stimulation, and comradeship, just when she needed them most.

Addams lived too far from Geneva to manage the WILPF's daily affairs, but she was intimately involved in its work. Among other things, she raised $500 a month to keep the organization solvent, and she presided at each of its conferences. All together, Addams made six trips abroad between 1921 and 1929. These included attending WILPF conferences in Vienna, Dublin, and Prague; peace conferences in Hawaii and the Netherlands; and a trip around the world with Mary Smith, during which she visited pacifists in many countries. (One of her stops was at Mahatma Gandhi's ashram in India.)

The extent of Addams' travel is the more remarkable because she was not in particularly good health during these years. Besides feeling generally worn down, she had an emergency kidney operation in Japan in 1923, followed by an angina attack in Dublin in 1926 that left her with heart problems the rest of her life. But the warmth of the reception she received in foreign countries must have made all the traveling seem worthwhile.

Issues of international peace and justice became Addams' major preoccupation during the 1920s. She served on a commission to help the new Irish Republic resolve its problems with the British Empire, spoke out against the United States' occupation of Haiti, wrote sympathetically about Mexico's right to fairer treatment from American oil companies, and praised Gandhi's nonviolent campaign to win India's independence from Great Britain. In addition, although she was well-aware of the Soviet Union's darker aspects, she insisted (in the face of intense American anticommunism) that it would be better for the United States to establish constructive dialogue with the Russians rather than to isolate them.

Addams' willingness to take on unpopular causes can also be seen in her continuing support of the League of Nations. In President Wilson's Fourteen Points speech during the war, he had described the formation of the league as an essential step toward ensuring international peace. In order to persuade the other Allied leaders to include the league in the Treaty of Versailles, Wilson had conceded virtually every other item on his agenda. Then, when the U.S. Senate appeared ready to reject both the treaty and the league, Wilson campaigned for them across the country with such intensity that the stress brought on a devastating stroke. Despite his efforts, the treaty went down to defeat, and when the league convened for the first time in November 1920, the refusal of the United States to participate cast a shadow over the proceedings.

Addams herself did attend the opening ceremonies, looking on with hope, if not total conviction. Her reservations were based on the fact that she believed the league was too much influenced by the wartime mentality that had shaped the Versailles peace treaty; for example, she thought that empowering the league to impose military sanctions was regressive, tying it to the old coercive methods that it had been created to replace. Nevertheless, Addams felt that the league was an experiment that must be supported, if only as a step toward something better. She campaigned for it in half a dozen states while the Senate was debating the peace treaty, attended many league meetings, and often wrote sympathetically about it. She agreed that the organization had its flaws, but "if you abolish the League, or if it dies, what is there to take its place? There is no answer."

As Addams worked to build support for the league and for the larger goal of world peace, she thought frequently of economist Simon Patten's observation that during the Progressive Era, reformers had developed a language that actually changed the way Americans thought about social justice. This, she said, was what pacifists had to do for peace. Somehow, they had to capture not only people's minds but their emotions—as William Stead had done in 1893 with his speech about Christ coming to Chicago and as Lewis Hine had done with his photographs of children laboring in the mills. Only in this way, Addams thought, could pacifists truly start building what she called an "international public" for peace.

Who would take the lead in this effort? Throughout the Progressive Era, Addams had seen women draw on their own distinctive worldview to make a compelling case for social reform. Now, she believed, it was up to them to play the same role on behalf of world peace. She remained convinced that, once the women of the world really understood that "war destroys everything that mothers have begun," they would join forces to make it impossible.

`In calling on women to act, Addams was buoyed by her conviction that, as she put it, "War is not a natural activity for mankind." People would prefer to act peaceably, she believed, but they could only feel safe in doing so if they trusted the social order within which they lived to treat them fairly, to meet their needs, and to reward them for acting on their own best instincts. Thus, the way to prevent war was not to focus on treaties and armies but to fight poverty and inequality and discrimination. This was Addams' fundamental plan for peace:

to build social institutions that were so strong and so just that they would make war and violence unnecessary.

As the 1920s drew to a close, Addams saw reasons for both hope and concern in the world around her. The League of Nations seemed to be finding its feet, the new World Court was functioning, and campaigns such as the No More War Movement in England suggested that the younger generation might do a better job of preserving the peace than their parents had. On the other hand, arms expenditures were soaring in western Europe, and compulsory military training was becoming increasingly common. Moreover, the United States remained resolutely isolated from the rest of the world—walled off by high tariffs, strict immigration laws, and its refusal to join either the League of Nations or the World Court. It was impossible to be sure which of all these tendencies would dominate in the years ahead.

Addams had many opportunities to mull over these uncertainties as she labored to complete her latest book: *The Second Twenty Years at Hull-House*. This volume was designed to carry the story of her life forward from 1909—the year when her previous memoir, *Twenty Years at Hull-House*, had ended. The writing went slowly, partly because it covered such a troubled period of her life and partly because there was no single compelling theme like the development of Hull-House to hold the narrative together. The effort of the writing shows in the book, and so does Addams' sadness. There are few of the anecdotes that enlivened her earlier work, and a good deal less humor. But the project did give her a chance to reflect again on her wartime experiences and to comment on many of her strongest interests during the postwar years, including world peace, women's roles, immigration, food relief, and Prohibition.

The *Second Twenty Years* did not deal with Hull-House in much detail, but Addams made clear in the book how proud she was that the settlement had survived and flourished. The timing was opportune because just as she was completing the manuscript in 1929, Hull-House celebrated its 40th birthday. The anniversary gathering was a huge and emotional occasion, but for Addams, it must have had a bittersweet flavor since it also marked the end of a remarkable era in her own life.

Another era came to a close that summer when Addams, because of ill health, retired from the presidency of the Women's International League for Peace and Justice, a position she had held ever since the first International Congress of Women in 1915. She would continue to contribute to the WILPF for the rest of her life, both organizationally and financially, but her days of overseas travel were over, along with her leading role as the international voice of female pacifism.

And so the 1920s ended on a valedictory note, with *The Second Twenty Years* going off to the printer, Hull-House moving gracefully into middle age, and the leadership of the WILPF passing into other hands. Throughout the decade, Addams had struggled to do her best as an author, a reformer, and a pacifist. But all three of these tasks had been more difficult because they were carried on in an environment of harsh and unrelenting criticism. Ellen Starr recognized as clearly as anyone what it had cost Addams to function in that atmosphere. "All, even the great," she observed, "naturally enjoy the sunshine of approbation and work more easily in its congenial warmth." Nevertheless, Addams had stood her ground throughout the 1920s, speaking out on one controversial issue after another, even when she knew that to do so would only invite more attacks. Would she ever regain the public standing she had enjoyed in the past? She could not imagine that she would.

11

Looking Forward, Looking Backward

By the time Jane Addams turned 70 in 1930, the American people were starting to remember why they had admired her so much in the past. Right-wing critics still attacked her from time to time, but their numbers had dwindled and their public influence was greatly diminished. Now organizations that had avoided her for years came forward to do her honor. Magazines vied with each other to publish her work, universities showered honorary degrees upon her, and she received more speaking invitations than she could possibly fulfill. Once again, it was safe to think well of Jane Addams, and even to call her a great American.

There were a number of reasons for this change of heart. The simple passage of time had certainly played a role; as the Red Scare faded into memory, people became more willing to forget the animosities of the 1920s and pay tribute to Addams' life of service. She herself recognized that her advancing years might also make her less controversial. "Perhaps," she suggested, "they think I am too old to make much trouble for any one any more." In addition, many of the ideas about peace and reform that Addams had been affirming for years had begun to sound more credible. By the early 1930s, Americans were growing more concerned about international peace, and the devastation wrought by the Great Depression gave new credibility to Addams' longtime stress on government support for the needy. For all these reasons, as she entered the 1930s, Addams found herself back in the good graces of the American public.

Month by month, the honors poured in. In just three years, between 1930 and 1932, Addams won Bryn Mawr College's annual $5,000 prize for a woman of eminent achievement; received a medal from the Greek government; was given $5,000 by *Pictorial Review* magazine as the woman who had made the most distinguished contribution to American life; and was even included by the inmates of San Quentin Prison in a list of the 12 greatest men of the century.

Addams herself regarded this blizzard of recognition with wry humor. She insisted that the Greek government had honored her simply because her Greek neighbors were fond of her, and when she heard that *Good Housekeeping* magazine had ranked her first among America's 12 greatest women, she observed that among the men who made the selection, one of them "formerly regarded me as a traitor, and I am quite sure that two at least of the others had never heard of me." But however skeptically she responded, the praise must have been a welcome change after her long years of ostracism.

Another indicator of Addams' return from the wilderness was the fact that she was once again welcome in the White House. Backing her friend Herbert Hoover for president in 1928 marked Addams' first vote for a major-party candidate since 1916, when she had endorsed Woodrow Wilson as a supposed peace candidate. Her choices in the years after 1916 made clear her frustration with mainstream American politics. In 1920, she voted for socialist Eugene V. Debs, who at the time was serving a federal prison term for opposing the draft. And in 1924, she supported Robert LaFollette, another much-vilified opponent of the war, who was trying to revive the Progressive Party. In 1928, many of Addams' friends voted for Democrat Al Smith, but she supported Hoover, primarily because she admired the dedication and competence with which he had administered European food relief during World War I. When Hoover won the election, Addams had a friend in the White House again for the first time in more than 10 years.

In November 1931, Addams received even more dramatic evidence of her return to favor: She learned that she had won the Nobel Prize for Peace. Year after year, she had seen this award go to others—even in 1920 to Woodrow Wilson, who in Addams' view had gravely undermined the cause of peace by bringing the United States into the war. Now the prize was hers. But her pleasure was marred by the news that she would be sharing it with Nicholas Murray Butler, president of Columbia University. Butler was being honored for his role in helping to launch the Carnegie Endowment for International Peace. But to Addams and many of her allies, his record was tarnished by the fact that during World War I, he had denounced peace activists and even persuaded the Columbia trustees to fire two faculty members for speaking out against the draft. Knowing that she would be sharing the Peace Prize with Butler dimmed its luster for Addams. Nevertheless, winning the award was a notable event in her life, particularly because she was the first woman ever to be so honored.

A month after getting the news of her Nobel Prize, Addams entered Johns Hopkins Hospital in Baltimore for lung surgery. The operation—including a disastrous reaction to the anesthetic—left her in such poor health that she was unable to go to Oslo the following spring for the award ceremony. But the eloquent presentation speech, hailing her as the "spokesman for all the peace-loving women of the world," must have warmed her heart. "She is the foremost woman of her nation, not far from being its greatest citizen," said the member of the Nobel Committee chosen to give the address. "When the need was greatest, she made the American woman's desire for peace an international interest." Whatever Addams' reservations about the circumstances of the award, it was an extraordinary honor, and she knew it. Perhaps the 1930s would be a better decade for her than the 1920s had been.

Hard Times Revive Reform

If things did improve for Addams in some respects during the 1930s, it was not because times were better economically. On the contrary, they were far, far worse. In the months following the stock market crash of October 1929, the U.S. economy went into a tailspin. By 1932, America's gross national product had fallen from $104 billion to $59 billion, farm prices had dropped 60 percent, railroads controlling one-third of the country's mileage had gone bankrupt, and more than 5,500 banks had closed their doors. Meanwhile, the nation's unemployment rate soared from 3 percent to 25 percent.

The economic crisis hit Chicago particularly hard. Within two years, the city's own relief fund had run out of money, and many private charities were also close to bankruptcy. Writer Edmund Wilson, who visited Chicago in 1932, described the heartbreaking scenes he witnessed around the city: an old man dying of cancer in an unheated house, a family of five camped out in a basement, a jobless young man staring listlessly into space, a tattered black banner fluttering over a squatters' camp. As for the neighborhood around Hull-House, Wilson described it as "a sea of misery."

Rising to the occasion, Hull-House dedicated itself almost entirely to providing assistance to the poor and the unemployed. Staff members raised every dollar they could find, bought food wholesale, and distributed it to needy families. They provided funds for those who did not qualify for official charity, loaned rent money to families about to be evicted, and handed out free milk for babies. In addition, in an effort to maintain the cultural life that had always been important at Hull-House, the staff ran art classes and discussion groups for the unemployed.

Addams herself had now taken up permanent residence at Mary Smith's house, and because she could no longer tolerate the cold, she generally spent most of each winter in Arizona or Florida. But when she was in Chicago, she nearly always spent the afternoons and early evenings at Hull-House, and her importance at the settlement was as great as ever. In 1932, a young resident wrote to a friend about the delight of hearing Addams' voice downstairs after a long absence. "There isn't any other voice like it, is there? Suddenly it seemed as if everything clicked, as if the tonic note had been struck and the chord was complete." Running downstairs, seeing Addams in the parlor again, the young woman felt as if "there must have been something unfinished about the room all the time she wasn't there. Her hair is whiter—that's all, and it's beautiful. Otherwise she looks so exactly the way she always did and always will. I think she has the most familiar face in the world."

Despite her limited hours at Hull-House, Addams took a strong interest in the neighborhood's problems and in the settlement's struggles to deal with them. To support these efforts, she donated the entire $10,000 of her American prize money to unemployment relief in the Hull-House neighborhood. At the same time, she used her writing and speeches to urge that the country look beyond emergency relief and begin instituting longer-term programs, such as unemployment insurance and old-age pensions. She chaired an unsuccessful effort to get government pensions enacted in Illinois, and she served as vice president of the American Association for Social Security, which campaigned at the national level for both unemployment insurance and pensions. In addition, she called for broader reforms, including better housing, safer working conditions, union rights, youth services, and improved public health.

Under ideal circumstances, Addams' friend President Hoover would have been campaigning for re-election in 1932 on exactly that platform. But the spiraling depression had far outrun his efforts to deal with it. Addams knew that Hoover was out of his depth, but after their long friendship, she could not quite bring herself to vote for his opponent, Franklin Roosevelt. In the end, having campaigned for neither candidate, Addams voted for Hoover. When—to no one's surprise—Roosevelt won the election (with nearly 60 percent of the vote), Addams wasted no time in regret but immediately began to consider how she could further the new administration's most progressive goals.

Her first effort, even before Roosevelt took office, was to help mobilize support for the appointment of the first female Cabinet member in American history. Soon after Election Day, a number of leading Democratic women made clear to Roosevelt that they felt he owed them something for their massive support during his campaign. And what they wanted, they said, was the appointment of Frances Perkins as Secretary of Labor.

A generation younger than Addams, Perkins' lifetime commitment to social justice had begun in college, when she heard a fiery speech by Addams' close colleague Florence Kelley. After graduating, Perkins volunteered briefly at Hull-House while teaching school in Chicago, earned a master's degree in political science at Columbia University, and later served as director of the New York Consumers' League. For the past 15 years, she had worked in New York State government, most recently as Governor Roosevelt's Industrial Commissioner. Perkins was driven by the same moral fervor that had animated Addams' generation of social activists, but she had also had professional opportunities that were not generally available when they were starting their careers.

Roosevelt indicated he was willing to name Perkins to the Labor Department, but he insisted that he would need a groundswell of support to prepare the way. Immediately, women's organizations began sending out the word through all the networks they had established over the years. Committees formed to promote the nomination, and letters and telegrams poured into the White House. The head of the New York League of Women Voters rallied her troops. Addams published an article in *Forum* magazine. Grace Abbott (a former Hull-House resident and Julia Lathrop's chosen successor at the U.S. Children's Bureau) made sure that Perkins met all the necessary members of Congress.

When the candidate herself showed signs of cold feet, she was taken firmly in hand by the woman who had been masterminding the whole process: Mary Dewson, a former colleague of Florence Kelley's and now director of the Democratic National Committee's Women's Division. "You owe it to the women." Dewson told Perkins. "You must step forward and do it." The candidate was persuaded, Roosevelt was assured that there was sufficient public support, and on February 28, he announced that Frances Perkins would be the new Secretary of Labor. She served with distinction until the president's death in 1945.

Addams' critics during the 1920s had often insisted that Hull-House was the hub of all female radicalism in the United

States and that the second such center—the U.S. Children's Bureau—was really the same thing because it was controlled by "a dynasty of Hull-House graduates." It was, of course, entirely false to suggest that these women and the larger networks to which they belonged were conspiring on behalf of America's enemies. But their loyalty to each other, their skill at collaboration, and their overlapping professional connections—these were never more evident than in the campaign to place Frances Perkins in the Department of Labor.

As New Deal programs spread out across the country, Addams was able to play a more direct role in the ongoing activity. In 1933, she was appointed to the Chicago advisory committee for the Housing Division of the Public Works Administration, and when a city housing commission was established the following year, she was asked to join that too. At the same time, she pressed for progress on other fronts, calling for higher wages, shorter working hours, larger public works programs, and a fairer division of corporate earnings.

As Addams watched the New Deal take shape during the final years of her life, she could see a national consensus starting to emerge, to the effect that, just as the federal government had an obligation to protect the country militarily and commercially, so it must ensure certain minimum social and economic standards in Americans' daily lives. This was the goal Addams and her fellow progressives had started pursuing at the city and state levels as early as the 1890s, and it had pulsed at the heart of the Progressive Party platform in 1912. Addams did not live to see the programs that embodied these ideas most concretely—such as the Social Security Act, the National Labor Relations Act, and the Fair Labor Standards Act (which finally outlawed child labor). But the direction was clear by the time she died, and she welcomed it. In a letter to a friend in 1934, she acknowledged that the problem of unemployment was still unsolved, but she observed, "It is really a wonderful time in which to live."

Uncertainty Overseas

As she had done ever since World War I, Addams continued to combine her social reform activities with intense involvement in the world peace movement. During the 1920s, the international situation had been her main source of hope and comfort. On the other hand, in the 1930s, things at home seemed to be improving while the picture overseas was becoming more complicated.

But we make a mistake if we imagine that Addams saw the events of those years as they appear to us now. When we look back from our own vantage point at the international situation of the 1930s, we tend to think of it as a mere prelude to World War II. But to people alive at the time, the future still seemed full of possibilities. In particular, pacifists like Addams clung to the belief that the horror of World War I had shown the terrible futility of using force to settle international disputes. Now if ever, they thought, it should be possible to persuade the people of the world that peace was not just desirable—it was the only possible way to live.

These were tantalizing years for Addams because the need to arouse the public seemed so urgent while her own physical resources were limited. But what she could do, she did. Although she delivered many fewer speeches than in her younger years, she did address the 1931 Conference on the Causes and Prevention of War in Washington, D.C., which drew delegates from 44 states. As principal speaker, Addams gave a stirring call for disarmament while sharing the platform with a retired general, the Chief of Naval Operations, the president of the Navy General Board, and the Secretary of Commerce. Later that year, Addams delivered to President Hoover a disarmament petition carrying 200,000 signatures. At the follow-up conference in Geneva (which she was not able to attend), petitions were presented bearing six million signatures from all around the world. One can understand why Addams and her fellow pacifists felt that world trends might at last be moving in their direction.

Despite having retired from the presidency of the Women's International League for Peace and Freedom, Addams continued to serve the organization as Honorary President. She corresponded widely on WILPF business, provided the new leaders with advice and counsel, and helped mediate occasional disputes. She also continued to raise money for the organization, including contributing a significant gift of her own: the entire $16,480 she had received for the Nobel Prize. Ever practical, Addams accompanied her contribution—the largest the WILPF had ever received—with a note stressing that there should be no publicity, as "it would be unfortunate to give the impression that we are now financially provided for and can spend with less careful consideration."

Besides her organizational work for WILPF, Addams devoted considerable effort to educating her fellow citizens about the cause of peace. She wrote more than a dozen essays on the subject for American magazines between 1930 and 1935 and gave a number of speeches. For example, in 1932, she addressed the platform committees at both the Republican and Democratic nominating conventions, enumerating the steps that the United States should be taking to foster peace; these included lowering its tariffs, recognizing Soviet Russia, joining the World Court, and nationalizing the American arms industry so the profit motive would have no role in decisions about the making and selling of arms. Addams also began giving radio addresses for the first time in her life. In all these ways, she tried to arouse the American public to share her own sense of urgency about averting the danger of war.

Reviewing Addams' speeches and writings on peace during the 1930s, one can see how her thinking had evolved since she first began speaking out against militarism more than 30 years earlier. Addams, like most of her contemporaries, seems to have had little sense in the early 1900s that a world war was imminent. Accordingly, her approach to peace at that time was developmental—almost leisurely—with her primary argument being that if the people of the world could learn to conduct their daily relationships without coercion or the abuse of power, then over time, they would outgrow the inclination to solve international problems by force. As Addams explained in later years: "I believed that peace was not merely an absence of war but the nurture of human life, and that in time this nurture would do away with war as a natural process."

Addams never abandoned this belief, but once World War I broke out, she devoted her attention to more immediate challenges—first trying to stop the fighting, then trying to keep the United States out of the war, and, in the 1920s, trying to mobilize support for structures that would maintain the peace. A number of these structures were in place by the 1930s, including some arms-limitation treaties, the League of Nations, the World Court, and the Kellogg-Briand Treaty against war. And yet it is clear from Addams' writing that as the 1930s progressed, she began to feel that the danger of war was growing larger, not smaller. She knew that many people all over the world longed for peace—the meetings and petitions, as well as the responses to her own speeches and essays, made that evident. But she saw more and more clearly how difficult peace would be to achieve.

One major obstacle, Addams believed, was fear. There was a new darkness in her tone as she described how fear could spark minor conflicts between nations that then spiraled out of control. In considering this problem, she saw a parallel between the insecurity that American families were feeling in the face of the Great Depression and the sense of insecurity that gripped many nations. "That clutch of cold fear is one of the hideous aspects . . . of human nature," said Addams. "People under fear will do almost anything to rid themselves of their panic." When nations felt this kind of vulnerability, they poured their resources into armaments. And yet, the more they spent on arms, the more vulnerable they felt because the other nations were all racing to keep up with them. This, Addams believed, was how wars started: from fears that festered and multiplied instead of being peaceably resolved.

Nationalism made this problem worse. Over the past century, she pointed out, many spheres of human activity—including finance, transportation, science, medicine, and culture—had developed strong connections across national borders. But politics remained mired in a world of separate nation-states, competing with each other for economic advantage and expending huge sums to protect themselves against each other militarily. More than any other force, she said, "excessive and exaggerated nationalism" posed a serious danger to the peace of the world.

Addams usually avoided singling out specific nations for rebuke, but by 1934, she was sufficiently concerned about the rise of Nazism to state that the problem of nationalism could be seen at its very worst in Germany, where it had "grown into a megalomania." Adolf Hitler had been in office just over a year when she wrote those words, but he had already used a fire in the Reichstag (the German parliament building) as a pretext for declaring martial law. And Addams had heard about the growing persecution of the Jews from her friend Alice Hamilton, who had recently traveled in Germany. At the same time, Benito Mussolini was consolidating his power in Fascist Italy, and Japan had made its first incursion into the Asian mainland, establishing a puppet state called Manchukuo in the Chinese territory of Manchuria.

In the case of Manchukuo, Addams noted with approval that both the United States and the League of Nations had refused to recognize the new state. This, she said, should be the trend of the future, using "moral energy as distinguished from physical force." But despite Addams' positive remarks, there was an unmistakable contrast between the largely theoretical nature of the response to Manchukuo—a sharp diplomatic note and a rebuke from the League of Nations—compared to the Axis Powers' soaring ambitions and their readiness to use military power to achieve those ambitions.

In confronting the rising dangers of the 1930s, Addams had two principal ideas to offer—the same ones she had been offering for years: international conflict resolution and disarmament. To her, they went hand in hand. Nations would be more willing to give up their arms if they knew there was a trustworthy system for resolving their grievances without war. On the other hand, the more progress they made on disarmament, the less likely it was that quarrels would escalate overnight into military confrontations. In 1932, Addams pointed out that during the previous year—despite a global depression and terrible poverty—the world had spent $5 billion on "useless armaments." "What might the present generation not achieve," she asked, "if it could be relieved of this old fear of war and cease preparations for war?"

For people who hated war and wanted to be done with it, Addams' proposals offered an appealing road to peace. The problem was that by the mid-1930s, there were a number of regimes in the world—most notably the Nazis—who saw war as not only necessary but inspiring. How could one appeal to such nations? And if one failed, how could one expect even peace-loving countries not to turn to war themselves?

One way Addams responded to this challenge was to reiterate the full hideousness of war. "Wars are not waged for honor, or for understanding," she said, "but for destruction." In an article in *Liberty* magazine, she reminded her readers that, however horrific World War I had been, the next one would be even worse. She warned: "Experts now conceive of the warfare of the future as *bound to involve whole populations* [her italics]." To Addams, it seemed so clear. War was terrible, and it was avoidable. How could people ignore the message? "A great Kingdom of Peace lies close at hand," she wrote almost pleadingly in 1935, "ready to come into being if we would but turn toward it."

Despite her efforts, however, Addams believed that a military mind-set was gaining ground in the world and that no organizational arrangements for peace could succeed as long as it prevailed. Perhaps, she said in early 1935, "we must wait for the subsidence of the war psychology for the vigorous prosecution of this great task." A few months later, in one of the last speeches she ever gave, she took a slightly more optimistic note, claiming to see evidence of "a rising tide of revolt against war as an institution." But her next sentence was far more pessimistic: "We are suffering still . . . from a war psychology; the armies have been demobilized, the psychology has not." The only hope, she concluded, was "an educated public opinion which shall fight this poison's spread."

Addams was still agonizing over these issues during the final years of her life—the mid-1930s—and the questions she could not solve continued to plague the Women's International League for Peace and Freedom in the years that followed. How do you face down, without the use of force, a militaristic government that is determined to crush you? Some of the

WILPF members (including most of the Americans) held fast to the idea of nonviolence. But many of the Europeans concluded that under the circumstances, the use of force was unavoidable. Even Addams' close friend Emily Balch, the organization's longtime staff director, reluctantly supported America's decision to enter the war after the Japanese attack on Pearl Harbor in 1941. "War seems to me as bad as it has always seemed," said Balch. Nevertheless, "a state may have to choose between two evil alternatives."

Would Addams have come to the same conclusion if she had lived longer? We can never know. Back in 1924, she had affirmed her conviction that "we are not obliged to choose between violence and passive acceptance of unjust conditions." To the very end of her life, Addams was still hoping to find a way to avoid that choice—to preserve both peace and justice.

The End of a Useful Life

During the final years of her life, amidst all her forward-looking work on behalf of peace and social reform, Addams also spent a good deal of time thinking about death and remembrance. For example, in 1932, she published a collection of 10 memorial addresses that she had delivered at the funerals of various people associated with Hull-House. Many of these speeches combined references to immortality with the more earthly assurance that those who had died would live on in the memory of their friends. Addams called the book *The Excellent Becomes the Permanent*, explaining that the people she had memorialized "exemplify the old statement that, though all else may be transitory in human affairs, the excellent must become the permanent."

In putting her book together, Addams decided to include a chapter that she had first published in *The Long Road of Women's Memory* in 1916. It described her emotional response when a trip to Egypt stirred up long-buried memories of her first childhood encounters with death. In her introduction to the new book, Addams explained that she was reprinting this chapter because it offered an answer to the many people who had written to ask "What do you believe? What is your attitude toward the future life?" In fact, the chapter did not really explain her beliefs about the afterlife. Instead, it conveyed her intense empathy with the fear and sorrow that people throughout human history have felt in the face of death.

Just a few months after Addams' book was published, she came face to face with death herself when two of her dearest friends—Florence Kelley and Julia Lathrop—died within a few weeks of each other. Addams had loved and admired both these women for more than 40 years, and their loss was a bitter blow. Then, in March 1934, came a heavier blow still, when her cherished Mary Smith died at the age of 65. Some months later, recalling that desolate spring, Addams told her nephew James: "I suppose I could have willed my heart to stop beating, and I longed to relax into doing that, but the thought of what she had been to me for so long kept me from being cowardly."

Addams' friend Alice Hamilton reached out to her in her grief and took her away to Connecticut for the summer. When Addams returned to Chicago that fall, she moved into Louise Bowen's house and resumed her usual work schedule. She also started writing a biography of Julia Lathrop. This project evoked another flood of memories—all the more poignant because Lathrop's life had paralleled her own in so many ways: the Illinois girlhood, the stalwart Republican father, the delight in college, the Hull-House years, the career in social welfare, and the life as a single woman. It almost felt, Addams said, as if she were rewriting her own memoirs from a different angle. She was never satisfied that her book was doing Lathrop justice. "I am too near her," she said, "and I miss her too much." Nevertheless, she continued to work at the manuscript, trying to give life to their shared history.

Addams took another excursion into the past when her nephew James Weber Linn started writing a book about her. She made all her papers available to him, answered questions about her life, and read through the first eight chapters of his manuscript. Her marginal comments made clear her fond skepticism about the project. "My dear, you mean well, but you exaggerate," she wrote on one page. And at the end of the first eight chapters: "This is all very well, but don't you think the

schoolboy who admires his old aunt is just a little evident?"
(Linn, a professor of English at the University of Chicago,
produced an affectionate but substantive account of his aunt's
life, which was published in 1935 under the title *Jane Addams:
A Biography*.)

In May 1935, Addams traveled to Washington, D.C., for one
of the most festive and emotional occasions of her life: the 20th
anniversary of the Women's International League for Peace
and Freedom. The gala events that week included a reception
given by Eleanor Roosevelt at the White House, and they
culminated in a dinner at which 1,200 guests gathered to pay
tribute to Addams. Among the galaxy of notables who spoke
that night, including the First Lady, one of the most eloquent
was Addams' friend Harold Ickes, Secretary of the Interior. He
said:

> Jane Addams has dared to believe that the Declaration of
> Independence and the Constitution of the United States were
> written in good faith and that the rights declared in them are
> rights that are available to the humblest of our citizens. She is
> the truest American that I have ever known, and there has
> been none braver. . . . Parents who want to develop the finest
> in their children will bring them up in the Jane Addams
> tradition and those so reared will be the best citizens of their
> generation.

When it was Addams' turn to address the crowd, she discarded
her prepared speech and spoke from the heart. First, she
assured her audience, "I do not know any such person as you
have described here tonight." So, she said, rather than deal with
this "alien celebrity," she would talk about peace. The mood of
her speech was sober, even dark in places, yet she urged her
listeners not to give up hope. "We may be a long way from
permanent peace, and we may have a long journey ahead of us
in educating the community and public opinion. Ours may not
be an inspiring role. But it tests our endurance and our moral
enterprise, and we must see that we keep on."

The next day, Addams had lunch with several of the women
who had been with her at the first International Congress of
Women 20 years before. An outdoor rally followed, with the

proceedings broadcast to London, Paris, Moscow, and Tokyo. The chilly weather kept Addams indoors, but she listened to the speeches and responded from the studio. That afternoon, Ickes wrote Eleanor Roosevelt to thank her for her tribute to Addams. He concluded: "I can recall some rather tragic periods when she was not greeted with the acclaim that was so spontaneous last night. It all goes to show that steadfastness and character will win out in the long run."

Addams returned to Chicago and spent the next 10 days working at Hull-House, going to committee meetings, and appearing before the Cook County Commissioners to talk about unemployment relief. She also completed her draft of *My Friend, Julia Lathrop*. On May 14, she visited friends in three different hospitals, and when one was unable to come downstairs to see her, she climbed two-thirds of the way up and sat on the steps so they could talk. That night, she had dinner at Hull-House for what turned out to be the last time. The next day, she felt a sharp pain in her side. An operation was recommended, and when the surgeons examined her, they discovered she had inoperable cancer. She died on May 21 at the age of 74.

All through the next 24 hours, Addams' body lay in state in the largest hall at Hull-House while an endless parade of mourners passed by—as many as 6,000 people an hour during the busiest part of the evening. Then, on the afternoon of the funeral, Addams' coffin was moved outdoors to the central courtyard. Long before the ceremony began, the area was packed to overflowing and every window was filled with people. Out on the street, loudspeakers were set up so the huge crowds gathered there could also share in the ceremony. The service featured singing by the Hull-House Music School and a sermon that started with architect Christopher Wren's famous epitaph: "If thou seekest a monument, look about thee."

The next day, Addams was buried in Cedarville in the cemetery established by her father. On her headstone was the simple inscription she had chosen herself:

JANE ADDAMS
OF
HULL-HOUSE
AND
THE WOMEN'S INTERNATIONAL LEAGUE
FOR
PEACE AND FREEDOM

Within hours of Addams' death, tributes to her life and work began pouring in from every direction. A resolution by the Chicago City Council pronounced her "the greatest woman who ever lived." A former Illinois governor compared her to the Virgin Mary. Kings and presidents sent their condolences, while ordinary people chimed in from all over the world with their own words of praise. Of them all, columnist Walter Lippman captured Addams' spirit with particular clarity and elegance. He wrote:

> She had compassion without condescension. She had pity without retreat into vulgarity. She had infinite sympathy for common things without forgetfulness of those that are uncommon. That, I think, is why those who have known her say that she was not only good, but great. For this blend of sympathy with distinction, of common humanity with a noble style is recognizable by those who have eyes to see it as the occasional but authentic issue of the mystic promise of American democracy.

What might have moved Addams even more than these eloquent words were the signs of mourning in the neighborhood she had thought of as home for more than 40 years. Up and down Halsted Street and all through the 19th Ward, shops and even saloons were draped in purple and black. "Purple for the nobility of her life," explained an Italian grocer; "black for our great loss."

12

Leaving a Legacy

Despite the accolades that poured in at the time of Addams' death, she received relatively little public attention in the decades that followed. In a country preoccupied with the approaching war, then with the war itself, and finally with the Cold War, the major concerns of Addams' life—peace and social reform—commanded less attention. And under these circumstances, Addams herself attracted less interest as an historical figure.

This situation changed during the 1960s, when the revival of interest in both peace and social reform made Addams' life seem relevant again. But readers of this new generation brought their own preoccupations to her work—particularly a sharper sensitivity to issues of race, class, and gender. Inevitably, these concerns influenced how they responded to Addams, leading to skeptical questions about her position on racial issues, her relationship to her immigrant neighbors, and the heavy streak of maternalism in her particular brand of feminism. In more recent decades, too, these issues have continued to receive close attention in analyses of Addams' life and work.

Such questions are well worth considering, as long as we explore them in the context of Addams' world rather than our own. For example, when we examine her racial attitudes, it becomes clear that she was not free of the prejudices of her time but that she surmounted them far more successfully than most of her contemporaries, even those within the progressive movement.

As for her feelings toward immigrants, her voluminous writings were, as historian Gary Dorrien observes, "strewn with just enough condescending statements to fuel the derision of her debunkers." Nevertheless, Addams' underlying regard for her immigrant neighbors showed in her tireless efforts on their behalf—expressed through her personal support, her advocacy for more enlightened government policies, and her continuing efforts to educate the public about the needs and admirable qualities of the country's immigrant population. Indeed, considering the high regard in which so many of the immigrants themselves held Addams, we owe them the respect of assuming that they knew a friend when they saw one.

In terms of Addams' views on women, she did indeed believe that their strongest claim to a public voice lay in their differences from men—their unique experience as mothers and nurturers. Her lifelong commitment to protective legislation for female workers was also based, at least in part, on her concern for their capacity to bear and raise children. This maternalist approach is less common today, and it has a slightly old-fashioned sound in an era when women more typically stress their right to be treated as equals. We also have the advantage of hindsight, knowing how often over the years the emphasis on gender differences has been used to keep women in a subordinate position. Nevertheless, it is worth noting that at a time when many men—and plenty of women as well—had real doubts about gender equality, Addams' progressive maternalism may well have been the most pragmatic and reassuring way she could possibly have chosen to justify women's involvement in public life and to encourage the first steps toward government regulation of working conditions.

More than a few observers have commented on the irony that Addams, an unmarried career-woman, should have placed such emphasis on women's role as nurturers. But most of the people who saw her in action seem to have agreed that her professional life was itself animated by a nurturing spirit. Her public image certainly reinforced that impression, and like her "difference feminism," it probably helped take the sting out of some of her more controversial positions. The soft voice, the modest manner, the demure bun, and the plain dark dresses—

all these must have affirmed the idea that this was not a woman interested in competing for male power. Thus, Addams took one of the greatest obstacles she faced—the taboo against women's asserting themselves on public issues—and defused it by embracing the most traditional expectations of how a genteel woman should look and speak. Recognizing the effectiveness of her style, philosopher William James gently teased her for being "all so quiet and harmless! Yet revolutionary in the extreme."

Besides Addams' capacity to present challenging ideas in a reassuring context, another distinctive aspect of her career was the diversity of her interests. It is hard to think of any leader today, male or female, who has actively participated in so many different kinds of social efforts. Addams was not only a major figure in the settlement movement and the peace movement; she was also a leader in efforts related to child welfare, women's suffrage, arts and culture, politics, housing, recreation, education, juvenile justice, labor relations, and civil liberties. To some extent, this diverse range of interests was a reflection of her times; the Progressive Era in particular was noted for its robust and overlapping networks of reform activity. But even in that context, the breadth of Addams' involvement was unusual; not one of her Hull-House colleagues covered so much organizational ground.

In its barest outlines, Addams' career followed a simple arc, starting in the 19th Ward and moving steadily outward— through activities at the city, state, and national levels until it encompassed the whole world. Each new initiative revealed the need for the next—from neighborhood garbage patrol to a city political campaign, to the drive for state factory laws, to the national fight against child labor, and, finally, to the grandest effort of all: the crusade against war. But however far she traveled, Addams never lost touch with the steps along the way. So, in her final years, she was still working regularly with the staff at Hull-House, even while she was simultaneously advocating for an expansion of city relief funds, pulling strings to help nominate the next Secretary of Labor, and writing essays about the need for world peace.

Through all Addams' many reform activities, a few key themes kept recurring: the need for mutual understanding, the value of collaboration, and the importance of applying our democratic ideals to daily experience. To start with the theme of mutual understanding, Addams believed that America could not function as a democratic society unless people in all walks of life learned to take seriously the hopes and fears of individuals who were not like themselves. This was the idea that first brought Addams to Hull-House in 1889, and it animated her continual efforts to build bridges between people from different social worlds—worker and boss, immigrant and native-born American, servant and mistress, charity visitor and client, man and woman.

One vivid expression of Addams' emphasis on empathy and understanding can be seen in her heartfelt advocacy on behalf of young people. She was convinced that most adolescents were filled with dreams of love and adventure that they simply did not know how to express. What these young people needed was not punishment but rather sympathetic guidance that would help them channel their dreams into constructive activity. Addams insisted that however self-sufficient or even rebellious young people might seem, they depended on the adults around them to confirm or deny their hopes of the world. The adults' responsibility was to understand those hopes, take them seriously, and help young people build on them to create satisfying and productive lives.

Addams' faith in the value of mutual understanding also shaped her approach to world peace. She was convinced that if people everywhere could learn to understand each other better, they could transcend the resentments that provoked wars and prevented social progress. "Much of the insensibility and hardness of the world," she wrote, "is due to the lack of imagination which prevents a realization of the experiences of other people." One of Addams' own great gifts was her imaginative insight into the feelings of others, and throughout her life, she did her best to share that gift with the world.

It is easy to see how Addams' call for mutual understanding applies to American life today. Like her, we know very well what it is to live in neighborhoods divided from each other by income and race. Furthermore, the hostility we see expressed toward Arab and Hispanic immigrants today is in many ways similar to what she saw directed toward Italians and Jews in her own time. Like Addams, we have seen differences over politics and religion rip communities apart. And like her, we have watched overseas conflicts rooted in old hatreds explode across the landscape. Even though Addams' ideas were developed in response to other quarrels and other wars, her call for "sympathetic understanding" is as relevant today as it was a century ago.

The second theme that reappeared continually in Addams' career was the importance of group effort. During the course of her career, she served on hundreds of different committees and coalitions, not to mention her lifelong dedication to that remarkable collective: Hull-House. She reveled in her collaborative comradeship with other reformers during the Progressive Era and with fellow pacifists in the peace movement. Addams was convinced that this kind of shared endeavor—"this wonderful unification of effort"—was by far the most effective way to move society forward. At the same time, she found it profoundly rewarding on a personal level because, as she said, it filled one with "the consciousness of participation and well-being which comes to the individual when he is able to see himself 'in connection and cooperation with the whole.'"

Addams' commitment to group effort explains her unswerving loyalty to the labor movement—even though she endured bitter criticism for her position and even though she did not always agree with the actions of specific unions. When the paternalistic businessmen of her day insisted that they themselves were best qualified to look out for their workers' interests, she gave them credit for good intentions but flatly insisted they were wrong. She was absolutely convinced that leaders must work with their people, not decide by themselves what was best for them. That way, whatever the outcome, it would be "sustained and upheld by the sentiments and aspirations of many others." To Addams, the labor movement embodied this principle of solidarity and shared effort. And it was because of this collaborative ideal—however imperfectly realized—that Addams always insisted the movement represented a "forward step in American democracy."

Addams' ideas on collaboration also had implications for her views on government. Like many progressives, she came to believe that under some circumstances, the best way for people to overcome the challenges they faced was to act collectively through government. From her perspective, government was not a distant external power; it was an instrument of the people through which they could work together to ensure a better quality of life for all Americans. Addams and her allies in the progressive movement spent years promoting this idea. The results were not always immediate, but those early efforts prepared the ground for scores of our most valuable laws and public programs today—including occupational health standards, the minimum wage, the prohibition of child labor, housing safety codes, and Social Security.

When we speak of Addams' commitment to group effort, her lifetime of collaboration with women merits special note. It is difficult to imagine how different her career would have been had she not had the companionship, stimulation, and support of hundreds of progressive women, including the remarkable Julia Lathrop, Florence Kelley, Lillian Wald, Alice Hamilton, and Emily Balch. These women came to maturity in an era when female organizational activity was at its height. Had they been born earlier, gender restrictions would not have permitted them so active a public life; had they been born later, they would have been more likely to join organizations that also included men. As it was, the times fostered the creation of a gigantic network of clubs, settlements, and other female associations that operated almost autonomously within a larger society controlled by men. This network was at its height during the Progressive Era, but its methods and values continued to shape Addams' approach to reform as long as she lived.

Over the years, Addams experienced the joy of seeing what dedicated women could accomplish together, as well as the frustration of being reminded periodically (for example, during World War I) that men still ruled the world. Through it all, her collaborative relationships with women remained one of her greatest satisfactions. Today, the two institutions to which she devoted her life remain as testaments to that collaboration and to the institution-building talent it evoked in Addams.

Addams' most famous creation, Hull-House, is still a visible presence in Chicago. The original house on Halsted Street is now the Hull-House Museum. And although the rest of the old settlement complex is gone (replaced by the campus of the University of Illinois at Chicago), the Hull-House Association continues to serve the city, with active programs in several newer immigrant neighborhoods. As for the Women's International League, it is now the oldest women's peace organization in the world, with a lively American branch and sections in 36 other countries.

The third recurring theme in Addams' worldview—so important that it ran through almost everything she did—was her determination to put America's democratic ideals into practice. As a pragmatist, she insisted that these ideals only had meaning when they were applied to the practical realities of life. "The sphere of morals is the sphere of action," she wrote. "A situation does not really become moral until we are confronted with the question of what shall be done in a concrete case, and are obliged to act upon our theory." A ward boss taking a bribe, an anarchist arrested for making a speech, a child laborer too beaten down to reach his or her potential— these were troubling in themselves, but they were the more disturbing because they were betrayals of American values. Addams was convinced that if American democracy did not work in a neighborhood like the 19th Ward, it did not work at all. So it was too with her work at the state and national levels. In every case, her focus was on bringing abstract ideals to life.

Applying this philosophy to the international scene, Addams believed that a nation's foreign policies should reflect its principles. She was therefore troubled when the United States used its superior power to oppress a smaller country, or acquiesced in an ally's military adventures, or ignored the role that its own arms merchants were playing in perpetuating foreign wars. As with the smallest abuse of power in the 19th Ward, so with the country's whole approach to international relations—the proof of America's ideals lay not in its rhetoric but in how it acted every day.

This, then, was Addams' vision for America: to apply the nation's bright democratic promise to the hard challenges of daily existence. In her career, we see that vision exemplified. Whether she was combating poverty or gender discrimination, censorship or corruption, conflict between classes or conflict between nations, her purpose was always the same: She was working to give practical reality to our highest ideals.

Addams was sustained in her efforts by her hope that long after she was gone, Americans of good will would continue to pursue the same democratic vision that had inspired her. So, as we consider how to respond to her life, we would do well to remember these words, which she wrote in 1903:

> Progress is not automatic. The world grows better because people wish that it should and take the right steps to make it better.

When Addams talked about progress, when she talked about making the world better, she meant that at every level of our existence—from the way our country operates overseas to the way we treat our own families—we should try to make our actions more democratic, more just, and more merciful. Surely nothing would make her happier than to feel that there are Americans today who share that vision and are still trying to make it a reality.

Study and Discussion Questions

Chapter 1: Finding the Path

1. How did Jane Addams' father and stepmother influence her early life?

2. What challenges did female college graduates of Addams' generation face if they wanted to get married and also have a career? Do you think women have an easier time today balancing work and family responsibilities?

3. Why was Addams so unsettled during the first eight years after she graduated from college?

4. What was life like in the 19th Ward, where Addams established Hull-House?

5. What were the most important factors in getting Hull-House launched successfully?

Chapter 2: Reaching Out to the Neighbors

1. Given the poverty of the people in the 19th Ward, why did Addams initially concentrate on providing them with cultural programs rather than economic assistance?

2. Imagine yourself living in the 19th Ward—perhaps as a working mother, or an aspiring teenager, or an immigrant grandfather. How do you think you would have felt about the various Hull-House programs and about Addams herself?

3. Settlement workers have been criticized for focusing too much on "Americanizing" their immigrant clients. How would you assess Addams in terms of this charge?

4. How did Addams bring college-level courses to her Hull-House neighbors? Why did she later develop doubts about them?

5. What problems did Addams see in the traditional "charitable relationship," and how did she try to avoid these pitfalls at Hull-House?

Chapter 3: Putting Democracy into Practice

1. What were some of the key goals of progressivism? Looking at the United States today, how well would you say the progressives' goals have been realized?

2. Given Addams' interest in the relationship between immigrants and the rest of American society, what do you think she would have to say about the position of immigrants in the United States today?

3. What were Addams' views about government's social responsibility to its people? How did she feel about the role that government services played in the lives of her immigrant neighbors?

4. What did Addams learn from the settlement's unsuccessful campaigns against political boss Johnny Powers?

5. How did Addams feel about such political radicals as socialists and anarchists? How did her relations with these groups reflect her ideas about democracy?

Chapter 4: Choosing Collaboration

1. Explain why you would have liked—or not liked—to be a resident at Hull-House.

2. Choose any one of the following—Julia Lathrop, Florence Kelley, or Alice Hamilton—and discuss how she benefitted from and contributed to Hull-House and its community.

3. Discuss Addams' changing relationship with the sociology professors at the University of Chicago.

4. What does *Hull-House Maps and Papers* tell us about the settlement's approach to social research?

5. Why were settlement workers like Addams initially wary of a connection with the social work profession? How did their feelings change over time?

Chapter 5: Focusing on Women

1. How did the "cult of domesticity" differ from the way American women had lived in earlier times? How did it interfere with the public role that Addams had in mind for women?

2. Why did an unmarried career woman like Addams put so much emphasis on women's role as mothers and nurturers?

3. What insights did Addams gain about the women in the Hull-House neighborhood from the Devil Baby incident?

4. According to Addams, why did women who simply wanted to take care of their own families still need to involve themselves in public issues?

5. Why did female activists like Addams feel that women needed the vote?

Chapter 6: Nurturing the Spirit of Youth

1. What special challenges did Addams' immigrant neighbors face in dealing with their teenage children?

2. According to Addams, in what ways were young people harmed when they started factory work too early? In what ways was society harmed? Given the drawbacks of child labor, why did parents allow their children to work?

3. How would you compare your own school experience to Addams' view of what education should be like?

4. What kinds of dangers did Addams believe awaited teenage boys and girls when they set off into the city in search of amusement? How would you compare those dangers to the ones facing teenagers today?

5. What kinds of programs did Hull-House organize to win teenagers away from commercialized recreation? Since the atmosphere at the settlement sounds stricter than at places of public amusement, why do you think so many young people went there?

Chapter 7: Speaking Up for Labor

1. What were some of the problems faced by factory workers in the late 19th century? In what ways would you say that workers today are better off or worse off?

2. In what ways did Hull-House residents support the labor movement? How did Addams justify these activities, and what was the public reaction?

3. Why was Addams so conflicted in her feelings about labor strikes?

4. Why did Addams hold industrialist George Pullman primarily responsible for the railroad strike of 1894?

5. What kinds of steps did Addams want the government to take in order to improve American labor conditions? Why could labor unions not improve matters on their own?

Chapter 8: Taking Progressivism to the Nation

1. What were the advantages and disadvantages of using women's role as mothers to justify laws that limited their working hours, as was done in the Supreme Court's *Muller v. Oregon* decision?

2. How did the U.S. Children's Bureau build on patterns of women's activism that had emerged in previous decades?

3. Discuss Addams' agreements and disagreements with the platform of the Progressive Party.

4. How did Addams feel about Theodore Roosevelt as the party's presidential candidate?

5. What did Addams expect to be achieved by the Progressive Party campaign in 1912, and how closely did the outcome match her expectations?

Chapter 9: Trying to Stop a War

1. Why did Addams' 1907 book *Newer Ideals of Peace* include chapters about such ordinary aspects of civilian life as urban government, immigration, and labor relations?

2. What do you think of Julia Wales' proposal to end World War I through "continuous mediation" by a council of neutral nations? Do you think that mechanism could be applied to any of the conflicts we see today?

3. What was the mission of the "envoys" sent from the International Congress of Women to the various European capitals in 1915? Did they achieve their goals?

4. Why did many members of the American peace movement abandon their opposition to the war once the United States entered the conflict in April 1917?

5. Why did Addams choose a different course? How did that choice affect her life?

Chapter 10: Searching for Hope in the 1920s

1. What were some of the factors that diminished public interest in social reform after World War I?

2. Why was Addams so troubled during the 1920s by the behavior of the younger generation? What do you think she would say about young people today?

3. Why did the threat of radicalism and subversion arouse such fear among Americans in the 1920s? How did Addams' critics connect her to these threats?

4. What was the "Spider Chart," and what was it designed to show?

5. What was Addams' opinion of the League of Nations? How do you think she would feel about the United Nations today?

Chapter 11: Looking Forward, Looking Backward

1. How and why did Addams' standing with the American public change in the early 1930s?

2. How did Addams respond to the problems of the Great Depression?

3. How did the women's campaign to make Frances Perkins the Secretary of Labor grow out of earlier female associations?

4. In what ways did President Roosevelt's New Deal build on the work that Addams and her fellow reformers had done during the Progressive Era?

5. By the mid-1930s, how did Addams feel about the prospects for world peace? Do you think she would have stuck by her pacifism if she had lived another five years?

Chapter 12: Leaving a Legacy

1. How has Addams' public reputation risen and fallen over the years? Do you think her career has relevance for us today?

2. How do you feel about the emphasis Addams placed on mutual understanding as the key to everything from labor relations to world peace? Do you think it was a realistic position in her time? What about in our world today?

3. What were the advantages and disadvantages to Addams of working so frequently through organizations composed all or primarily of women?

4. Imagine a young woman today establishing a social agency in a poor immigrant neighborhood, as Addams did. What conditions would make it easier—or harder—for her to build the kind of career that Addams built a century ago?

A Note on the Sources

Of the 11 books that Jane Addams wrote, only *Twenty Years at Hull-House* has been continuously in print since it first appeared, but most of the rest have been reissued in recent years. The titles are as follows:

1902: *Democracy and Social Ethics*

1907: *Newer Ideals of Peace*

1909: *The Spirit of Youth and the City Streets*

1910: *Twenty Years at Hull-House*

1912: *A New Conscience and an Ancient Evil*

1915: *Women at the Hague: The International Congress of Women and Its Results* by: Jane Addams, Emily G. Balch, and Alice Hamilton)

1916: *The Long Road of Woman's Memory*

1922: *Peace and Bread in Time of War*

1930: *The Second Twenty Years at Hull-House: September 1909 to September 1929*

1932: *The Excellent Becomes the Permanent*

1935: *My Friend, Julia Lathrop*

The bulk of Addams' literary output and the source material for most of her books lie in the outpouring of essays, speeches, and other short pieces that she produced during her lifetime. No single definitive list of this work exists, partly because Addams published and lectured so widely and partly because scholars deal differently with the many cases in which she reworked the same material for use in different forms. Louise Knight's *Citizen: Jane Addams and the Struggle for Democracy* (2005) lists about 100 of the more significant short pieces. The list in John C. Farrell's *Beloved Lady: A History of Jane Addams' Ideas on Reform and Peace* (1967) runs to 514 items, and he asserts that even this is incomplete. These shorter writings appear in three published collections. Two of the collections—*The Social Thought of Jane Addams* (1965), edited by Christopher Lasch, and the *Jane Addams Reader* (2002), edited by Jean Bethke Elshtain—include selections from each period of her career, while the material in *Jane Addams' Essays*

243

and Speeches (2005), edited by Marilyn Fischer and Judy D. Whipps, focuses more specifically on her writings about war and peace.

In terms of archival resources, the large Jane Addams Collection (part of the Swarthmore College Peace Collection) includes most of Addams' personal papers and correspondence, as well as family documents, news clippings, materials about Hull-House, and many photographs. The Jane Addams Memorial Collection at the University of Illinois at Chicago provides an excellent overview of Hull-House and the Chicago reform environment within which Addams worked. Additional information is available at the Hull-House Museum, located in the original settlement building on Halsted Street in Chicago. Drawing on these and other archives, Mary Lynn McCree Bryan has compiled an 82-reel microfilm collection—The Jane Addams Papers, 1860–1960—which is available in many college libraries. Bryan is also working with Barbara Bair and Maree de Angury on *The Selected Papers of Jane Addams*. Two 700-page volumes in this series have appeared so far, carrying Addams' story up to the year Hull-House opened; more volumes are planned.

Addams' nephew James Weber Linn wrote the first biography of her, which appeared shortly after her death in 1935. His *Jane Addams: A Biography* lacks the documentation and professional distance of more scholarly works, but it is well-written and tells a compelling story. Nearly 40 years later, Allen S. Davis wrote another major biography: *American Heroine: The Life and Legend of Jane Addams* (1973). A bit more critical than Linn's, this book is still among the best introductions to her life. Five new Addams biographies have appeared within the past decade or so. Two carry her only into her 30s, culminating in her early years at Hull-House. They are: Gioia Dilberto's *A Useful Woman: The Early Life of Jane Addams* (1999), and Victoria Bissell Brown's *The Education of Jane Addams* (2003). Louise W. Knight has divided the story of Addams' life into two books—*Citizen: Jane Addams and the Struggle for Democracy* (2005), which takes her up through the founding of Hull-House, and *Jane Addams: Spirit in Action* (2010), which covers the rest of her career. The fifth recent account, Jean Bethke Elshtain's *Jane Addams and the Dream of American Democracy* (2002), covers the full span of Addams' life. There are also more than half a dozen biographies for younger readers, most designed for grades 5–8.

A number of books about Addams focus on specific aspects of her work. For example, in *Beloved Lady: A History of Jane Addams' Ideas on Reform and Peace* (1967), John C. Farrell devotes more attention than any other biographer to Addams' career as a pacifist. Katherine Joslin's *Jane Addams: A Writer's Life* (2004) concentrates on Addams as an author. And in *Jane Addams and the Men of the Chicago School, 1892–1918* (1988), Mary Jo Deegan explores her relationship with Chicago sociologists and the evolving field of sociology. The essays in *Jane Addams and the Practice of*

Democracy (2009), edited by Marilyn Fischer, Carol Nackenoff, and Wendy Chmielewski, discuss Addams' ideas about democracy in relation to various contemporary schools of social theory.

Much of the zest of life at Hull-House derived from the remarkable women who congregated there. Eleanor J. Stebner's group biography, *The Women of Hull-House: A Study in Spirituality, Vocation, and Friendship* (1997), focuses particularly on the role of religion in the various residents' careers. Longer accounts of individual women's lives include: *The Autobiography of Florence Kelley: Notes of Sixty Years* (1986); Kathryn Kish Sklar's *Florence Kelley and the Nation's Work: The Rise of Women's Political Culture* (1995); Alice Hamilton's memoir, *Exploring the Dangerous Trades: The Autobiography of Alice Hamilton* (1943); Barbara Sicherman, ed., *Alice Hamilton: A Life in Letters*, (2003); Jane Addams' *My Friend, Julia Lathrop* (1935); Lela B. Costin's *Two Sisters for Social Justice: A Biography of Grace and Edith Abbott* (2003); and Kathleen Banks Nutter's *The Necessity of Organization: Mary Kenney O'Sullivan and Trade Unionism for Women, 1892–1912* (2000).

Of the books describing Hull-House as an institution, one particularly useful publication—now unfortunately out of print—is *One Hundred Years of Hull-House* (1990), edited by Mary Lynn McCree Bryan and Allen F. Davis; this anthology of short reminiscences and contemporary news reports paints a portrait of the settlement from its founding to its centennial. Other analyses of the Hull-House experience include Shannon Jackson's *Lines of Activity: Performance, Historiography, Hull-House Domesticity* (2000); Rivka Shpak Lissak's *Pluralism and Progressives; Hull House and the New Immigrants, 1890–1919* (1989); and an account by Addams' protégé Hilda Polacheck, *I Came a Stranger: The Story of a Hull-House Girl* (1989).

For information on the neighborhood around Hull-House, one might start with the remarkable *Hull-House Maps and Papers* (latest edition, 2007), a collection of articles about the area that was produced in 1895 by a team of people associated with the settlement. There is also a useful historical website entitled "Urban Experience in Chicago: Hull-House and Its Neighborhoods, 1889–1963" at www.uic.edu/jaddams/hull/urbanexp. Another perspective on life in Chicago appears in Erik Larson's historical novel *The Devil in the White City: Murder, Magic, and Madness at the Fair That Changed America* (2003); it takes place during the World's Fair of 1893.

James Green provides useful historical background on the labor environment in Addams' Chicago in his book *Death in the Haymarket: A Story of Chicago, the First Labor Movement, and the Bombing that Divided Gilded Age America* (2000). Other helpful sources on different aspects of labor during this period include: James P. Barrett's *Work and Community in the Jungle: Chicago's Packinghouse Workers, 1894–1922* (1987); Josiah Bartlett Lambert's *"If the Workers Took a Notion:" The Right to Strike and American Political Development* (2005); and Cynthia

R. Daniels's essay, "Between Home and Factory: Homeworkers and the State," in *Homework: Historical and Contemporary Perspectives on Paid Labor at Home*, Eileen Boris and Cynthia R. Daniels, eds. (1989).

Among the various general treatments of progressivism, Maureen A. Flanagan's *America Reformed: Progressives and Progressivism, 1890s–1920s* (2007) and Steven J. Diner's *A Very Different Age: Americans of the Progressive Era* (1998) provide fairly sympathetic overviews, while Michael McGerr's *A Fierce Discontent: The Rise and Fall of the Progressive Movement in America, 1870–1920* (2003) and Robert H. Wiebe's *The Search for Order, 1877–1920* (1966) are more critical. Lewis L. Gould offers a lively account of progressivism at its peak in *Four Hats in the Ring: The 1912 Election and the Birth of Modern American Politics* (2003). There are also two collections of short biographies of progressives, each featuring two or three Hull-House residents: Steven L. Piott's *American Reformers, 1870–1920: Progressives in Word and Deed* (2006) and Cecilia Tichi's *Civic Passions: Seven Who Launched Progressive America* (2009).

Alan Dawley explores the later phases of the progressive movement in *Changing the World: American Progressives in War and Revolution* (2003), showing how some reformers (including Addams) continued to promote key progressive concepts throughout World War I and into the 1920s. Progressive ideology is discussed in more detail in Dawley's *Struggles for Justice: Social Responsibility and the Liberal State* (1991); Marc Stears' *Progressives, Pluralists, and the Problems of the State: Ideologies of Reform in the United States and Britain, 1909–1926* (2002); and Gary Dorrien's *Social Ethics in the Making: Interpreting an American Tradition* (2009).

Allen F. Davis's book on the settlement movement—*Spearheads for Reform: The Social Settlements & the Progressive Movement, 1890 to 1914* (1985)—remains the classic introduction to the subject, while Mina Carson's *Settlement Folk: Social Thought and the American Settlement Movement, 1885–1930* (1990) looks more specifically at the leaders' ideology. Other perspectives on the settlement movement during Addams' time appear in the early chapters of Judith Ann Trolander's *Professionalism and Social Change: From the Settlement House Movement to Neighborhood Centers, 1886 to the Present* (1987) and Elizabeth Lasch-Quinn's *Black Neighbors: Race and the Limits of Reform in the American Settlement House Movement, 1890–1945* (1993).

The role of women in Progressive Era reform is thoughtfully explored in Robyn Muncy's *Creating a Female Dominion in American Reform 1890–1935* (1991) and Daphne Spain's *How Women Saved the City* (2001). Maureen A. Flanagan's *Seeing With Their Hearts: Chicago Women and the Vision of the Good City, 1871–1933* (2002) describes the specific environment within which Addams' career developed. Progressive women's political and suffragist activities are analyzed in Rebecca Edwards' *Angels in the Machinery: Gender in American Party Politics from the Civil War to the Progressive Era* (1997); Sara Hunter Graham's *Woman Suffrage and the New Democracy* (1996); and Rebecca J. Mead's *How the Vote Was Won: Woman Suffrage in the Western United States, 1868–1914* (2004). Nancy Cott's classic *The Grounding of Modern Feminism* (1987) provides a valuable picture of how these events intersected with the emergence of modern feminism.

Women's role in child-related reform is discussed in Elizabeth Clapp's *Mothers of All Children: Women Reformers and the Rise of Juvenile Courts in Progressive Era America* (1998); Linda Gordon's *Pitied But Not Entitled: Single Mothers and the History of Welfare* (1994); Molly Ladd-Taylor's *Women's Child Welfare and the State, 1890–1930* (1994); and Kriste Lindenmeyer's *"A Right to Childhood:" The U.S. Children's Bureau and Child Welfare, 1912–1946* (1997). Further perspective on the juvenile court movement appears in Michael Willrich's *City of Courts: Socializing Justice in Progressive Era Chicago* (2003), while Viviana A. Zelizer's *Pricing the Priceless Child* (1985) provides thought-provoking context for the whole topic of child welfare with its discussion of the changing view of childhood during the 19th century.

On the topic of immigration, the country's tensions and debates over assimilation and exclusion are described in Ellis Cose's *A Nation of Strangers: Prejudice, Politics, and the Populating of America* (1992) and Roger Daniels' *Guarding the Golden Door: American Immigration Policy and Immigrants Since 1882* (2004). As for race relations, David W. Southern's *The Progressive Era and Race: Reaction and Reform, 1900–1917* (2005) describes progressivism's generally poor record in this area. Gary Gerstle's *American Crucible: Race and Nation in the Twentieth Century* (2001) covers a longer time period, but his treatment of the Progressive Era also highlights the limitations of the reformers' democratic vision when it came to race. Pulling the issues of race and immigration together, Jonathan M. Hansen describes in *The Lost Promise of Patriotism: Debating American Identity, 1890–1920* (2003) how certain Progressive Era leaders (including Addams) articulated a more inclusive concept of American identity.

For readers seeking background on Addams' work in the peace movement, Thomas J. Knock's *To End All Wars: Woodrow Wilson and the Quest for a New World Order* (1992) provides a useful overview of America's involvement in World War I and the various elements of the American peace movement. Books on women's work for peace include: Harriet Hyman Alonso's *Peace As a Women's Issue: A History of the United States Movement for World Peace and Women's Rights* (1993); David Patterson's *The Search for Negotiated Peace: Women's Activism and Citizen Action During World War I* (2007); and Linda K. Schott's *Reconstituting Women's Thoughts: The Women's International League for Peace and Freedom Before World War II* (1997).

Index